OUR
PREHISTORIC
ANCESTORS

ALSO BY
HERDMAN FITZGERALD CLELAND

PHYSICAL AND HISTORICAL GEOLOGY

PRACTICAL APPLICATIONS OF GEOLOGY

PLATE V

La Tène pottery. (1), (2) and (3) Pottery from Southern Germany
which shows the influence of Hallstatt traditions in their designs;
(4) a vase of buff ware with scrolls which resemble the ornamentation of some of the jars from Glastonbury, England; (5) a pedestal
vase of reddish ware covered with scrolls in a brown pigment; (6)
a vase painted on two sides with rosettes, and red bands around
the neck and foot; (7) a carinate vase with zigzag designs. (8)
This fine lustrous black jar with a raised band painted red on the
shoulder, was in a grave with the skeleton of a warrior whose
equipment for his journey in the life after death was an iron sword,
a lance, a large wooden shield, an iron knife, and a pair of shears.
(9) A black pedestal vase with red designs. (1), (2) and (3) are
from South Germany, and (4) to (9) are from France.

OUR PREHISTORIC ANCESTORS

BY HERDMAN FITZGERALD CLELAND
PROFESSOR OF GEOLOGY, WILLIAMS COLLEGE.

"I have seen mankind begin lower nor
the gibbering ape, and I've seen them end
the striving sons of God, millions on millions, on millions of years, multiplied into
dizziness, crawling, infinitesimal work overcoming Nature, overcoming themselves,
overcoming the princes of the powers of
darkness."—*Marco Polo*, DONN BYRNE

GARDEN CITY PUBLISHING COMPANY, INC.
GARDEN CITY, NEW YORK

Printed in the United States of America by

TO

M. J. C. AND E. D. C.

PREFACE

The purpose of this book is to describe as briefly as clarity will permit the events in man's prehistory which have been of greatest significance in his progress toward civilisation. All civilised peoples owe much the same debt to the men of the Stone Ages. In their upward climb all passed through these stages, but when metals came in use the cultures of different regions diverged. Because of this, the discussion here given is confined largely to Europe.

The Neolithic or New Stone Age is stressed because in it man made the great fundamental inventions, compared with which, the greatest achievements of to-day, though more spectacular, are relatively unimportant. Greater changes in man's physical well-being and mental attitudes took place in this age than in all preceding and subsequent ages.

In the preparation of this work the writer studied the collections in the British Museum, the Museums of Gothenburg, Stockholm, Copenhagen, Berlin, Halle, Leipzig, Vienna, St. Germain-en-Laye, and Madrid, as well as numerous local museums.

Special mention should be made of a number of works upon which the author has freely drawn: Déchelette's "Manuel d'Archéologie"; Schumacher's "Siedelungs- und Kulturgeschichte der Rheinlande"; many articles in Ebert's "Reallexikon der Vorgeschichte"; V. Gordon Childe's "The Dawn of Civilization"; and H. Obermaier's "Fossil Man in Spain." Although the writer can not accept some of the conclusions of Mr. W. J. Perry and Prof. G. Elliott Smith, he has found the works and lectures of these authors most thoughtful and stimulating.

Grateful acknowledgment is made for special photographs

to the National Museum, Stockholm; the Irish National Museum, Dublin; the Museum of Ethnology, Berlin; the Museum of Halle; The National Archaeological Museum, Madrid; M. Paul Vouga, Neuchatel and for the permission of the trustees of the British Museum to use illustrations from the Guides to the Antiquities of the Stone, Bronze, and Iron Ages.

Appreciative thanks are due to a number of European prehistorians, and especially to the late Dr. Walther Bremer of Dublin, Dr. Arne and Mr. Lindquist of Stockholm, and Dr. Unverzagt of Berlin. The writer is under obligations to Mr. V. Gordon Childe, author of "The Dawn of European Civilization," and to Dr. Bremer for reading chapters of his manuscript and for making many helpful suggestions. The writer recalls with pleasure and profit visits to East Anglia, England, to study the work of J. Reid Moir, to Stonehenge, and Avebury, to Brittany, to Amiens, and to the Dordogne, with Professor George Grant MacCurdy, Director of the American School of Prehistoric Research.

Special acknowledgment is due my wife, Emily Wadsworth Cleland, whose ability to accurately translate German, French, and Italian has made it possible to go to the original sources for most of my material. Her knowledge of Classical Archæology has also been freely drawn upon. I also desire to thank Dr. E. F. Greenman, Curator of Archaeology in the Museum of the Archaeological and Historical Society of Ohio, for reading the proof.

CONTENTS

LIST OF ILLUSTRATIONS

OUR
PREHISTORIC
ANCESTORS

OUR PREHISTORIC ANCESTORS

CHAPTER I

THE CONTRIBUTIONS OF THE MEN OF THE OLD STONE AGE

WHEN OUR ANCESTORS AND THEIR RELATIONS WERE IN THE HUNTING STAGE

IF WE are to understand how modern civilisation arose, we must know the motives which impelled man to change his habits, to invent new tools and ornaments, and finally to acquire the advantages and disadvantages of civilisation. The interest of the lower animals is fundamentally one of food, of mating, of safety, and, in some, of companionship. These motives are equally fundamental in man. Novels are popular because they tell of the technique of lovemaking —which is mating—or of adventure and prowess. Prowess is the ability, by brute force, or cunning, to protect one's self or one's mate, to secure food, to find shelter, to overcome one's enemies, and to mate. These are the motives that go back through the ages for millions of years. The first mammals had them and their ancestors, the amphibians, and their ancestors, in turn, back to the dawn of life. No mental traits can be stronger than these, for they have been passed on by inheritance for tens of thousands of generations. The individual who lacked any of them either did not survive or left no descendants. It is evident, therefore, that the motives which led man to struggle for what we call civilisation are as old as life itself. The fundamentals of civilisation: agriculture, the domestication of animals, the building of houses, social

1

organisations, are but the results of motives which are common to all animals.

If this is true, why are man and his works unique? Why is his career a new departure in the history of organic evolution? Throughout the long ages of the geologic past, Nature seized upon all structures capable of useful development: in some animals the feet and legs were developed for speed; in some the teeth became adapted for special food; in some both feet and teeth became extraordinary organs of locomotion and mastication; in some minute bony particles in the skin gradually increased in size until the animal was fully protected from its enemies by a heavy armour; in some the bulk increased so that by mere weight they were able to overcome their competitors.

Finally, in the earliest Tertiary, a weak, lemur-like creature appeared (Fig. 35, p. 67) which, though affording few possibilities of evolution along the lines followed by other animals, had a brain with a capacity for great improvement. During the course of the Tertiary, the brain of the descendants of this potential ancestor of man increased in size and improved in quality until a new and higher type of animal was evolved, whose descendants were to become the rulers of the universe (Fig. 1). But it is only in mental development that man can justly claim preëminence, for in other respects he is inferior to many animals.

Where Man Originated. The question: "Where did man originate?" has been answered in many ways. Europe, Asia, Africa, Australia,[1] and even Antarctica have been suggested and arguments have been brought forward for each. Europe [2] has been suggested because the remains of the earliest true men of which we have any record have been found in Eu-

---

[1] Otto Schötensack: "Die Bedeutung Australiens für die Heranbildung des Menschen aus einer niederen Form," *Zeitschrift für Ethnologie,* XXXIII [1901], p. 127. Quoted by R. A. S. Macalister: A Text-book of European Archaeology, p. 572.

[2] A. Hrdlicka: "The Peopling of the Earth." *Proc. Am. Phil. Soc.,* vol. LXV, no. 3, 1926, pp. 150-156.

rope, and because large anthropoids—suitable ancestors—lived in Europe in the Tertiary. Africa[3] has been favoured because man's nearest living relatives, the gorilla and chimpanzee, are living there now, and because of the physical characteristics of some of the Africans. Southern Asia has been favoured because the "number and diversity of the

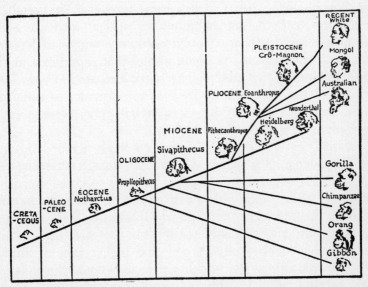

FIG. 1.—Genealogical tree to show man's ancestry and his relation to races of submen. If this chart were more detailed it would show that a number of other human species arose, only to disappear after a short or long existence. Of all these species only Homo sapiens (modern man) has survived. After American Museum of Natural History.

forms of the fossil apes give the impression that (in the Middle and Upper Tertiary) Asia was the laboratory where the differentiation of the ancestors of mankind must have been in the process of elaboration."[4]

The available evidence points more strongly to Asia as the place of man's origin than to any other continent, and

[3] Charles Darwin: "The Descent of Man."
G. Elliot Smith: "Essays on the Evolution of Man," London, 1924, pp. 81-82.
[4] M. Boule: "Fossil Men." 1923. p. 458. Trans. by J. E. and J. R. Ritchie.

to the central plateau of Asia, north of the Himalayas,[5] rather than to any other part of that continent. The fossil life of Asia with its many and diverse species of apes is favourable to the suggestion, and the physical and climatic conditions were such as to force animals that lived in trees to adapt themselves to a terrestrial habit. Osborn's [6] argument on this point is excellent. "This high plateau country of central Asia [in the Tertiary] was partly open, partly forested, partly well-watered, partly arid and semi-desert. Game was plentiful and plant food scarce. The struggle for existence was severe and evoked all the inventive and resourceful faculties of man and encouraged him to the fashioning and use first of wooden and then of stone weapons for the chase. It compelled the Dawn Men—as we now prefer to call our ancestors of the Dawn Stone Age—to develop strength of limb to make long journeys on foot, strength of lungs for running, and quick vision and stealth for the chase. Their life in the open, exposed to the rigours of a severe climate, prompted the crude beginnings of architecture in their man-made shelters, and the early use of fire for bodily warmth and for the preparation of food.

"This conception of the early development of man in a high plateau country accords with all principles of human evolution, and is well-established by observations in the Holocene or recent period of the Age of Man. In support of this view we may note: *First:* That the evolution of man is arrested or retrogressive in every region where the natural food supply is abundant and accessible without effort; in tropical and semi-tropical regions where natural food fruits abound, human effort—individual and racial—immediately ceases: *Second:* That all precocious intelligence and early civilisation in mankind were fostered in open regions where

---

[5] W. D. Matthew: "Climate and Evolution." *Annals of the New York Academy of Science,* XXIV, 1915.
[6] Henry Fairfield Osborn: "Why Central Asia?" *Natural History,* vol. XXVI, 1926, pp. 263-269.

the food supply is scarce and impossible to obtain without individual effort and resourcefulness. The corollary of these two principles is the *third:* That during Tertiary times all the lowlands of Asia were relatively well forested and well watered, with a relatively accessible food supply—conditions altogether favourable not to man but to the continued development of the great anthropoid apes, as well as to the retention of arboreal or semi-arboreal habits of life. In brief, while the anthropoid apes were luxuriating in the forested lowlands of Asia and Europe, the Dawn Men were evolving in the invigorating atmosphere of the relatively dry uplands."

When Man first began to Improve on Nature's Tools

Man's early ancestors used the tools Nature had prepared: the stones of the river bed and of the gravel bank, and the shingle of the seashore. But after a time they began to use some discrimination in selecting their stones. If they wanted a cutting tool they searched for a sharp-edged flake of flint or rock. If they wanted to break a nut or smash the skull of an animal they chose a nodule or pebble that fitted the hand comfortably. In time they learned that flint was the best material for their use and thereafter they used stone only when flint or obsidian was not available. The first stone knife and hammer were ready-made.

After using such tools for thousands of years, it occurred to some bright individual that he might resharpen the dulled edge of an unusually good, natural flint knife by striking off small flakes. He also learned that if his stone hammer or sharp-edged flint did not fit the hand, the troublesome points or edges could be removed or reduced by flaking. Flint fragments which may have been modified in this way are called eoliths (Fig. 2).

Eoliths. Eoliths (Greek, *eos* dawn; *lithos* stone) are defined as "primitive flint implements, consisting of splinters or fragments of flint nodules whose natural form is but little altered by human handiwork. The aptitude to serve as instruments for cutting, striking, boring, sawing, etc., which they already possess by nature, is intensified by retouching." [7]

The discovery that he could improve fortuitous flakes enabled man to take a long step forward. It led to a technique

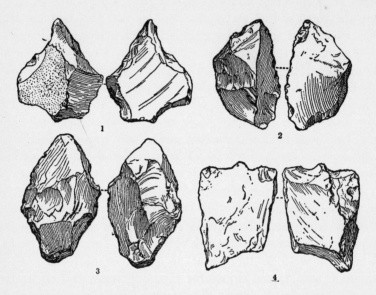

Fig. 2.—Eoliths. The first stone implements used by men or submen were fortuitous flakes slightly modified in shape by use or intent. The flakes here shown from Foxhall, England, have some of the characteristics of (1) a borer, and (2) a scraper for cleaning hides. After J. Reid Moir. Reduced in size.

in flint-working, which some thousands of years later (in the Neolithic) was brought to a high state of perfection. It increased man's effectiveness, and stimulated his inventiveness. Moreover, as the less intelligent and less inventive individuals of his own kind were now at a distinct disadvantage in getting food and in protecting themselves from their enemies they tended to disappear. The result was a gradually

[7] H. Klaatsch: *Zeitschrift für Ethnologie.* XXXV (1903) p. 116.

improving race. It is difficult to distinguish these first attempts of man to improve natural flakes from flakes which were made by natural forces. The flood waters of streams and the heavy surf of the seas batter pebbles against each other and break off flakes which, in turn, are chipped along their edges. It is such secondary chipping that often looks as if it were the work of human hands. Pebbles and flint nodules are also broken and their edges chipped by the pressure of overlying rocks, by the feet of animals, and in other ways. As a consequence, few persons are willing to say positively whether a so-called eolith is the work of natural forces or of man.[8] It is certain, however, that primitive tools of this character must have been made by early men or submen. Although time has destroyed all wooden tools and implements that Eolithic man used, there is no doubt that wood was often employed.[9]

Habits of Eolithic Man or Subman. We can learn much about the probable habits of Eolithic man by studying the habits of his nearest living relations. We are at least safe in assuming that man's ancestors of the late Tertiary or early Pleistocene were as intelligent as the Apes of to-day. The baboon is said to use stones for breaking nuts, and sticks to pry up stones in its search for insects. The chimpanzee also has many human habits. If man's ancestors began with such habits, it is easily seen how they could have passed through an eolithic stage to a tool-making one.

Eolithic Man. Theoretically, men with the same intellectual gifts as modern man could have passed through successive stages during which they used ready-made flakes, natural flakes which they had slightly improved by crude flaking,

[8] J. Reid Moir, who has made a careful study of eoliths, has no hesitancy in identifying them. J. Reid Moir: "Further Discoveries of Humanly-fashioned Flints in and beneath the Red Crag of Suffolk." *Proceedings of the Prehistoric Society of East Anglia,* Ipswich. 1920-1922.

Abbé H. Breuil: "Les industries pliocènes de la région d'Ipswich." *Rev. Anthropologique,* XXXII, July-Aug., Paris, 1922.

[9] For a bibliography of the literature on eoliths, see H. Obermaier: "Fossil Man in Spain," pp. 373-375.

and finally stone tools of definite design. Chance discoveries have brought to light parts of skeletons of creatures closely akin to man, who were probably makers of eoliths.

Pithecanthropus Erectus. One of the most important early human creatures, or submen, was the famous *"Ape Man"* or Pithecanthropus (Fig. 3 and Fig. 9), one fragmentary skeleton of which was discovered in Java in 1891. Of this creature, G. Elliot Smith [10] says: "No one who has seen the cast of the interior of the brain-case, and is capable of interpreting

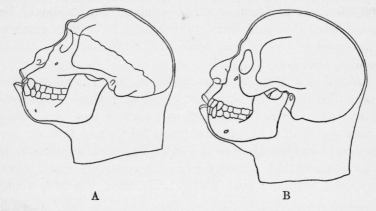

A   B

FIG. 3.—(A) Restoration of the skull and face of Pithecanthropus erectus, the so-called Ape-man. The size and shape of the brain shows that the animal was truly a member of the human family, though a lowly one.

(B) Restoration of the skull and face of the Piltdown Man (*Eoanthropus dawsoni*). The skull is as much as two-fifths of an inch thick. The brain is more human than that of Pithecanthropus. After Lull and McGregor.

its obtrusive peculiarities of form and proportions could have any hesitation in deciding that Pithecanthropus was truly a member of the Human Family, if a very lowly one. The capacity of the brain-case of the Javan specimen was probably about 950 cubic centimeters (that is, about 100 cubic centimeters greater than Professor Dubois's estimate), which brings it within the range of variation even of *Homo sapiens;* whereas 650 cubic centimeters is the biggest record for an ape, even

[10] G. Elliot Smith: "Essays on the Evolution of Man," pp. 84-85.

of a gorilla twice the body-weight of a human being." A study of the shape and development of the brain of this creature leads to the conclusion that the power of speech [11] was developed to such a degree as to enable him to transmit information and ideas. Pithecanthropus had a long, apelike skullcap. The teeth are distinctly human. In stature, shape, and weight of body, Pithecanthropus was human. The body characteristics had an earlier development than the brain.

Many estimates of the time at which Pithecanthropus lived have been made. Some writers state that 400,000 to 500,000 years is a conservative estimate, but it should be remembered that such estimates are little more than guesses. The evidence that he may have lived 1,000,000 years ago is perhaps stronger.

Heidelberg Man. A very primitive, heavy, and massive jaw, called the Heidelberg Jaw, found near Heidelberg, Germany, may also have belonged to a race of men or submen who made eoliths. The most striking features of this jaw are its weight and the absence of a chin. The teeth are human in type and although actually large are relatively small when compared with the jaw. Without the teeth the jaw would probably have been considered that of an ape, but the teeth indicate clearly that the creature belonged to the human stock. No eoliths were found with the jaw.

Piltdown Man.—The fragments of a very ancient skull, the Piltdown man (*Eoanthropus dawsoni*), found in Southern England, show that the skull was extremely thick-walled, averaging about two-fifths of an inch in thickness. With the exceptions of a jaw which was found in the deposits with the

---

[11] A study of the external form of the brain of extinct animals is possible because a cast of the inside of the skull gives a nearly perfect representation of the shape of the brain, even the convolutions and positions of the blood vessels being shown. The reason for this is that the brain completely fills the cavity, and that during the growth of the skull and brain, bony ridges grow into the depressions of the soft brain, and the pressure of the blood vessels on the outside of the brain makes depressions in the bone. This principle is used by dentists in changing the position of children's teeth: a slight pressure, long applied, will bring the teeth into the desired positions.

skull and which resembles closely that of a chimpanzee, the skull is of a rather high type. The brain though small comes definitely within the range of variation in size found in modern man, but it is to be noted that those parts of the brain which develop latest in our skulls were defective in the Piltdown man. It is an interesting and suggestive fact that the gravels which contained the Piltdown skull have also yielded flint flakes which have been identified as eoliths. In addition to these so-called eoliths, there was found a remarkable object, nearly seventeen inches long, made from a part of the leg bone of some such animal as an elephant. One end is artificially pointed to a chisel edge.

Eolithic Man's Contributions to Civilisation. One great debt of civilised man to Eolithic man or subman was the acquisition of the ability to make a tool with which to make something else. This was an important advance, a momentous step. Apes and related animals have no such ability. They can use sticks and stones as tools to help them reach objects or to protect themselves, but they cannot make a tool, for example, with which to shape a stick to be used for some special and useful purpose. If it were necessary to call in Special Creation to account for man's appearance on earth, an appropriate time for the exercise of this power would have been when, by the growth and improvement of the brain, man's ancestors needed only the added ability to make tools to start them on the road to humanity. If apelike creatures were endowed with the ability and perseverance to make a tool with which to make a weapon or other useful implement, the ascent of man would almost certainly have been assured.

EARLY PALEOLITHIC

When Man First Made Tools of Definite Design—the Early Old Stone Age (Chellean and Acheulean)

Geography. During a large part of the Paleolithic, men and animals could migrate freely to and from Great Britain

and the continent, because the English Channel and Irish
Sea were not then in existence. At times there were land con-
nections between Europe and Africa: (1) where the Strait of
Gibraltar is now, and (2) by way of Italy which was joined
to Sicily and Tunis by a broad peninsula. At this time the
Mediterranean Sea was restricted and formed two or more

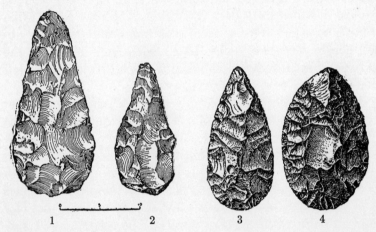

1   2   3   4

FIG. 4.—Hand-axes or *coups de poing*. The favourite tool of the Early Paleolithic was the hand-ax which probably combined the functions of ax,
scraper, borer, knife, and saw. It was the *chef d'œuvre* of Early Paleolithic man and was in use for many thousands of years. The usual length
was from three to five inches but some a foot long have been found. The
average length was about five or six inches. (1) and (2) (*Chellean*) are
older than (3) and (4) (*Acheulean*) and show that the later peoples had
acquired greater skill in flint working. (1) and (2) after St. Germain
Museum; (3) and (4) after Capitan. Reduced in size.

lakes. These land connections explain the presence in Great
Britain and Europe of elephants and other great beasts and
also the repeated migrations of Paleolithic tribes to and from
Europe and Africa.

The maximum elevation probably did not occur everywhere at any one time; nor did it last throughout the entire
Paleolithic period. Great Britain, however, seems to have
been a part of the continent at least during the Third Inter-

glacial, the Fourth Glacial, and the Post Glacial Stages, as is shown by the free migrations of animals and man.

Implements. The oldest known implements of man are of crude workmanship. They differ from eoliths in showing without question that they were the work of intelligent beings who were endeavouring to make tools of definite shapes. The most distinctive and common of these early implements are called *coups de poing* or hand-axes (Fig. 4). These are large almond-shaped tools, four to ten inches long, which are in appearance not unlike two hands with the palms touching. The shape of this implement can best be understood by studying the figure. The form of the early hand-ax varies considerably as it depended to some degree on the shape of the flint from which it was made. This was the indispensable, all-round, early Paleolithic tool. When the thick end was held in the hand the pointed end could be used for hacking or cutting, for drilling holes, for scraping hides, and for many other purposes. When held by the pointed end it could be used as a hammer. Others with the same general shape were more specialised and may have been hafted for axes, used as scrapers or for other purposes. Some of the flakes which were broken off in making the hand-ax were slightly modified by chipping and in this way a small variety of tools, such as scrapers for cleaning hides, and awls for perforating skins, were obtained (Fig. 5).

The invention and perfection of the hand-ax had a remarkable effect on the inventiveness of man. The heavy hand of tradition now limited or nearly stopped initiative, and man's delight was in making more skilfully made tools of the same type. A hundred thousand years is probably a conservative estimate of the time during which this was man's most prized implement and his highest artistic achievement.

Man of the Early Paleolithic. What manner of man lived in the early Paleolithic (*Chellean* and *Acheulean*) and made hand-axes is not known, as no skeletal remains have been found. The discovery of hand-axes in Europe, especially in

Great Britain, France, and Spain; in many parts of Africa; in Asia, especially in Syria, India, Indo-China, Japan, and on the island of Ceylon, shows the wide distribution of these

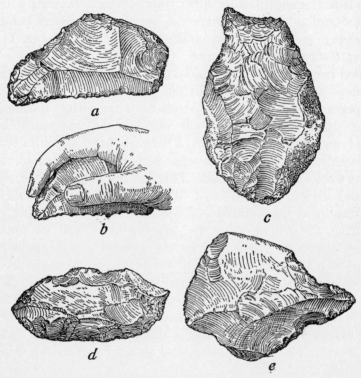

Fig. 5.—In addition to the hand-ax, other flint tools were made and used by Early Paleolithic man. Most of these were wrought from flakes that had been struck off in making hand-axes.
(a) A scraper for hides which could also be used as a knife. (b) shows how the implement was probably held and explains the blunt back and sharp edge. (c), (d) and (e) are flakes that have been worked into points and were probably for boring holes in wood and skins. After Commont. Reduced in size.

people. It is improbable that Paleolithic man lived in North or South America, or rather that the New World was inhabited by human creatures during the vast Paleolithic period. The evidence which has been offered to support the theory that Paleolithic man lived in the Americas is not convincing.

Distribution. It is evident from what has been said that the men of the Early Paleolithic inhabited large areas in the Old World, in Europe, Asia, and Africa. Many regions were uninhabited because of the absence in them of flint or other material suitable for the tools which formed such an important part of the equipment of the period, because of forests and swamps and for other reasons. The population, however, was not large at any time.

Habits. We can be sure that the Early Paleolithic peoples were wandering hunters who, in a warm climate, required little protection. They made stone implements of some variety. With these they were able to supply their needs for food and clothing. Whether or not they made baskets, were able to plait or weave, and how they dressed the skins of the animals they killed, is unknown. The wooden implements they may have used crumbled to dust long ago.

Without doubt they protected themselves with skins. The abundant flint scrapers (Fig. 5, a) seem certainly to have been used for scraping and preparing the skins of animals. The absence of needles, pins, or other implements for fastening skins together suggests that the body was covered with single pelts. Such was the beginning of the manufacture and wearing of clothing.

THE MIDDLE OLD STONE AGE (MOUSTERIAN)

Habits. For some reason, probably because of the increasing cold of the beginnings of the last great ice sheet, the poorly clad men of the Middle Paleolithic were forced to go to caves (Fig. 6) for shelter. This new habit of life brought about a rather rapid change in flint tools, and in the technique of flint-working. Instead of trimming a large flint nodule to make a hand-ax, the craftsman made his tools from the flakes which were struck from a nodule. In this way a single flint nodule could be made to furnish many tools. The people,

FIG. 6.—The cave of Spy, Belgium, where skeletons and implements of Neanderthal men were found. The cave is dry and could easily be made comfortable. It was inhabited for a long time by Neanderthalers. Photograph by the Author.

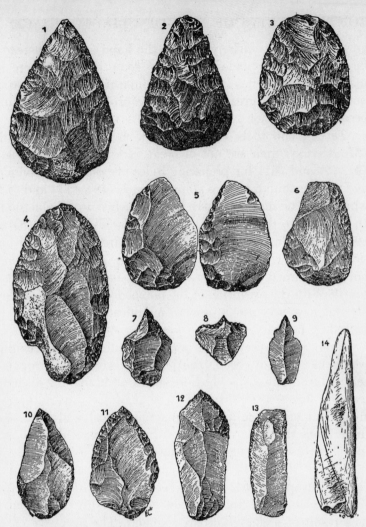

Fig. 7.—Flint implements used by Middle Paleolithic (*Mousterian*) man. (1), (2), and (3) miniature hand-axes carefully dressed on both sides. Such implements are rare. (4), (5), and (6), scrapers for hides; (7), (8), and (9), piercers; (10), (11), and (12), characteristic Mousterian "points"; (13), flake retouched as a knife; (14), piece of bone with striations, probably used as a compressor to chip off flakes. The technique used in manufacturing flint implements was different from that of the Early Paleolithic in that the implements instead of being made by shaping a core, were made from flakes struck from a core, and were retouched by the pressure of bone (14) or wood. The hand-ax was still made in the old way. After Commont. Reduced in size.

however, did not entirely discard the hand-ax but, instead of larger ones, they made small ones, some of which were not more than two inches long. These miniature implements could not have been of great use and were probably manufactured because of tradition.

Tools. The tools (Fig. 7) made by Middle Paleolithic (*Mousterian*) man are not of great variety. Scrapers (Fig. 7, (4), (5) and (6)) for preparing hides are especially common, and next in abundance are points (Fig. 7, (10), (11) and (12)) which may or may not have been attached to javelin shafts. In addition to these tools, there are awls (Fig. 7, (7), (8) and (9)) for piercing hides; long thin flakes, dressed on one or both sides, which were used as knives (Fig. 7, (13)), saws and notched scrapers which were probably for smoothing javelin shafts. With the exception of the notched scrapers the artifacts are not new inventions but are modifications of tools of the preceding period.

There was, however, the important difference in technique which has already been mentioned. Lower Paleolithic man selected from the chips which he struck off in making his hand-ax such flakes as could readily be manufactured into small tools. But as the chips were generally short and thick they differ from the tools made from the more carefully prepared and more useful Mousterian flakes.

If the Middle Paleolithic (*Mousterian*) culture had its rise in Europe (which has not been proved), the explanation for the change in flint-working could readily be explained as a result of a change in environment. The necessity of living in caves gave man a fixed place of abode, and also compelled him to carry flint nodules to his cave to be worked. Because of this, he learned to economise his raw materials, and, because he lived in one place for many days at a time, he experimented in his idle hours with discarded flints and thus learned to make better tools and to invent a new technique. The new flint technique was a great invention which was used for many thousands of years thereafter. It consisted of breaking a flint nodule so as to have a flat surface or "striking platform" from which large flakes could be struck by sharp blows.[12] The advantage of making implements from large flakes was that it saved time and material since it was usually necessary merely to trim off the edges of the flake to make a tool of a desired shape. There is no evidence that Middle Paleolithic man made bone tools—an astonishing fact. The sole use of bone, as far as known, was for anvils which were employed in manufacturing flint tools.

Hunting. The manner in which Neanderthal man (*Mousterian*) hunted cave bears is known from a study of the Drachenhöhle or Dragon's Hole, in Styria, Austria. When the bears came from the innermost recesses of the caves where they had been hibernating, the Neanderthal hunters stationed themselves in such a position that, when the bears passed, they could strike them with long-handled clubs at the end of which sharp stones were fastened. This is proved by the numerous wounds on the skulls of the cave bears which are always on the left side of the skull or jaw, that is, on the side exposed to the attack of right-handed men.

Man of the Middle Paleolithic (Mousterian)

Although almost the only knowledge we have of the Early Paleolithic peoples is obtained from a study of their stone implements, we are more fortunate in our knowledge of the men of the Middle Paleolithic. A considerable number of skeletons and skulls of these people have been found in Europe, as well as one in Palestine. The most important race of the Middle Paleolithic (and it is possible that it is the same that made the Early Paleolithic implements) is called the Neanderthal race (*Homo neanderthalensis*) because of the discovery of their skeletons in a cave in the side of a deep gorge, known as the Neanderthal, near Düsseldorf, Germany.

[12] It is possible that the "Mousterian" technique was developed elsewhere and that its invention may have been the result of necessity brought about by increasing cold. Cf. *Man*, 1926, p. 116.

A study of the skeletons of this race makes it possible to reconstruct a fairly accurate picture of the appearance of these ancient hunters.

Physical Appearance of the Neanderthal Race. Picture to yourself a small, stocky man, about five feet four inches in height, with a head too large for his body. His sloping shoulders are stooped and his thick, bull neck is bent forward in the same curvature as the back, that is, in an ape-like posture.

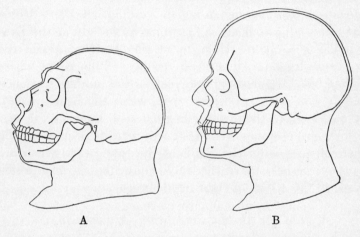

A   B

Fig. 8.—(A) Restoration of the skull and face of Neanderthal man.

(B) Restoration of the skull and face of Cro-Magnon man. This skull is of the modern type, *Homo sapiens*, but the brain is larger than that of modern man. After Lull and McGregor. Compare the sections of the skulls of Neanderthal and Cro-Magnon men (Fig. 9).

His legs are stout and are bent at the knees and hips giving him a shuffling, awkward gait. His hands are large and coarse and do not have the power of delicate manipulation possessed by the hands of modern man. His feet are better adapted for grasping and climbing than those of modern man. A closer view (Figs. 8 and 9) brings out even greater peculiarities. The skull is long and flat, and the almost complete lack of a forehead and the great projecting ridge over the eyes give a look of stupidity and brutishness. (A similar development of the forehead and eyebrow ridges is seen in the chimpanzee and gorilla, but not in modern man). This appearance is further intensified by the large, broad, but not flat, nose; for the nose of Neanderthal man did not possess negroid characteristics. The enormous development of the face and the absence of a chin are also striking. Nothing is known of the colour of the skin and hair, or of the cast of countenance, but it is generally assumed that the skin was not black. The lower jaw is heavy and differs from that of modern man, among other characteristics, in having the wisdom teeth the largest and most useful of the molars, and not the least useful as in ours. The general impression is of a creature of low intelligence, notwithstanding the large brain, and of great physical strength. A shaggy covering of hair which probably covered the body increased the brutish appearance. The great size of the brain, which exceeds that of modern Europeans, was due to a great development of that region which was probably concerned primarily with the mere recording of the fruits of experience, rather than with the acquisition of great skill in the use of the hand and the attainment of the sort of knowledge that comes from manual experiment.[13]

Love of Ornament. Even in the Middle Paleolithic there seems to have been some love of ornamentation. The evidence for this is not strong but is indicated by the presence in caves of nodules of the black oxide of manganese, which was probably used to paint the body.

Care of the Dead. The care of the dead—whether to protect the living from malevolent spirits, to show affection and honour for the departed, or for other reasons—has occupied an important place in man's thought, and has inspired some of man's most stupendous and beautiful examples of architecture. Because of the warm climate of the Early Paleolithic, man seems to have lived in the open. If he buried his dead he did so in the soil of the river valleys and other places where he lived. Bodies so buried would soon disintegrate into dust

[13] G. Elliot Smith: "Essays on the Evolution of Man," p. 70.

and nothing would remain which could now be recognisable. When, in the Middle Paleolithic, man was forced by a cold climate to live in caves, he buried some of his dead in them. Burials in caves are much more favourable for preservation than those in the open. One of the oldest sepultures of man was discovered at Le Moustier, France. (Hence the term *Mousterian.*) For this reason it is very important. It is of a youth who was laid to rest in an attitude of sleep. The head rested on a small mound or pillow of flint fragments, and the right side of the face on the elbow of the right arm. Near the left hand, which was extended along the body, were a hand-ax, and a scraper of Mousterian type.

A family sepulture at La Ferrassie (Dordogne), France, discovered in 1909-11, is important in showing that a custom, which prevailed for many thousands of years thereafter, was in use then—namely, of flexing or folding the arms and legs against the body. This burial at La Ferrassie consisted of a man, a woman, and two children.

The people who made these burials must have had a belief in a life after death. Did they bind the limbs to the body to prevent the spirit of the dead from troubling the living? Was there a mixed feeling of fear, affection, and reverence?

Cannibalism is possibly indicated, but by no means proved, by the discovery of partly calcined human bones at Krapina, Croatia, which may have been the refuse of feasts on human flesh.

Distribution. The Middle Paleolithic (*Mousterian*) peoples ranged over a wider territory than did those of the Early Paleolithic. Their implements have been found in many parts of Europe, Africa, and Asia.

THE LATE PALEOLITHIC

The Late Paleolithic Peoples (Aurignacian, Solutrean, Magdalenian)—Man of the Modern Type Appears

Date. The evidence upon which to base an estimate of the duration of the Upper Paleolithic periods, and the dates of their beginning and close is so uncertain that all figures must be taken with reservation. According to one writer[1] the Upper Paleolithic began in Southwestern France about 12,000 B.C. and lasted until about 6,500 B.C., that is, it extended over a period of 5,000 or 6,000 years. According to another writer[2] the Upper Paleolithic began in Southwestern France about 18,000 B.C. and lasted about 7,000 years.

Cro-Magnon Race. Civilisation made a great bound forward when the Late Paleolithic peoples appeared in Europe. In physical characteristics and in brain, the dominant race of that time was modern in all essential features and is con-

FIG. 9.—Skull and brain sections of Chimpanzee, Pithecanthropus, Neanderthal, and Cro-Magnon Man. After McGregor. Note the increasing size and depth of the brain, the progressive elevation of the forehead, the forward growth of the brain cavity above the face, the reduction in size of the bony face and the retraction of the front part of the jaws. "No structure found in the brain of an ape is lacking in the human brain, and, on the other hand, the human brain reveals no formation that is not present in the brain of the gorilla or chimpanzee. The only distinctive feature of the human brain is a quantitative one." "The difference is only quantitative but its importance can not be exaggerated. In the anthropoid brain are to be recognized all those parts which have become so enormous in the human brain. It is the expansion of just those parts which have given man his powers of feeling, understanding, acting, speaking and learning."

sidered by all anthropologists as belonging to the same species as modern man, that is, to *Homo sapiens*. It is called the Cro-Magnon race because the first skeletons of these people were found in a rock shelter in a hamlet of that name near Les Eyzies, in the Dordogne, France. With a very few exceptions the men were tall, averaging about six feet, one and one-half inches in height, and of athletic build. The forehead typical

[1] Peake and Fleure, "Hunters and Artists," page 91.
[2] Montelius as quoted by Osborn and Reeds, Old and New Standards of Pleistocene Division in Relation to the Prehistory of Man, *Bull. Geol. Society of America,* vol. 33, 1922, page 470.

of this race is what we would term a fine one, and the top of the skull is high and well-rounded and not flattened as is the Neanderthal head (Fig. 9). The brain is much larger than the average to-day. The face is short and broad at the cheeks and the nose is narrow. The brow ridges are inconspicuous and very different from the beetling brows of the Neanderthal people (Fig. 8). The lower jaw is strong and the chin well-moulded. It was, in short, a superb race, both physically and mentally.

Against such a race as this the dull-witted Neanderthalers, who depended more on brute strength than on cunning, had little chance, and the new immigrants with their greater intelligence were soon able to exterminate them. It is possible that the Neanderthalers were covered with shaggy hair and were so repulsive in appearance that even the females were never taken by the Cro-Magnon men but were hunted like undesirable wild beasts.

Předmost Race. Skeletons of at least two other races have been found in Late Paleolithic deposits. The skeletons of one such race were discovered at Předmost, Moravia (see p. 27). The male skulls are large and have retreating foreheads and heavy brow ridges. However, in addition to these Neanderthal characteristics, they have well-developed chins and a shin bone which is typical of the Cro-Magnon people. The Předmost women were more modern in appearance and were not unlike many English and Scandinavian women of to-day.

Grimaldi Race. What may be another strain has been called by some authorities the Grimaldi race. Although possessing negroid characteristics it is closely allied to the Cro-Magnon race.

Origin of the Cro-Magnon Type. There is so much difference of opinion among anthropologists as to the origin of *Homo sapiens,* of which the Cro-Magnon race seems to have been the first to inhabit Europe, that it would be idle in this introductory chapter to do more than to state the problem. The great majority of anthropologists believe that the Later

Paleolithic peoples had their development in some continent
other than Europe, and did not reach the latter until the beginning of the Late Paleolithic. One writer,[14] however, im-
plies that *Homo sapiens* may have been evolved from the
Neanderthal race in Europe. He also states that "the Neanderthal form is a necessary stage of man's evolution; it is not
uniform in type either as to skull or skeleton, it shows plain
indications of progressive differentiation toward modern man;
and it is met with in a more or less dilute but still recognisable form in later humanity, even down to the present
day." [15]

Another writer has recently advanced the theory that
man and all his ancestors belonged to a superior line of beings which, throughout the whole of geologic time preceding
the Late Tertiary, had kept itself aloof from other verte-
brates. These creatures he calls "Dawn Men." [16]

If the Neanderthal type evolved into man of the modern
type, the intermediate stages must have been evolved before
the Middle Paleolithic (*Mousterian*).[17] It seems more probable that Neanderthal man was one of a number of offshoots
that left no descendants, and that modern man arose, long
before, from some other and common ancestor.

Weapons and Implements of the Late Paleolithic. Cro-
Magnon families were obliged to live in caves and rock-shelters because of the cold. Excavations in their caves have
brought to light many thousands of flint tools, and many
carved bone and reindeer horn objects. Because of this, we
probably have a fairly complete knowledge of their stone
and bone implements (Figs. 10 and 11). Of their wooden
implements, of which they must have had many more, we
know almost nothing.

[14] H. Hrdlicka: "The Peopling of the Earth." *Proc. Am. Phil. Soc.*, vol.
LXV, no. 3, 1926, pp. 150-156.
[15] Ibid.
[16] H. F. Osborn: "Why Central Asia?" *Natural History,* vol. XXVI, 1926,
pp. 263-269. See also W. K. Gregory and J. H. McGregor. Ibid., pp. 270-271.
[17] Arthur Keith: "The Antiquity of Man," 2nd ed., 1925 vol. I, p. 223.

As their weapons and implements were made of flint, bone, and wood, it is not surprising that the Cro-Magnon people invented many flint, horn, and bone tools for making, rounding, and straightening arrow and spear shafts, and for manufacturing other implements of wood and bone. As they were hunters and depended largely on the chase for food and clothing they needed tools to prepare the skins of the animals they

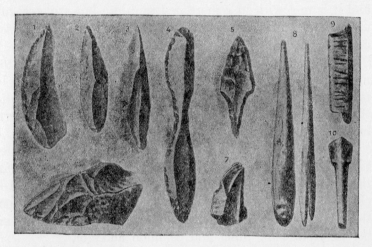

Fig. 10.—The characteristic tools made by Late Paleolithic man in the first half of this stage (*Aurignacian*). Flint implements such as those shown in this figure are found by the hundreds mixed with kitchen débris, in the caves and rock-shelters of France. (1) and (2) flint points of the type known as Châtelperron, (3) a cutting tool, (4) a notched flake, (5) a flake with a tang, (6) a thick scraper with a keel, (7) a graver, (8) a bone javelin point with a split base for the insertion of a wooden shaft, (9) and (10) bone objects. Note that the "retouching" is accomplished by "pressure flaking" and not by percussion. After Breuil. The figures are about one-half actual size.

killed, and consequently they made flint knives to cut the skins and scrapers to dress them. Small flint splinters and pointed bone tools were used for piercing the skins they made into clothing. They invented bone needles (Fig. 12) which they made from splinters of bone sawed to a convenient shape, burnished on sandstone, and pierced with fine flint drills. The bone needles were wonderfully well made, and some are, indeed, superior to those used in Roman times. Our steel needles are merely made of a different material. There is little doubt

FIG. 11.—Implements used near the close of the Paleolithic (*Magdalenian*). When Late Paleolithic man had attained his greatest skill as a painter and engraver, many of his flint implements were rather carelessly made. They are generally small, and many are but slightly retouched. Tools such as (2) and (3) are very common. They are called gravers (*burins*); the transverse chisel-end is believed to have been used to engrave ivory, bone, and stone. Many tools such as (2) and (3) were adapted for two uses; one end was used for engraving and the other for scraping. (1) is a double-ended scraper, (4) has a drill or piercer on one end and a scraper on the other, (5) is notched and was possibly used for smoothing small, cylindrical objects such as arrow shafts, (6) is a small flake trimmed for cutting, (7) is a javelin point, (8) is a bone piercer, (9) and (10) are bone needles, (11) is a javelin point, bevelled and curved, (12), (13), and (14) are bone harpoons, (12) is the older and (14) is the younger type. After Boule. About one-half actual size.

that wooden knives and many other tools and implements of wood were invented and used. These people also invented a harpoon which, in a modified form, was employed in Neolithic times.

Habits of the Mammoth Hunters at Předmost. Remarkable discoveries in brick clays at a depth of seven to eight feet, at Predmost, Moravia, give a picture of the life of the early part of the Late Paleolithic (*Aurignacian*) which is so accurate that it should be described here. These discoveries show that these ancient hunters were skilful in killing the

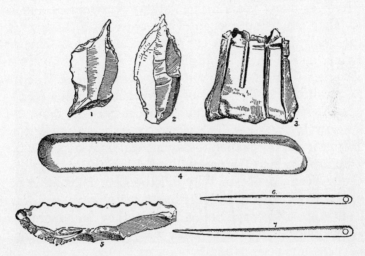

Fig. 12.—Tools for making needles consisted of (5) a flint saw for cutting out a splinter of bone, (4) a smooth piece of sandstone for polishing, and (1) and (2) fine pointed drills for making the eye. (3) shows a piece of bone from which splinters have been sawed, and (6) and (7) the finished needles.

mammoth and other large animals such as the cave bear, as the bones and tusks of more than 1,000 mammoths and many bones of the cave bear indicate. To hunt with the weapons they had required not only great courage and resourcefulness but also "team work" of a high order.

Předmost was an ideal place for the hunter because it was situated on one of the game routes of Prehistoric Europe. As the rigours of winter began to fall on the plains of Silesia and Poland, great herds of game were compelled to trek southward. One of the few routes open to them was the valley which led past the limestone shelters of Předmost. In the late spring and early summer when the return trek set in, and when the herds of mammoth and reindeer, accompanied by their camp followers, the bear, lion, and wolf, left the plains of the Danube and the central plains of Moravia, the Předmost lane again became a hunter's paradise.

Here for many years a population of perhaps a hundred lived. Here are found enough of the objects which they used in their daily life to enable one to tell something of their way of living, and of their intelligence.

Physical Characteristics of the Předmost People. The men were powerfully built [18] and of medium height, five feet, six inches. Although of the same species as modern man, they had heavy brow ridges. The women were more modern and their type is not uncommon to-day in Scandinavia and Britain. The brain was about ten percent larger than the average brain of the modern European. Why did the Late Paleolithic peoples, the Cro-Magnon and Predmost races, have such large brains? A possible explanation is that they had more need for them than does modern man, who, under modern conditions, does not need as much brain as he has to enable him to live in comfort. Contrast the conditions under which these ancient hunters lived with those of the average man of to-day. The mammoth hunter had to solve problems just as urgent and just as intricate as fall to our statesmen. Almost every day of his life depended on the quickness and effectiveness of his mental responses in the face of danger. Not only this, but he must make, not buy, his ornaments and his clothes. He must be his own physician and entertainer. He was on the broadcasting end of the radio; we are on the receiving end.

The Předmost peoples, moreover, were not satisfied with a mere existence but had commenced to embroider human life and make it a more lovely thing. They carved and engraved on bone and ivory; they used paints of at least three

[18] Modified after Sir Arthur Keith.

colours, as the pigments on stone palettes show; they made bone pins for the hair; they wore necklaces, pendants, and bracelets.

The Solutrean Technique. With the Upper Paleolithic deposits in Western Europe, especially in France and Northern Spain, are intercalated deposits which contain wonderfully

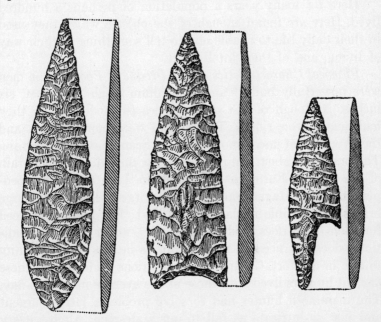

FIG. 13.—For a relatively short time finely wrought "laurel leaf" blades, and "shouldered points" were made. The technique is remarkable for the time. The flints are flaked on both sides and in skill and technique closely approach those of Neolithic times. (See Fig. 41, p. 88.) After Obermaier. Reduced in size.

fine flint blades (Fig. 13), rivalling those of the Neolithic in workmanship. These deposits are called Solutrean after the type station at Solutré, France. One can be quite sure that the earlier (*Aurignacian*) peoples of Europe did not gradually acquire this skill, and also that the flint technique of the later Magdalenian tribes was not derived from them. It is distinctly the work of a people with a high skill in working

flint who, for a comparatively short time, were in many parts
of Europe. There are two possible explanations: either it is
the work of a people who rapidly spread from the East into
Europe and who failed to reach Italy and Southern Spain, or
it is the work of slaves who were forced to labour for an alien
people. This last explanation is suggested by the fact that,

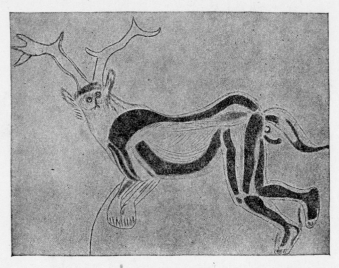

FIG. 14.—The sorcerer seems to have played a large part in the lives of the
Late Paleolithic hunters. This figure is in the cave of Les Trois Frères in
the foothills of the Pyrenees. It has the horns of a stag, an owl-like face,
ears of a wolf, the tail of a horse, and the feet of a man. It seems to
symbolize strength, fleetness, keen vision, and wisdom. After Count de
Bègouen and H. Breuil.

*Reproduced by the courtesy of The Hispanic Society of America from Obermaier's
"Fossil Man in Spain" (Yale University Press).*

with the exception of such implements as those shown in
Figure 13, most of the flint implements are no more skilfully
made than those of Aurignacian times.[19]

The Great Art of the Late Paleolithic. Religion and superstition seem to have played a large part in the life of Late

[19] H. Breuil suggests that the Solutrean technique was developed in Hungary and Slovakia and that the laurel leaf flint was developed from the
hand-ax. Peake and Fleure suggest that it may well have occurred in the
steppe-lands of western Asia.

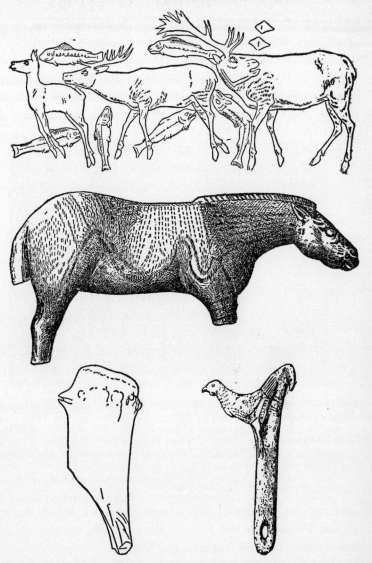

Fig. 15.—Some of the best engravings and carvings of the Late Paleolithic hunters. (*Top*) A restoration of what has been termed "the earliest picture in the world." After Lankester. (*Center*) Figure of a wild horse carved in ivory, Lourdes. (*Bottom left*) Figure of a bird's head on reindeer horn. After R. Schmidt. (*Bottom right*) A spear thrower carved in the form of a bird. After Breuil.

31

Paleolithic man and led to the development of an artistic skill which is the wonder of all artists and students. There seems little doubt that the people of that time were weighed down under a heavy load of superstitions and magic. Elaborate rites and ceremonials were developed, and probably the life and movements of the people were determined by the sorcerer (Fig. 14) or medicine man.[20] Cro-Magnon man carved and engraved the figures of animals, such as horses, reindeer, musk oxen, mammoths, foxes, stags, lizards, and fish on bone and horn (Fig. 15). The work varies greatly in merit: some of it is poorly executed, but some is truly remarkable. One of the best pieces of carving has been called "the earliest picture in the world" because it is a "composition." [21] It is an engraving on the antler of a deer representing a group of deer in movement. The largest stag is on the right; he is commencing to advance, and turns his head backwards to see what the thing is which has alarmed him and his companions. His mouth is open and he is "blowing." Next to the stag is a younger animal, and leading the group is a hind jumping on all four feet as young heedless deer do. The action is lifelike, and the drawing is true.

Remarkable sculptures of horses in high relief were found in the rock-shelter of Cap Blanc near Les Eyzies, France, buried in deposits of Magdalenian Age.

CAVE ART

Interesting as are these objects of art, the paintings and engravings on the walls and ceilings of the caves are much more so. To understand the art of Later Paleolithic times, and to form a judgment of the motives that led the artists to work in the well-nigh inaccessible recesses of caves, it is nec-

[20] An interesting novel "Bison of Clay" by M. de Bègouen, based on a knowledge of the Upper Paleolithic, gives a graphic picture of the probable power of the sorcerer, and the influence of superstition.
[21] Sir E. Ray Lankester: "Secrets of Earth and Sea," p. 10 ff.

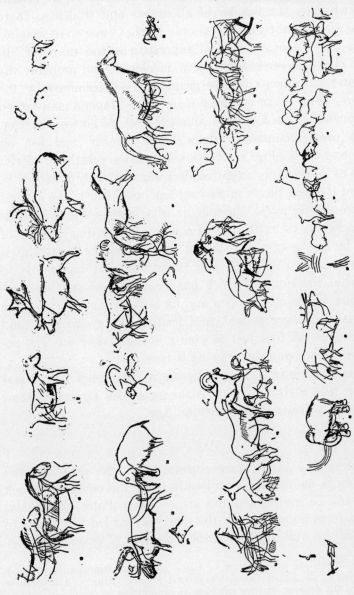

Fig. 16.—Some of the drawings in the Cave of Les Combarelles; horses, bison, reindeer, mammoths, and other animals. After H. Breuil.

essary to visit the caves in which this art is preserved. Only four of the many caves which contain the art of this ancient time will be described.

Cave of Combarelles. The first is that of Les Combarelles in the Dordogne, France.[22] This cave is a tortuous tunnel about 720 feet long, and so narrow and low in places as to make progress difficult. In this damp, difficult passage the artists made their drawings. But it should be noted that no figures are nearer the entrance than about 375 feet, that is, they were drawn where the light of day could never have penetrated. The artist was obliged to make his drawings from memory and by the dim light of a torch or of a wick fed by melting grease. In this cave are more than 400 drawings (Figs. 16 and 17) and engravings, many of which are well executed (but no polychrome paintings). The animals portrayed are 116 horses and asses, 37 bison, 19 bears, 14 reindeer, 13 mammoths, besides ibexes, wild oxen, stags, does, and lions, and a fox and a woolly rhinoceros. There are also a few poorly-drawn human figures with grotesque heads, which probably represent ceremonial masks or hunter's disguises.

Cavern of Font-de-Gaume. One of the most famous caves and, from the point of view of the development of art, the most important is that of Font-de-Gaume [23] (Fig. 18) at Les Eyzies in the Dordogne. On the sides and ceiling of a long, high, and wide smooth-walled cave, the artist engraved and painted in black, red, and brown, figures of more than 80 animals of which there are 49 bison, much like the American buffalo, 15 mammoths, 4 horses, a woolly rhinoceros, and 4 reindeer.

[22] L. Capitan; Abbé H. Breuil; D. Peyrony: "Les Combarelles aux Eyzies." 1924. A brief article by Abbé Breuil is to be found in Natural History, vol. XXVI, 1926, pp. 227-237.

[23] The splendid monograph, "La Caverne de Font-de-Gaume," by L. Capitan, Abbé Breuil, and D. Peyrony (1910), should be studied. The beautiful coloured plates give a vivid picture of the art. It is only after careful study that one can distinguish some of these engravings and paintings in the caves.

FIG. 17.—Photograph of an engraved figure of a woolly rhinoceros on the limestone wall of the Cave of Les Combarelles in the Dordogne, France. After H. Breuil.

This cave is especially important as it shows the development of Paleolithic art. It is possible to determine which are the older paintings because many of them are superposed: later artists paying no attention to earlier drawings, paintings, and engravings (Fig. 19), but engraving and painting new figures on a smooth or sacred surface with no regard for the pictures already there. The earliest pictures are the crudest and are merely in outline. From this beginning, successive generations of artists learned to make black frescoes of the

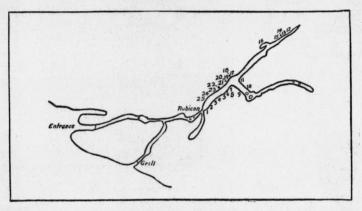

Fig. 18.—Map of the Cave of Font-de-Gaume. The drawings and paintings indicated by the numbers were made by the faint light of a grease lamp or a torch and were drawn from memory. After Capitan.

horse, reindeer, and bison with lifelike accuracy. Later, after engraving the outlines and some of the details, they coloured the figures in red, brown, and black. There was no apparent attempt to produce the colour or surface markings of the animals.

Cave of Altamira. To the author's mind, two of the most impressive sights in Europe are to be seen in two other caves: one in Northwestern Spain and one in the foothills of the Pyrenees in France. The first of these is the Cave of Altamira, near the town of Santillana, in Spain. In this cave, there is a low chamber about forty by sixty feet and three to

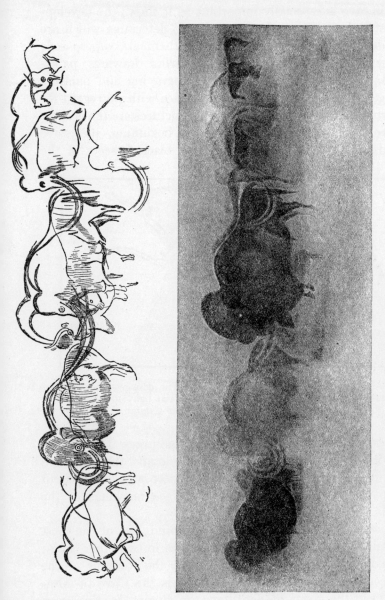

Fig. 19. The artist first made an engraving of the animal he wished to paint as is shown in this illustration. Note how earlier drawings are marred by later ones. It has been suggested that the artist may have covered the earlier paintings and drawings with blood and on this as a background made new pictures as on a new canvass. After H. Breuil.

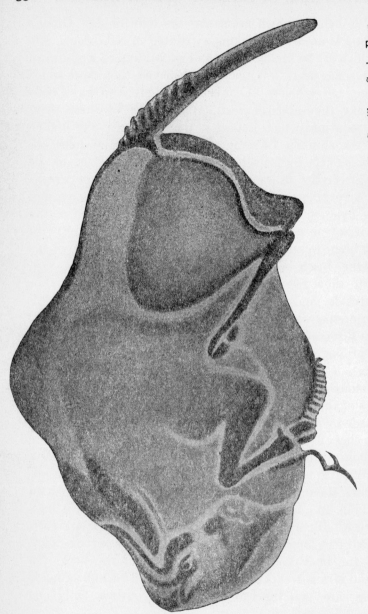

FIG. 20. This polychrome painting is to be seen on the ceiling of the Cave of Altamira, Santillana, Spain. Four shades of colour were used. The artist first engraved the outline and some of the details and then applied the colours. The posture of the animal was adapted to an irregularity of the rock surface. This painting is about five feet two inches long.

Reproduced by the courtesy of The Hispanic Society of America from Obermaier's "Fossil Man in Spain" (Yale University Press).

six feet in height, which never saw the light of day. On the low ceiling is an array of animals painted in red, brown, and black which are so lifelike in pose (Fig. 20) and so well-drawn that for some years few scientists believed they were old.[24] They are, nevertheless, the work of artists who have been dead many thousands of years. One feature of these polychrome paintings which impresses the observer is the lifelike pose of the animals. In some of the paintings the artist obtained this effect by utilising the natural irregularities of the roof to give relief to his paintings. As some of these irregularities were pillow-shaped bosses four or five feet long, and three or four feet wide, they were admirably adapted to the artist's use. One painting shows a bellowing bull bison with his back arched and limbs drawn under him as if to expel the air; another bison is portrayed as lying down in such a position as to show the soles of his feet. A wild boar, in a running attitude, and other striking paintings attest the skill of these prehistoric artists.

Clay Bison of Tuc d'Audoubert. The second of these caves is that of Tuc d'Audoubert in the foothills of the Pyrenees. About a half mile from the present entrance of the cave is a large chamber with a clay-covered floor. Claw marks and the imprints of the great paws of the cave bears, and the impressions made by their hairy hides where they had leaned against the soft clay of the walls, and even where they had lain down, are plainly visible. Some jaw bones of cave bears which had been broken so as to remove the teeth, probably for charms, were lying about. Near the centre of the chamber are two bisons (Fig. 21) modelled in clay: a bison cow and a bull, and beneath them a little calf. The bull and cow are each about two feet long. The cow is carefully modelled: the contour of the body and legs, the long hair of the neck, the horns and straight ears are skilfully made. The bull is made with less care, and the calf is merely in outline. Only one

---

[24] H. F. Cleland: "Weathering under Constant Conditions." *Science,* vol. LVI, no. 1458. 1922, pp. 660-661.

side of each bison is completely modelled, the other side, which is leaning against a rock fallen from the roof, is not finished. No doubt these bison—a bison cow followed by a bull half-rearing on its hind legs, and a calf—symbolised the fertility of the herd, and the little calf represented the calf the cow was to bring forth. By making these images, the tribe assured a plentiful supply of bison for the coming season. The opening into the cave was probably closed at the time

FIG. 21.—Models of bison found in the Cave of Tuc d'Audoubert. The statuettes are modelled in clay. The bison cow in front is more carefully executed than the bull. After Count de Bégouen.

Reproduced by the courtesy of The Hispanic Society of America from Obermaier's "Fossil Man in Spain" (Yale University Press).

the models were made, for there is no evidence that it was again visited by man until its discovery in 1912 by the sons of the Count de Bégouen.

The figures are slightly cracked but probably are in nearly the same condition they were a month after their making. It is evident that artists who could make these statuettes from memory, by dim artificial light, must have had much experience, and it is probable that scores of models were made by them in different places, but, being of so perishable a material as clay, only those modelled in a moist, undisturbed

This famous painting which shows the costumes of women, apparently dancing about a nude male idol is from the rock-shelter of Cogul, Lerida, Spain. The women are shown wearing skirts and caps. The figures of animals of the chase, which probably have no relation to the human figures, are well executed.

About ½ natural size. After J. Cabré. Reproduction by the courtesy of the Hispanic Society of America from Obermaier's FOSSIL MAN IN SPAIN (Yale University Press)

cave like that of Tuc d'Audoubert were preserved. This wonderful cave and the sight of these statuettes of extinct animals, made of the most perishable materials, by artists who lived thousands of years before the dawn of the Egyptian civilisation, is to-day one of the most impressive sights in the world.

Mutilated Models of Montespan. In the cavern of Montespan (Haute Garonne), France, there are clay models of

FIG. 22.—A hunter following the tracks of an animal. From the Cave of Morella la Vella, Castellón, Spain. After E. Hernández-Pacheco.

Reproduced by the courtesy of The Hispanic Society of America from Obermaier's 'Fossil Man in Spain" (Yale University Press).

bears and other animals which have been mutilated by javelin thrusts. Here, again, a magical significance is evident. The artist purposely mutilated his models in order to put the animals represented into the power of the hunters of his tribe.

Art in Southern and Eastern Spain. An Upper Paleolithic people who lived in Eastern and Southeastern Spain, but with different traditions and religious rites, also left a realistic art. One marked difference between this art and that of Northern Spain, and France is the frequent occurrence of human figures. The lifelike action of many of these paintings is striking (Figs. 22 and 23). Not infrequently, the artist combined human figures and animals in groups or compositions (Plate II). The pictures, with few exceptions, are painted, not engraved. They are on the rear walls of shallow recesses in rock-shelters, probably because deep caves are rare in that region. The human figures are only about two and a half to six inches in height.

Why Paintings Were Made. Attention has been called to the fact that the Cro-Magnon artist made one drawing on

Fig. 23.—Two stags painted in red on the wall of a rock-shelter at Calapatá, Teruel, Spain. Note the lifelike pose and drawing. One-sixth natural size. After J. Cabré.

Reproduced by the courtesy of The Hispanic Society of America from Obermaier's *"Fossil Man in Spain"* (Yale University Press).

another, the earlier being ruined (Fig. 19) by the later. Another significant fact is, that with few exceptions, the animals portrayed are those especially prized for food, chiefly bison, reindeer, and horses. One writer [25] in discussing this matter says: "When we find them piling reindeer upon reindeer, bison upon bison, till there are hundreds of such figures spread with no apparent purpose over the cave walls; when we find these drawings made in the dark where no one can see them, and when we find them recklessly mutilated after

[25] R. A. S. Macalister: "A Text-book of European Archaeology. pp. 508-509.

they have served their purpose, we may be sure some more recondite explanation than mere æsthetics must be sought for them." Most students of the subject believe that the motive which inspired these artists is to be found in sympathetic magic. They hold that the Cro-Magnon people believed that a desired result could be accomplished by mimicking it. Consequently, when the men were about to go on a hunt, they made a picture of the animal they hoped to kill because they believed that by so doing an animal like that portrayed would be found and would succumb to their skill. The explanation most in favour, then, is that these drawings were made because these remote ancestors of ours thought by so doing they could so charm the animals of the chase as to put them in their power.

Belief in the Hereafter. It is not surprising to find evidence that these people had a belief in the existence of a life after death. The evidence for this belief is based largely upon their burial customs. The dead were reverently interred with the weapons, ornaments, and implements they had used during life. In some cases, the flesh was removed from the bones, the bones painted red, and after being placed in the grave in a position as nearly relative or natural as possible, were buried. The evidence of a belief in a future life can best be presented by describing a grave which was excavated in the Cave of Grimaldi near Mentone, France. "There were three persons in the grave; a tall man, a young woman, and a boy of about 15 years. A pit had been dug and lined with red ochreous powder; in it the bodies were stretched at full length, or only slightly bent. On the man's head were canine teeth of deer, drilled for suspension; fish vertebræ and small shells, also perforated, the whole being the ornaments of a sort of cap or crown. On the neck was a breast ornament of the same materials, and a flint knife about ten inches long. The boy's skeleton had an elaborate crown of fish vertebræ and shells on the head and a collar consisting of two rows of fish vertebræ (Fig. 24) and one of nassa shells, divided into groups by deer's teeth. On the foreheads of the skeletons were some remarkable ornaments of bone, shaped like two eggs end to end." [26]

It does not seem probable that people would bury with their dead the finest of their flint tools, implements and ornaments, unless they believed these possessions would be used in a future existence. An alternative suggestion is that the tools, weapons, and ornaments of the dead were buried with their owners because it would be unlucky for the living to use them.

FIG. 24.—Necklace of fish vertebræ, deer teeth, and shells found in a grave at Mentone, France. After A. J. Evans.

Of the many races of prehistoric men, including our Neolithic ancestors, none appeals to the imagination as does this race of tall, big-brained, artistic hunters, men who lived when the mammoth and woolly rhinoceros, the reindeer, the bison, and herds of wild horses roamed over Southern Europe, and when Sweden was still covered with a great ice sheet, men who, long before the beginnings of art in Egypt and Greece, had, with the crudest tools, but impelled by an overwhelming desire to portray faithfully the animals they hunted, created an art of a high order.

CLIMATE

How Climate is Determined. The climate of the Paleolithic is known chiefly from the animals which were man's con-

[26] R. A. S. Macalister: "A Text-book of European Archæology," p. 356.

temporaries (see table, p. 46). The animals whose bones are found in deposits containing his artifacts, the plants of his time, his skeletons, his drawings and paintings on cave walls, and his engravings and carvings on horn and bone, show the life of his time. When the reindeer, the mammoth (whose body was protected by long hair and a thick undercoating of wool), the woolly rhinoceros, and animals that now live in the arctic regions were present, we say that the climate was cold. If there are many bones of horses and bison, we say steppe conditions, somewhat like those of the high plains of the United States or the steppes of Russia and Mongolia, prevailed. When elephants (other than the mammoths), rhinoceroses (other than the woolly rhinoceros), hippopotami, and other animals that now live in tropical or subtropical regions were present, it is evident that the climate was warm.

Man's principal development and prehistory took place during the Ice Age or Pleistocene. Now, the Ice Age (see table, p. 46) was not a time of continuous cold but, in Europe, was made up of four cold stages of great duration separated by three long warmer interglacial stages. In fact, the second interglacial stage lasted possibly 100,000 years. The climate in Europe at that time was warmer than now, and Southern England was almost tropical.

When Paleolithic Man Lived. Upper Paleolithic man is known to have lived (see table, p. 46) in the last, or fourth glacial stage. He was contemporaneous with the reindeer, the mammoth, and the woolly rhinoceros. Middle Paleolithic man (*Mousterian*) lived at the beginning of this last glaciation and probably during the close of the third interglacial stage. There is a general agreement among prehistorians and geologists on this point. However, an accurate correlation of the Early Paleolithic (*Prechellean, Chellean,* and *Acheulean*) with the earlier glacial and interglacial stages is impossible in the present state of our knowledge. It is seldom that two investigators agree. It seems probable to the writer that the

CHRONOLOGICAL TABLE OF

Climate	Animal Life
Climate nearly as at present.	Animals of living species. Domesticated animals.
Slightly cooler than now.	No domestic animals except (possibly) the dog.
Cold of the last phases of glaciation. Man lived in caves.	Reindeer abundant during most of this time, woolly rhinoceros, mammoth.
4th and last glacial stage (Würm). Life in caves. Cold and moist.	Mammoth, woolly rhinoceros, reindeer.
3rd interglacial stage (Riss-Würm). Climate mild. Life probably in the open.	Hippopotamus, straight tusked elephant, Merck's rhinoceros.
3rd glacial stage (Riss).	Mammoth, woolly rhinoceros, reindeer, arctic fox, lemming.
2nd interglacial stage (Mindel-Riss).	Straight tusked elephant (E. antiquus), Merck's rhinoceros, deer, bison.
2nd glacial stage (Mindel).	Arctic mollusks on English Coast.
1st interglacial stage (Günz-Mindel).	Warm flora and fauna.
1st glacial stage (Günz).	Arctic fauna.
Pliocene.	

* The length of the Pleistocene or glacial period is in doubt but at least 1,000,000 years seem to be a fair estimate.
† H. F. Osborn and C. A. Reeds [1] place the Lower Paleolithic in the 2nd interglacial stage, and the Eolithic in the 1st interglacial and 2nd glacial stages. R. A. Smith [2] places the Lower Paleolithic in the 2nd interglacial and 2nd glacial stages.

age of the hand-ax (*coup de poing*) (*Chellean* and *Acheulean*) was during the long third interglacial stage. It may, however, have begun much earlier. The above-given table is perhaps as definite as the known facts warrant.

DETERMINATION OF THE SEQUENCE OF CULTURES

There are several kinds of evidence that enable the student of prehistory to determine the period or stage in which human artifacts were used: (1) the order of superposition, (2) the preservation, and the amount of the mineralisation

EARLY MAN IN EUROPE *

Human Periods	Men of Prehistoric Times
Iron, Bronze, and Neolithic Ages.	Modern Man (Homo sapiens).
Epipaleolithic (*Azilian, Maglemose*).	Homo sapiens.
The larger part of the Late Paleolithic (*Magdalenian, Solutrean,* and possibly part of the *Aurignacian*).	Homo sapiens: Cro-Magnon, Grimaldi, Předmost, etc.
Aurignacian, and part of the Middle Paleolithic (*Mousterian*).	Neanderthal Man (Homo neanderthalensis).
Probably Early Mousterian. Early Paleolithic (*Acheulean* a n d *Chellean*)†	
Possibly the Chellean began as early as the 2nd interglacial stage.	The time at which Heidelberg, and Piltdown men lived is in doubt. Some authorities consider them to have been nearly contemporaneous, others believe they were separated by thousands of years.
Eoliths and crudely shaped tools.	
Eoliths are found in late Pliocene deposits at Cromer, Ipswich, etc., England, and elsewhere.	Pithecanthropus lived either at the close of the Pliocene or early in the Pleistocene.

[1] *Bull. Geol. Soc. Am.*, vol. 33, p. 471, 1922.
[2] "Stone Age Antiquities of the Brit. Mus.," 3rd ed., 1926.

of bones, (3) the contemporary animals, (4) the kinds and technique of implements, (5) the art, (6) the skeletons of man himself.

Deposits in Caves. It is fortunate for the study of prehistoric man that, for 20,000 years and more, man lived in caves for at least a part of the year. While he lived in such habitations he brought in mud on his feet, he left scattered about the bones of his meals, the ashes of his hearth-fire, and the rubbish of a none too clean family. By such accumulations, the floor was slowly raised. In the dirt of the floor, flints were embedded as they were lost and trampled on in the semi-darkness of the cavern. This happened also to great quantities of flakes chipped off in making tools. After living in a cave for a time, the family would be compelled to move because of the scarcity of game, and perhaps for many years the cave would be unoccupied except by wild animals. During this interval, a layer of dirt would accumulate on the floor which would contain no human artifacts; in other words, a sterile layer would be formed. Again the cave would be occupied by the same race or by a later one and another layer containing flints and the bones of animals would be added to the floor. By intermittent occupation for thousands of

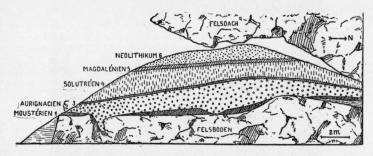

Fig. 24a.—Profile of Grotto du Trilobite. This cave was intermittently occupied by prehistoric man until it was nearly filled with débris. It was the home successively of Mousterian, Aurignacian, Solutrean, Magdalenian, and Neolithic families.

years, some cave floors were built up layer by layer until the openings were nearly filled (Fig. 24a). It is evident that these layers are the leaves of the great book of Prehistory and their contents the language of the past. By their study, the kinds of tools used by successive races are known. When skeletons were buried with flint tools it is possible to learn what tools were used by their possessors. A study of the bones of the animals in any layer tells what animals were contemporaneous with the man of the time. The animals and plants give a definite clue to the climate.

The Dordogne of France is a region of thick limestone strata in which streams have cut deep valleys with steep sides (Fig. 25). These limestone cliffs contain rock-shelters and caves from some of which springs of clear water flow. The conditions were ideal for a people who were obliged to live in natural rock-shelters as a protection from the cold of a

FIG. 25.—A typical view along the Vézère River, Les Eyzies, France. The conditions were favourable for hunters who required a natural shelter. There were rock-shelters and caves under the cliffs, fish in the river, and flint in the rocks. Photo by the Author.

glacial climate (Fig. 26). It was here that man lived for an immense stretch of time. Some of the rock-shelters of the Dordogne were intermittently inhabited for thousands of years, and in some of them man is living to-day.

Fig. 26.—How Paleolithic man kept warm in open rock-shelters during the cold winters is puzzling. The opening of the shelter shown in the illustration is nearly closed by icicles and may explain how some rock-shelters were made habitable. After T. C. Brown.

During a large part of the Early Paleolithic, man apparently did not often live in caves and rock-shelters. This was because of a congenial climate which enabled him to live in the open, especially on the terraces bordering rivers. On these terraces he lost some of his flint tools which were later covered by deposits of gravel and rainwash. On these new surfaces he also lost flints. When the gravels of such terraces (Fig. 27) are excavated for the use of modern man some of

Fig. 27.—In the sand quarry at Chelles in the Marne valley, there are two alluvial deposits, one below the line x-x containing crude Chellean flint implements and the upper containing Acheulean and later flints. Photo after D'Acy.

these lost tools are recovered, the older and cruder Chellean hand-axes occurring in gravels which underlie those containing the younger and more skilfully made Acheulean ones. In this way the relative age of the flints is determined. Consequently, when flint tools are picked up on the surface of the ground, in river gravels, or elsewhere, it is possible to determine their age by comparing them with implements the age of which is definitely known.

One of the most complete records known from a single cave is that from the cavern of Castillo, near Santander, Spain. From the top to the bottom, the deposits built up on the floor of the cave yielded twenty-five layers, as follows:[27]

25. Recent detritus.

24. *Early Bronze or Copper Age.*

23. *Epipaleolithic.* Azilian industry with flat harpoons.

22. Stalagmitic deposit.

21-19. *Late Paleolithic.* Two deposits containing Early and Late Magdalenian industries separated by a nearly sterile layer. The earlier of the two was nearly six feet thick with many bone and horn artifacts, some of which were engraved. There were also human remains.

18. A nearly sterile clay layer.

17. Solutrean.

16. A clay layer.

15-8. Four layers containing Aurignacian industries separated by clay layers.

7. Stalagmitic layer.

6-4. *Middle Paleolithic.* Two Mousterian layers separated by a clay layer.

3. Stalagmitic deposit.

2-1. *Early Paleolithic.* (2) A layer containing Acheulean hand-axes and other tools. (1) Resting on the original floor of the cave was a layer of clay containing a few poorly worked flints and the remains of hearth-fires.

Such a series of deposits as this of the Cave of Castillo is unique. It was only by comparing the deposits of many caves that the history of the Paleolithic was first obtained. It is as if one were attempting to obtain a complete story from a dozen or more copies of a history, from each of which many leaves had been torn. If none of the copies contained certain pages, some of the facts would necessarily be in doubt.

[27] Modified from H. Obermaier's "Fossil Man in Spain." pp. 162-163.

THE DEBT OF THE NEOLITHIC TO THE LATE PALEOLITHIC

Civilisation's debt to the Late Paleolithic peoples is large but difficult to estimate. A people depending upon hunting for food cannot attain a high culture, no matter how intelligent, nor how great their innate mental capacity. They may, nevertheless, invent many of the fundamental arts and crafts of civilisation and may need but a new environment to bring them to full fruition. Consequently, when agriculture was invented, and animals were domesticated, the change from the life of a hunter to that of a farmer would be made with hardly a break.

Neolithic man's knowledge of hunting was largely acquired from his Paleolithic ancestors. The use of the javelin, the bow and arrow, the harpoon, the construction of traps and other hunting lore, were all known before Neolithic times.

Their excellent and numerous bone needles show that the Late Paleolithic peoples sewed skins together, probably after they had been cut to a pattern. It is also probable these skins were either tanned or chewed to pliability, as the Eskimo women treat them to-day. There is reason for thinking that some of the garments were decorated with artistic coloured designs such as that shown in Figure 15, page 31. The eyed needle was one of the important inventions which the Neolithic owes to the Paleolithic.

Another invention was the kindling of fire by the use of flint and pyrite. Before this method was acquired, fire could only be obtained from some other hearth.

The Late Paleolithic peoples doubtless made many wooden utensils, such as bowls, spoons, ladles, boxes, mortars, and pestles, and they may have sewed skins to make containers for liquids, calking the seams with resin or asphalt to make them water-tight.

The ornaments used in Early Neolithic times did not differ greatly from those of the preceding age. The practice of wearing necklaces, partly for ornament and partly as amulets, was an inheritance from the past. Paleolithic man used red and yellow ochre to paint his body, and perhaps for tattooing. This may have been for adornment, for tribal symbols, or as a protective charm. How much of this custom was passed on is not known.

Elaborate coiffures (Fig. 28, (1) (2)) are shown on Paleolithic statuettes and may have been invented by the Cro-Magnon people.

The fact that the Cro-Magnon races had ceremonial dances indicates that some sort of music was produced. They probably had rattles, drums, whistles and flageolets, but as such instruments would have been made of perishable materials no record of them would be left.

The religion of Neolithic times was, in part at least, a modification of that of earlier times. In it the sorcerer was, with little doubt, an important personage and the use of spells and magic were essential features. Ceremonial dances were probably as important as in Paleolithic times, but were of a somewhat different character as the harvest had become more important than the hunt. As a result, a host of new traditions and rites had developed.

The Paleolithic female statuettes (Fig. 28) were either idols or fetiches and were the forerunners of the Neolithic idols (Fig. 54, p. 123).

Attention should be called to the use of red—the life-giving colour—in painting the bodies and skeletons of the dead, a custom which continued for many centuries after the Paleolithic.

What can be said about the truly extraordinary art of the Upper Paleolithic? Did it leave no impress upon the Neolithic agriculturists? Did artistic skill disappear with the Paleolithic? There is not a shred of evidence that this great art was handed down to the newer peoples. The art of the Cro-Magnon race was developed because of the necessity (so they thought) of making lifelike images of the game animals they wished to put under their power or whose fecundity they wished to increase. When this necessity was no longer felt the artists turned to other work. The decadence of Paleolithic art may also have been due to its replacement

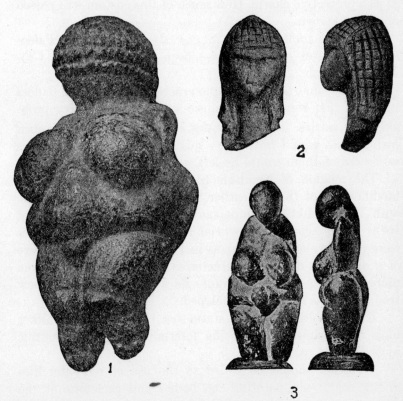

FIG. 28.—These three female figurines from the Late Paleolithic (Aurignacian) are characteristic of the idols or fetiches of this early period. (1) The Willendorf statuette, 4½ inches high, is from the loess of Willendorf, Lower Austria, and is called the Willendorf Venus. (2) A carved ivory head showing the arrangement of the hair. After E. Piette. (3) A statuette of a woman carved from soapstone, about 2 inches high. Mentone. After S. Reinach.

by other arts and industries. It is well known that when the development of the art of making stone vases was in progress in Egypt, there was a corresponding decline in the skill of the potter, and that with the introduction of metals, a marked

decadence in the working of flint set in. So in the Neolithic
Age, when pottery, agriculture, cattle-raising, and weaving,
were first introduced, the attention of the people was focused
on these things, that is, on the learning and perfecting of the
new arts and crafts. Another and important reason for the
decadence of art was the arrival of new immigrants with their
own interests and with, perhaps, little artistic feeling. The
best does not always survive.

Chapter II

THE EPIPALEOLITHIC [1]

THE AGE OF PYGMY FLINTS. THE INTERVAL BETWEEN THE
PALEOLITHIC AND NEOLITHIC

$Equivalents:$ The Epipaleolithic consists of:
Tardenoisian (France)
Azilian   " $\Big\}$ = Maglemose (Scandinavia)
Final Capsian (Spain)

Dates: It began about 5500 B.C. in Scandinavia, and perhaps as early as
6500 B.C. in Spain. Some writers date the beginning in France 11000 B.C.

THE Epipaleolithic (Greek, *epi* upon, *paleolithic*) is
termed the Age of Bone by some Swedish prehistorians but
although the term is appropriate in Scandinavia where bone
was the principal material used in making tools, it is not
descriptive of the culture of Southern France where, with the
exception of harpoons, bone was little employed. A more descriptive term is the "Age of Pygmy Flints or Microliths," since
minute, carefully worked flints were generally used not only in
Northern and Southern Europe but also in Northern Africa.

Hardly had the great Paleolithic cave artists reached the
climax of their artistic skill when nearly all record of them
ceases. Instead of finely carved bone and horn objects and a
truly marvellous mural and plastic art, the objects discovered
in the next later deposits are those of inartistic hunters and
fishermen. Moreover, when the skulls of these people are
studied it is found that they differ from those of most of the
Paleolithic races of Europe. This does not mean that the

[1] The term Epipaleolithic is preferable to Mesolithic because this age is
in no sense a period of transition but "merely represents the last activities
of hunting tribes while it never appears as the preliminary settlements of
Neolithic Man."

Upper Paleolithic type was entirely obliterated, for it has been shown that, in the Cévennes of France, as late as the Neolithic, the inhabitants belonged exclusively to the Upper Paleolithic race. (The geological age of the skeletons is proved by the Neolithic arrows (Fig. 29) which pierce them.) It is probable that many of the Late Paleolithic peoples followed to the North the reindeer and other game to which they were accustomed, as an ameliorating climate forced these animals to migrate to colder regions. The total number of the Late

Fig. 29.—A part of the backbone of a Late Paleolithic man which is pierced by a Neolithic arrow. After Boule.

Paleolithic inhabitants could not have been large at any time. It was not until a constant supply of food from agriculture and domestic animals was available that a large population could exist. It is not surprising, therefore, that the late Paleolithic peoples left so little impress on the physical type and mental qualities of their successors.

THE INDUSTRIES OF THE EPIPALEOLITHIC

When compared with the handiwork of the Late Paleolithic peoples, the implements of this later stage seem poor indeed. The larger flint tools are rough; the bone implements in Southern France, with the exception of the flat harpoon (Fig. 30) which, though crude in appearance, was probably more effective than the more artistic Late Paleolithic harpoons (see Fig. 11, p. 26), are of inferior workmanship. In Scandinavia, however, these people used a considerable variety of small bone and deerhorn implements as well as deerhorn hammers, axes, and harpoons (Fig. 31).

FIG. 30.—Characteristic Epipaleolithic harpoons of Southern Europe with a hole for the attachment of a thong. Fig. 31 shows a somewhat different type which was used in Scandinavia at about the same time.

Reproduced by the courtesy of The Hispanic Society of America from Obermaier's "Fossil Man in Spain" (Yale University Press).

"It is possible that if we knew more about the Azilians we should find that they were not so retrograde as their relics would seem to imply. There is reason to believe they had succeeded in taming the dog, and the assistance of this faithful companion in the hunt might well compensate for a want of finish in their weapons. Their poverty in art may be admitted and deplored, but it would be unfair to judge them by this alone; indeed, we might ourselves as a practical people protest against any criticism of our civilisation which should be based exclusively on, say, our sculpture or our architecture.

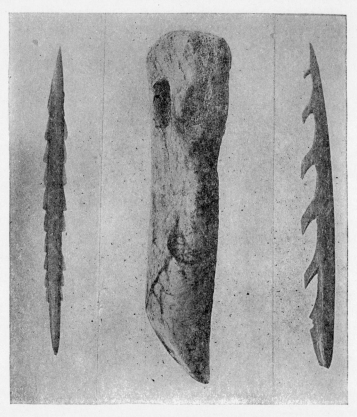

Fig. 31.—Harpoon set with pygmy flints, a deerhorn ax, and a deerhorn harpoon, Scandinavia. After Lindquist. Reduced in size.
Courtesy of the National Museum, Stockholm, Sweden.

"There is a difficulty in determining by what standard the civilisation of a hunting race is to be judged. If for the sake of illustration we take the social organisation, then on the whole the Red Indian might rank before the Eskimo. Yet if all we knew about these two races was derived solely from such of their implements as are likely to be preserved to future ages, we might fairly give the palm to the Eskimo. As to their work in flint the Indian is no doubt the superior, but in ivory all the advantages are on the other side. The Eskimo also has the needle, while the Red Indian is content with the awl. Pottery of course must be reckoned to the Indian, but the vessels carved out of soapstone by the Eskimo are an ingenious substitute and much better adapted to the conditions under which he lives.

"The Eskimo, however, does not work in ivory from choice, but because wood is a rare and costly substitute; the Indian uses wood because, while satisfying all his requirements, it is at the same time easily obtained and easy to work. So it may have been with the people of the Azilian age."[2]

It should be borne in mind that the Late Paleolithic peoples had an excellent material in reindeer horn which the Epipaleolithic peoples lacked. Reindeer horn is solid throughout and can be worked and carved much as ivory, whereas staghorn has a spongy centre and only the outside is dense and suitable for implements. It is also probable that the Epipaleolithic peoples of France and Spain made use of some tough, dense wood instead of the more intractable bone and horn. The absence of such a wood in the north may have forced the Scandinavians to use the more durable bone and horn.

The most striking characteristic of the age and one of the most puzzling is the abundance of small, carefully-made flint objects. These are called *pygmy flints* or *microliths* (Fig. 32) and found in many parts of the Old World. They are of a number of shapes: some are tiny blades; some are knife edges; some have a curved back and a straight sharp edge, in shape like a half-moon; some are like little graving tools and scrapers; and some are minute triangles with trimmed edges. Many of the pygmy flints were probably inserted into wooden han-

[2] W. J. Sollas: "Ancient Hunters," 3rd ed., pp. 596-7.

dles or in rows in wooden shafts (see Fig. 31), and were held in position by resin or some other cement. Some light is thrown on the subject by the discovery in England of thirty-five such flakes arranged in a line at intervals of one and a half to two inches. The suggestion is that they were the teeth of a saw or the barbs of a large harpoon, set originally in a grooved piece of wood, of which no trace remains,[3] Bone har-

Fig. 32.—Characteristic pygmy flints or microliths of the Epipaleolithic. Some of these carefully chipped flints were used in harpoons (see Fig. 31) but the use to which most of them were put is in doubt. This is called the Age of Pygmy Flints because these strange objects are characteristic of the time. After H. Breuil.

Reproduced by the courtesy of The Hispanic Society of America from Obermaier's "Fossil Man in Spain" (Yale University Press).

poons of the Neolithic age with a groove on one or both sides in which a row of flints had been inserted have been found. Pygmy flints continued in use in Neolithic and Bronze age times, but, after the Epipaleolithic, they were not made with care nor in great variety. Although few uses for pygmy flints, except for harpoons, saws, and other similar tools, has been suggested, their great variety, and the great care expended in

[3] "British Museum Guide to Stone Age Antiquities," 3rd ed., 1926, p. 89.

their manufacture leads one to think that the principal uses are not known. If they were used for tattooing, as some prehistorians suggest, the operation would not have required a great number of sharp points.

Art of the Epipaleolithic. The art of the Late Paleolithic had completely disintegrated and now consisted merely of crude geometric designs painted on pebbles (Fig. 33) and cave walls. The painted pebbles were found in the Department of Ariège, Southern France, in the natural tunnel of Mas d'Azil, through which the River Arise flows. They were painted either with the tip of the finger or a brush in lines and simple patterns. The paint employed is red ochre, probably mixed with fat, as the thickness of the colour shows. Scallop shells on which the paint was mixed, with the colour adhering, were also found in the cave. Similar painted pebbles have been found elsewhere. The designs painted on these pebbles and on cave walls in Spain are interpreted as representing various generalisations of human figures. A comparative study of the petroglyphs and the designs on the painted pebbles seems to prove this (see Fig. 33). Conventionalised animals were also made. It is possible that some of the designs may represent the beginnings of hieroglyphics.

Maglemose. While the Epipaleolithic peoples of France, Spain and elsewhere in Southern and Central Europe were making and using pygmy flints, a people with a similar culture was living in the lands about the Baltic. This was when Lake Ancylus was in existence and when it was possible to go on dry land from Denmark to Sweden.

The best known station of this culture is that of Maglemose (Great Bog) in Denmark and the culture is therefore called the Maglemose. Here, on rafts of pine logs anchored to the bottom of a shallow lake (which has since become a bog by the accumulation of peat) there lived a community of fishermen who also trapped wild fowl, and hunted the aurochs and elk. The kitchen refuse from the rafts was thrown into the lake, and many implements were dropped

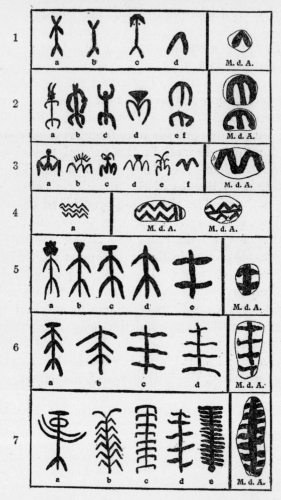

FIG. 33.—A comparison of the figures on painted pebbles from Mas d'Azil and the petroglyphs found on cave walls in Spain. Some of these may be the first hieroglyphics. (1) Conventionalised female figures. (2) Male figures. (3) Seated male and female figures. (4) Seated figures. (5) Standing male figures. (6) Standing male figures showing head, torso, arms, girdle, legs and penis. The Mas d'Azil design shows a purely geometric figure. (7) Standing figures. Perhaps this Mas d'Azil painting represents several persons. M. d. A.=Mas d'Azil. After Obermaier.

Reproduced by the courtesy of The Hispanic Society of America from Obermaier's "Fossil Man in Spain" (Yale University Press).

into the water and lost. As a consequence, many examples of their work have been preserved. They consist of bone and horn implements such as harpoons, spears, and chisels, and of pygmy flints, some of which were set in bone harpoons. There is some reason for thinking that their implements were derived from Upper Paleolithic types "while the survivals

FIG. 34.—A group of skulls found at Ofnet, Bavaria. The heads had been severed by stone knives, and were carefully arranged with the faces toward the west. They were buried at different times, and by loving hands as the ornaments and the arrangement of the skulls show. What the cult of the dead was is unknown. It is possible that it may have been a skull altar like those of New Caledonia. After R. R. Schmidt.

Reproduced by the courtesy of The Hispanic Society of America from Obermaier's "Fossil Man in Spain" (Yale University Press).

of Paleolithic art are recognisable in engravings on bone or horn." For this reason most authorities agree in considering the fisherfolk of Lake Ancylus as descendants, in part at least, of Upper Paleolithic tribes.

Peoples. Our knowledge of the peoples who lived in Europe in the interval between the Paleolithic and Neolithic is not as full as one could wish. The most important evidence

comes from Ofnet, Bavaria, and Mugem, Portugal. At Ofnet
were found two groups of human skulls arranged like eggs in
a nest, and buried in red ochre. The larger nest (Fig. 34) was
thirty inches in diameter and contained twenty-seven human
skulls, and the smaller one six skulls. The skulls were all
orientated to the west and as the mouth of the cave does not
face the west, the placing of the skulls with their faces toward the setting sun doubtless had some important significance. The skulls retained the lower jaws and one or two
vertebræ. As the vertebræ show the marks of stone knives
it is evident that the bodies were decapitated. Men, women,
and children are represented: five men, nine women, and
nineteen children. The children range in age from about five
to eighteen years. Buried with the dead were ornaments made
of perforated teeth of the stag and perforated snail shells.
The skulls of the men were unornamented; but the women
had deer-teeth necklaces or chaplets, and the skulls of the
children were adorned with snail shells. "On the skull of a
little child hundreds of shells lay close together, placed there,
no doubt, by some sad, affectionate hand." Of the twenty-one
skulls which are sufficiently preserved for study, some are
long heads (dolichocephalic), but with long faces (instead
of the broad face of the Cro-Magnon type); some are short
heads (brachycephalic), and some are intermediate (mesaticephalic). The dolichocephalic skulls do not differ greatly from
those of the modern Mediterranean type, and the brachycephalic skulls are like those of the widespread Alpine type.
These people were not descendants of the European Paleolithic tribes but of stocks that had their development elsewhere.

A considerable number of skulls of Epipaleolithic age
from shell heaps at Mugem, Portugal, includes both long
and short heads, but the dolichocephalics are the more numerous. They differ from the Cro-Magnon type in their size
—five feet three inches—and their faces, which are long instead of broad. These people were, in other words, not unlike

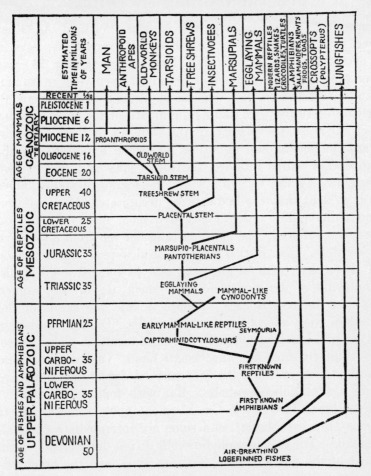

Fig. 35.—Dr. W. K. Gregory's diagram showing the evolution of the human stock. Note especially the estimates of geological time, the lines of descent and the time at which the human and anthropoid stock split off.

the modern Mediterranean type. It will be seen from these two discoveries that the population of Epipaleolithic times did not differ greatly in physical characteristics from that of to-day. Already the Mediterranean type predominated in the South, and the Alpine in Central Europe. They were immigrants, and were not descendants of the European Paleolithic races.

Duration of the Epipaleolithic. How long these hunters and fishermen lived in Europe is a mooted question. Did they, as one writer suggests,[5] survive for about 3,000 years, from about 6000 to 3000 B. C.? Or did the Paleolithic pass directly into the Neolithic by the partial extermination and partial absorption of the older peoples? [6] Were the so-called Epipaleolithic peoples merely tribes of hunters and fishers on the outskirts of the Neolithic civilisation?

The Debt of Civilisation to the Epipaleolithic. It is not clear that civilisation owes anything to the Epipaleolithic, except the invention of the stone hatchet or tranchet, and the stone pick. Not only were the people of this interval no more advanced than the Late Paleolithic men, but they seem to have had an inferior culture: they did not have the needle nor many of the useful flints of the Magdalenians, and they had little artistic skill. Their culture, such as it was, seems to have been derived from the Aurignacian (Early Late Paleolithic) or the Magdalenian.

[5] T. D. Kendrick: "The Axe Age," p. 172.
[6] G. Elliot Smith.

CHAPTER III

THE NEOLITHIC OR NEW STONE AGE

Equivalents: $\begin{cases} \text{Early (or delayed) Neolithic} \\ \text{Late or Full Neolithic} \end{cases}$ $\begin{cases} \text{Campignian} \\ \text{Ertebolle (Kitchen Midden)} \end{cases}$

Dates in Northern Europe: $\begin{cases} \text{5000-2000 B.C.}[1] \\ \text{3000-2000 B.C.}[2] \\ \text{Before 4000-1800 B.C.}[3] \end{cases}$

THE Neolithic (*neos* new; *lithos* stone) or New Stone Age was in many ways the most important through which the human race has passed. It is called the New Stone Age because then, for the first time, man ground and polished his stone tools. He did not, however, cease to make and use chipped flint tools for they were better for many purposes than were the polished ones. On the contrary, he developed, especially in the north of Europe and in Egypt, remarkable skill in the manufacture of chipped flint daggers and knives. But the Neolithic stands for much more than the manufacture of stone implements shaped and smoothed by rubbing and whetting. Man was no longer wholly dependent on hunting: he was a farmer; he reared domestic animals; he made pottery and wove cloth; and he had permanent villages of well-made houses. Even without metals, he might, in time, have attained a high civilisation such, for example, as that of Mexico, Central America, and Peru, for the mental capacity of the men of the Neolithic in Europe probably did not differ greatly from that of the men of to-day.

[1] Karl Schumacher: "Siedelungs- und Kulturgeschichte der Rheinlande."
[2] T. D. Kendrick: "The Axe Age," p. 172.
[3] Hans Reinerth: "Pfahlbauten am Bodensee."

CHRONOLOGY OF THE NEOLITHIC,

Date	Egypt [1]	Crete [1]	Greece [1]	Italy [2]
500				Iron Age VI 600-480 B. C.
				Iron Age V 700-600 B. C.
				Iron Age IV 800-700 B. C.
				Iron Age III 900-800 B. C.
1000				Iron Age II 1000-900 B. C.
	20th Dynasty Iron	Geometric Decoration	Geometric Decoration (Dipylon)	Iron Age I 1125-1000 B. C.
				Bronze Age V 1225-1125 B. C.
1250	19th Dynasty	Late Minoan III (palaces destroyed)	Late Mycenean (new palaces at Tiryns)	Bronze Age IV 1325-1225 B. C.
1400				Bronze Age III 1500-1325 B. C.
1500	18th Dynasty	Late Minoan II	Middle Mycenean	
1550				Bronze Age II 1625-1500 B. C.
	Beginning of 18th Dynasty Hyksos Period	Late Minoan I Middle Minoan III	Early Mycenean (gold ornaments —shaft graves)	
1700	13th Dynasty	Middle Minoan II	So-called *Urfirnis* and Marina ware	Bronze Age I 1850-1625 B. C.
	12th Dynasty	Middle Minoan I		Neolithic Culture
2000	6th to 11th Dynasties	Early Minoan		
2500	3rd to 5th Dynasties	Bronze		
3000		Neolithic Culture	Neolithic Culture	
3300	1st Dynasty [4] Pre-dynastic			

[1] Fimmen, D. "Die Kretisch-mykenisch Kultur."
[2] Montelius, O. "Die vorklassische Chronologie Italiens."
[3] Girke, G. "Zeitvergleichende Tabelle für Mittel und Nord Europa." (Mannus-Bibl.)
[4] Déchelette, J. "Manuel d'Archéologie."

Central Europe [3]	Western Europe [4]	Great Britain [5]	Scandinavia [6]
		La Tene IV (1-50 A. D.)	
La Tene III 125 B. C.-0	La Tene III 100 B. C.-0	La Tene III 100 B. C.-1	Iron Age III 150 B. C.-1
La Tene II 300-125 B. C.	La Tene II 300-100 B. C.	La Tene II 250-100 B. C.	Iron Age II 300-150 B. C.
La Tene I 500-300 B. C.	La Tene I 500-300 B. C.	La Tene I 400-250 B. C.	Iron Age I 500-300 B. C.
Hallstatt IV 675-500 B. C.	Hallstatt II 700-500 B. C.	Hallstatt 700-400 B. C.	Bronze Age VI 775-500 B. C.
Hallstatt III 850-675 B. C.	Hallstatt I 900-700 B. C.	Bronze Age V 1000-700 B. C.	Bronze Age V 1000-775 B. C.
Hallstatt II 1000-850 B. C.	Bronze Age IV 1300-900 B. C.		
Hallstatt I 1200-1000 B. C.		Bronze Age IV 1200-1000 B. C.	Bronze Age IV 1175-1000 B. C.
Bronze Age IV 1400-1200 B. C.	Bronze Age III 1600-1300 B. C.	Bronze Age III 1400-1200 B. C.	Bronze Age III 1400-1175 B. C.
Bronze Age III 1600-1400 B. C.		Bronze Age II 1700-1400 B. C.	Bronze Age II 1700-1400 B. C.
Bronze Age II 1800-1600 B. C.	Bronze Age II 1900-1600 B. C.		Bronze Age I 1800-1700 B. C.
Bronze Age I 2200-1800 B. C.	Bronze Age I 2500-1900 B. C.	Bronze Age I 2000-1700 B. C.	Late Neolithic
Neolithic Culture	Neolithic Culture	Neolithic Culture	

[5] Hoernes, M. "Urgeschichte der bildenden Kunst im Europa." Walther Bremer places the beginning of the Bronze Age in Great Britain at about 2500 B. C.

[6] This chronology is based on Montelius and Girke. The influence of the Bronze Age was felt in Scandinavia earlier than 1800 B. C., as is shown by the beautiful flint daggers made in imitation of bronze daggers.

[7] Breasted places the discovery of metal in Egypt at about 4000 B. C.

Geography and Climate. The geography and climate of the Neolithic in Europe was modern. It will be recalled that in part of the Paleolithic the English Channel and the North Sea did not exist, and that it was possible to go dry-shod from Europe to Africa by more than one route (p. 10). With the adjustments which followed the disappearance of the Great Ice Sheets, the lands were lowered, Great Britain was separated from the continent, and Europe from Africa. With minor details such as the formation of sand dunes, sand spits, and bars, and the wearing back of cliffs, and the filling up of estuaries, the coast lines were, in general, like those of to-day. Slight changes in the level of the land in Denmark have driven back the sea so that the shell heaps (p. 80) are now some distance inland. But as the land there is nearly flat, the vertical elevation was but a few feet. Since the beginning of the Neolithic, many of the lakes of Northern and Central Europe have disappeared, either by draining as the result of the erosion of morainic dams which formed their basins, or because of the accumulation of peat which converted many shallow lakes into marshes or into dry land. It is possible there were twice as many lakes in Europe during Neolithic times as there are now. The climate of the Neolithic in Europe is attested by the seeds and nuts which are found in the Pile Dwelling deposits and elsewhere. There are seeds of strawberries, blackberries, raspberries, elderberries, wild grapes, crabapples, dog-rose, and cherries of several species. There are nuts of the beech, hazel, and walnut, and acorns. All these plants now grow in the same regions as they did then.

There were extended periods of wet and dry, during which conditions were abnormal and people situated in unfavourable places were obliged to migrate. One such dry period was so acute and so prolonged that the level of the Swiss lakes was lowered several metres. The lowering of the surface reached its maximum in the Bronze Age when the Pile Dwellers built their houses further from the present shores than did their Neolithic forebears.

The similarity of the climates and geography of the modern and Neolithic world makes it possible to arrive at more definite conclusions than was possible in the discussion of the earlier stages of man's cultural development.

Distribution of the Neolithic. The Neolithic arts and crafts: agriculture, domesticated animals, polished and flaked tools, and pottery, spread over nearly the entire world. From the place of its origin, wherever that may have been, the new culture replaced the Paleolithic over the whole of Europe. It spread over Asia to Japan; from island to island to Australia; over the islands of the Pacific to Hawaii, and to distant and lonely Easter Island and to North and South America. This wide distribution was brought about in several ways, of which the increase and resultant crowding of populations was probably the most important. Famines doubtless caused many migrations. Expeditions for precious objects, and criminals or unpopular men escaping from punishment, would also spread the culture of the homelands. In many regions, however, "culture creep" was doubtless as important as any other factor in the dissemination of this civilisation, that is, backward peoples, by barter, war, and theft, would acquire household objects, implements, and weapons, and in time would learn to make them. In these ways, the Neolithic arts and crafts were spread far and wide.

The Neolithic civilisation was not the same everywhere, for it was influenced by the capacity of the people, by the fertility of the soil, by the natural resources, by proximity to other cultural centres, and in other ways.

In Europe and Asia, it lasted until after the introduction of copper and bronze; in Central and Southern Africa until iron was introduced; it was flourishing in the Pacific Islands, and in the Americas when Columbus made his voyage of discovery.

THE NEOLITHIC OF THE MEDITERRANEAN BASIN

The countries on the shores of the Eastern Mediterranean —Egypt, Asia Minor, Greece, and Crete—attained a high Neolithic civilisation much earlier than did those of Central, Western and Northern Europe. If our supposition is correct, it was in the Eastern part of the Mediterranean basin or in Central Asia (p. 77) that the Neolithic civilisation originated. The older estimates of 18,000 and 14,000 B. C. for the earliest industries of the Neolithic in Asia, Africa, and Crete seem much too high. It is possible these cultures may not have been in existence before 6000 B. C.

The Neolithic peoples of the Eastern Mediterranean made better pottery than those of Central and Northern Europe. For example, the Cretans made vessels with handles and spouts, and on the mainland of Greece, we find dishes, and globular vessels with necks, and strap handles. Some of this pottery shows high craftsmanship. It is very thin, and polished, and is decorated with stamped points, with lines, and with designs in white paint. Shortly before the introduction of bronze, jars covered with a white slip on which red designs were drawn, were manufactured.

In Egypt, and Asia Minor, flint working reached a high stage of excellence. If the decorated and highly polished axes of the second city of Troy [4] are examples of Neolithic craftsmanship handed down to the Bronze Age, it is safe to say that the art of stone working reached its zenith there. Stone technique was not of this high character everywhere in the Mediterranean basin. In Southern Italy, for example, it was crude.

Chronology. It is not known when the New Stone Age began in Europe. Did the art of grinding stone implements, first by chipping the rolled stones of the brook and then mak-

---

[4] Some of these axes are on exhibition in the Museum für Völkerkunde, Berlin. For beauty of design, and skill of workmanship they surpass any other work of the Neolithic or Early Bronze Age of which the author is aware.

ing them sharper by whetting and grinding, arise independently in Europe? Was it brought there by the slow infiltration of peoples from the South or East? Were the arts and crafts slowly spread by contact? A definite answer cannot be made. There is little doubt, however, that man made polished stone implements in Asia long before he did in Europe. It is for this reason that the date of the beginning of the Neolithic in Europe is so uncertain. Possibly the earliest Neolithic cultures—the Ertebolle, and Campignian—are not those of people who were inventing a new stone technique, but were those of aborigines who had not yet acquired much of the culture of a higher civilisation. It is for this reason that one writer [5] states that "the Neolithic is not really part of the Stone Age at all but rather a forerunner of the Metal Era" and that in Europe, it represents "part of the identical renaissance of human activity that enlivens the centuries that saw the first diffusion of metal instruments."

Unfortunately, there are no stratified Neolithic sites such as are found in the Paleolithic caves of Europe nor are the types of tools and utensils datable with certainty. Since data for determining the age of Neolithic deposits and objects in Europe are so uncertain, the dates assigned to "finds" or "caches" of this age, and to the age itself, should not be considered as established. The age in Europe, as far as our present knowledge shows, may have begun as early as 5000 or as late as 3000 before the Christian Era. Certain it is, that a people of the mental capacity of the Northern Europeans of that time, once they knew of its existence, would not have allowed many centuries to elapse before they would have acquired the ability to make their stone implements with the new technique.

The length of the Neolithic is also a debatable question. One recent writer [6] estimates that the Full Neolithic in Great Britain was very short, possibly not longer than 500 years.

[5] T. D. Kendrick: "The Axe Age," 1925, pp. 3-4.
[6] *Idem.*

Another [7] gives its duration in Europe as some 2800 years. Montelius estimated that the Megalithic period lasted about 1000 years (3000-2000 B.C.) (this does not include the earlier part of the Neolithic period) but does include the hallcists, megalithic monuments of the Early Bronze Age. The tendency seems to be to consider the Neolithic in Europe as of moderate rather than of great duration.

The Neolithic did not end abruptly, but gradually merged into the Bronze Age (Fig. 66, p. 146), as copper and bronze implements were imported, and the technique of copper smelting was acquired. Nevertheless, the spread of the superior cutting material was relatively rapid and, although in some out-of-the-way places its introduction was delayed, it was in general use in a comparatively short time. The Neolithic Age may be said, therefore, to have given way to the Bronze Age in Europe about 1800 B.C. (see table, p. 169) although universal in the Americas until the fifteenth century of our era.

After its introduction in Europe, the Neolithic developed along different lines until unique civilisations came into being, such as those of Scandinavia and of the Pile Dwellers of Switzerland and neighbouring lands.

Whence Came the Neolithic Cultures of Central Europe? The oldest Neolithic civilisation in Europe, so far as known, was in the fertile valleys of the Danube and its tributaries, where the soil was tilled and cattle, sheep, pigs, goats, and probably horses, were reared. The abundance of stone hoes (shoe-last celts [8]) show that the people were agriculturists, and the rarity of weapons, except disk-shaped mace heads, indicates that they were peaceably inclined. Their pottery was well made, and ornamented with simple scratched meanders, and later with other designs. Their religion may be surmised from their female idols (see Fig. 54, p. 123) of baked clay.

[7] Julius Andree: "Bergbau in der Vorzeit," *Vorzeit,* 1922.

[8] *Celt and Ax.* As used in this work, a celt (Latin, *celtis,* a chisel) is an ax-shaped implement without a perforation for a handle. The principal difference, then, between a celt and an ax is that the ax has a hole for the insertion of a handle and the celt has none.

They buried their dead in a contracted position. Bracelets made from Mediterranean shells show that there was some trade between the Danube basin and the South. After a time, the population became too large for the valleys and the people began to spread to unoccupied lands and make new settlements. They occupied Galicia and spread along the Oder, the Elbe, and the Rhine valleys. To the east their penetration reached Serbia and probably Hungary.

Another Neolithic culture, called Bell Beaker (*Zonenkeramik*) because of the characteristic pottery, was in the meantime moving from Northern Africa through the Iberian peninsula to France and Great Britain. This civilisation eventually reached the Danube valley and mingled with the one it found there. A characteristic vase of this culture may be seen in Figure 46 (4).

Origin of the Danube Culture. If the Neolithic civilisation of Europe came from the Danube valley, whence did the latter come? There is no evidence that it was a creation of the aboriginal Paleolithic peoples. The earliest Neolithic civilisation with its agriculture, its domesticated animals, and its pottery, seems to have been introduced fully developed in all its essentials. It is possible that the homeland of this culture was in the vicinity of Troy or Anatolia but the evidence is by no means convincing.

It will be seen from the above that the introduction of the Neolithic arts and crafts into Western Europe had nothing miraculous about it. "It was due to the gradual expansion of early agriculturists in obedience to perfectly natural laws and every step of their progress from the Danube valley can be traced with perfect accuracy in the implements, vases, and ornaments they have left behind them." [9]

THE BIRTHPLACE OF THE NEOLITHIC.

Wherever the Neolithic arts and crafts may have been invented, it is probably safe to say that the birthplace was

[9] V. Gordon Childe: "The Dawn of European Civilization," 1925, p. 183.

not in the New World nor in Europe. In other words, the Neolithic civilisations of Europe were not indigenous [10] but were
brought there by migrating peoples.

When we attempt to find the home [11] of the earliest Neolithic culture—the birthplace of civilisation—we enter the
realms of speculation. This must necessarily be so because of
the small number of sites in Asia and elsewhere which have
been excavated. Excavations in new sites may cause the modification or entirely change present theories. It is certainly
true that whether the early settlements of Susa, of Anau, of
Sumer, or of Asia Minor be examined, it will be found that,
in all essentials of culture, they resemble one another.[12] All
moreover, resemble the cultures of Egypt of late predynastic
and early dynastic times.

Was the Neolithic spread from Central Asia to the Plateau
of Iran and to Syria and Egypt? [13] Were the Neolithic arts
and crafts developed in Egypt [14] as the result of the discovery
of irrigation, and, consequently, is Egypt the homeland of
the Neolithic? Did Northern Asia foster the development of
the Neolithic and was it spread thence to Europe and

[10] It is held by some eminent prehistorians that the Neolithic civilisation
of Scandinavia arose spontaneously. The basis for this theory is the evolution
of the Scandinavian flint implements from simple Ertebolle forms. G. Kossina:
Die Indogermanen. *Mannus Bibliothek,* vol. 26, 1921.

[11] Recent discoveries in the United States point to a much greater antiquity
for Neolithic man in the New World than has previously been supposed possible. The evidence consists, in Florida, of human remains associated with the
skeletons of extinct animals, and of arrow heads associated with skeletons of
extinct bison in New Mexico, Oklahoma, Kansas and Texas. If the evidence
proves to be well-founded it would appear that Neolithic man inhabited
North America thousands of years before he reached Europe. If this is true
the theories that either Central Asia or Egypt was the birthplace of the
Neolithic culture may have to be modified. The fact that the arrowheads
are of European Neolithic type or at best of Solutrean technique does not
agree with the claim of great antiquity as even the Solutrean does not go
further back than the last glaciation, whereas the fossils are of animals that
lived during the first interglacial stage.

[12] W. J. Perry. "The Growth of Civilization," p. 26.

[13] Stephen H. Langdon: Cambridge Ancient History, vol. I, p. 362.

[14] W. J. Perry: "The Growth of Civilization," pp. 28-31.

America? [15] Such a diversity of opinion is due to the scantiness of the material and a lack of positive evidence. Possibly we may never know the answer to the question but it is equally possible that new excavations may unearth convincing proof.

The impossibility, as yet, of determining the exact age and often even the relative age of deposits has been a serious barrier in a study of the origin of the Neolithic. For example, if, as at Anau, in Russian Turkestan, the deposit containing Neolithic painted pottery is at a depth of 64 feet below the top of the mound and 24 feet below the present level of the plain, how may the age be determined? The rate of deposition changes with variations in climate. On a delta oasis such as that at Anau the rate of growth might vary greatly from time to time as the climate is wet or dry. Consequently, when an estimate of 9000 B.C. for the first settlement of Anau is given,[16] or 20,000 years [17] for the whole series at Susa, on the edge of the Persian (Iranian) Plateau, or 14,000 years [18] for that at Cnossus, Crete, are given, they must not be accepted as even relatively correct. They are probably the best estimates that can be made from available data. The same difficulty is encountered in estimating the antiquity of ancient deposits of the flood plain of the Nile. The climate of Northern Africa has varied greatly from time to time and with it the amount of silt carried by the river and spread over its valley.

The scantiness of the evidence is shown in the fact that for the whole of Central and Western Asia, careful excavations have been made only at Anau, in Russian Turkestan, at Suza on the edge of the Persian (Iranian) Plateau, and in a few places in Mesopotamia, and Asia Minor.

[15] N. C. Nelson: Archaeological Research in North China, *American Anthropology*, vol. 29, p. 200.
[16] Pumpelly and Huntington.
[17] De Morgan and Montelius.
[18] Evans and Montelius.

SHELL HEAP, KITCHEN MIDDEN, OR ERTEBOLLE CULTURE

Long, low ridges, or mounds, composed largely of oyster, and other shells, intermingled with the bones of mammals, birds, and fishes, and with crude flint implements, occur on the coasts of Jutland, Denmark. These shell ridges (Fig. 36)

Fig. 36.—A section in a Danish shell heap. The kitchen middens are composed of the accumulated shell refuse of a people who lived on the shore throughout the year. After Madsen.

are from ten to twenty feet high and some are as much as 150 feet long. They were first thought to be raised sea beaches but a study of them soon showed that they were formed of the discarded refuse of a people whose principal food was shellfish. Several names have been given to these deposits: the Danish names *Køkken Møddinger* or kitchen middens, *Affaldsdynger* or refuse heaps, and *Skaldynger* or shell heaps are all descriptive, but Ertebolle, the name of the place near which the shell heaps were first studied, is growing in favour as the name for this culture. An objection to the term Kitchen Midden is that some of the people of this culture (Nøstvet culture), as for example in Norway and Sweden, did not live on shell heaps.

Distribution of Shell Heaps. Kitchen middens occur in Great Britain and Ireland, in Japan, on the Atlantic and Pacific coasts of North America, and elsewhere, but they are

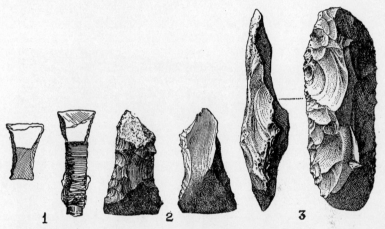

Fig. 37.—The characteristic flint implements of the people of the shell heaps are shown here. The variety was very small. (1) Transverse arrowhead used for shooting birds which shows the original binding. (2) Tranchet or hatchet, and (3) a pick.

(1) *Courtesy of the Trustees of the British Museum.* (2) *and* (3) *After Madsen.*

not all of the same age, and most of them are much more recent than the Danish ones. Some, indeed, were being made within the memory of man. Moreover, they are not characteristic of any one race or culture, and the only feature in common is the habit of living largely on shellfish and consequently of leaving shell or refuse heaps.

The Danish shell heaps are composed chiefly of the shells of edible shellfish such as the oyster, scallop, mussel, and periwinkle. Bones of the cod and herring, of geese, ducks, swans, gulls, partridges, roe deer, stags, and wild boars indicate some variety in the diet of the people. Long bones of the larger animals were broken in order to extract the marrow.

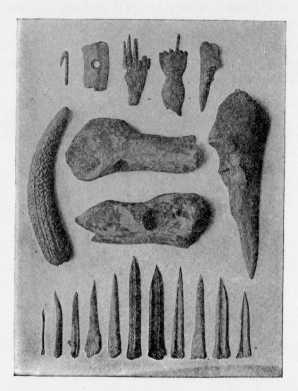

Fig. 38.—Bone and horn implements: piercers or awls, hammers, combs (broken) and a fishhook. After Madsen. Reduced in size.

No polished flint axes have been discovered but there are many roughly flaked flint knives, scrapers, borers, arrowheads with a broad edge (transverse arrowheads), Fig. 37 (1), tranchets, or chisel-axes (Fig. 37 (2)), and picks (Fig. 37 (3)). The tranchet is considered typical of this stage. Its broad, horizontal cutting edge was produced by striking off a large transverse flake by a single blow. This is a new tech-

nique. Bone combs (Fig. 38) with short handles and long
teeth, pins, needles, and awls were used.

The occurrence of fragments of thick, extremely crude
pottery, and of one complete jar, is important as it may prove
to be the oldest pottery made in Northern Europe. The jars
(Fig. 39) were large and somewhat globular, with a rim, and
a pointed base, but with practically no ornamentation, except
finger-tip impressions on the upper edge of the rim.

Fig. 39.—The only complete shell heap jar found. Denmark. Reduced in
size.

A fairly accurate picture of the life of these people can
be drawn. They were a poverty-stricken race who lived
throughout the year on the shores of the sea. Their food
consisted of shellfish, fish, game, roots, and herbs. In the
course of time long mounds of kitchen refuse were built up,
just as in Tierra del Fuego to-day certain tribes with similar
habits are leaving a like record of their customs. In addition
to the shellfish, which was the basis of their diet, they also
ate such birds and mammals as they could trap or kill, and
they were sometimes successful in hunting the stag, roe deer,

and wild boar. They probably used their broad-edged arrows (Fig. 37 (1)) to bring down the swan, gull, duck, and partridge. Periods of famine, when storms prevented them from getting shellfish, are indicated by bones of the fox and wolf, which would hardly have been eaten if other foods were available. Depressions in the mounds and hearths made of flat stones indicate the sites of huts or tents.

These shore settlements, which gave rise to the shell heaps, were not temporary summer camps but were permanent homes. This is proved by the bones of the swan which was a winter resident of Denmark, and by the bones of young, immature, and old deer. It would seem that these people must have had boats and fishlines to catch cod and herring. There is some evidence of the use of nets. There is no proof of the domestication of any animal except the dog, and none that they tilled the soil.

The Danish shell heaps belong to the earliest Neolithic. This is indicated in several ways: (1) They were accumulating when the Baltic Sea was more extensive than it is now (Littorina Sea, p. 134), that is, when the region was depressed. This is proved by the larger size of the shellfish, such as the oyster, which grew to the normal sea water size. (2) Moreover, there was a difference in vegetation. Since that time, the pine has given way to the oak. (3) The climate was slightly warmer then than it is now. This indicates a considerable lapse of time, for the change from a warmer climate to the present cool one was probably slow. (4) The absence of polished flint implements, except some which show a little grinding on the edge, indicates that the inhabitants lived earlier than the Full Neolithic. There is, however, a possibility that they were an isolated, backward people to whom the knowledge of grinding and polishing flint tools was slow in coming.

Ertebolle people also lived in Sweden (Nøstvet culture) on the shores of the sea but their record is preserved in sediments and not in shell heaps.

THE CAMPIGNIAN CULTURE

The Campignian culture is generally regarded as an early phase of the Neolithic and as contemporaneous with the Ertebolle culture, although some authorities place it in the Epipaleolithic period. The culture derives its name from a hut site on a hill on the lower Seine. Here a funnel-shaped pit, a little less than four feet deep and about fourteen feet in diameter, evidently the underground part of a dwelling, was excavated. On the bottom of the pit was a bed of ashes, and the remains

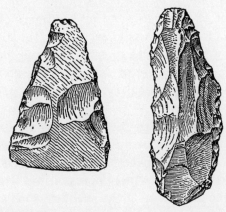

FIG. 40.—Tranchet or chisel-ax, and pick. Campigny, France.

of a hearth. No polished implements were found on the floor of the pit, although some occurred near the surface, but a number of flint knives, scrapers, engravers, and borers, which resemble flint implements of the Upper Paleolithic, were obtained. Besides these Paleolithic-like flints, there were found two types of flint tools which are regarded as typical of the Campignian and Ertebolle cultures: (1) the pick, a roughly-shaped implement whose form bears a resemblance to some unpolished Neolithic celts, and (2) the tranchet, or chisel-ax, a roughly-chipped celt with a broad blade (Fig. 40). Associated with these flint artifacts were a number of fragments of pottery. The size of the jars, the presence of lugs for suspension, and the efforts at ornamentation, certainly do not indicate the first crude attempts of a people who were beginning to learn the art of pottery making, but those either of a people who had learned the art from neighbouring peoples or who had had long practice.

The fact that the pick and tranchet occur in Ireland, as well as in widely separated places in Europe, shows that the culture was widespread. Two possibilities have been offered to explain this culture: (1) that it was the culture of indigenous peoples who had but recently invented pottery, but the size and quality of the vessels would seem to make this suggestion improbable, (2) that it was the work of isolated tribes of wretched people who had nothing but poor tools and poor pottery, although their neighbours may have had an advanced civilisation. Since the Neolithic culture of Europe spread from the East, the second explanation is the more probable. It has recently been insisted that we have no real proof that the Campignian industry, which now passes as an early phase of the Neolithic,[19] is in reality older than the polished celt culture, and, on the other hand, some fairly good reasons for supposing that it is contemporaneous; that the miniature hatchet or pick is a cheap imitation of the celt proper, and was used in agriculture, mining, or other work for which the polished ax was an unnecessary luxury.

THE FULL NEOLITHIC

Perhaps the best working hypothesis to explain the spread of Neolithic cultures in Europe is that the cultures were not indigenous but came from the East or Southeast and were introduced by agricultural tribes with domesticated animals. The cultures were extended partly by invasion but largely by "culture creep." After being introduced the culture was slowly or rapidly modified to meet new conditions or as a result of the influence of tradition or the genius of the people.

The aboriginal Epipaleolithic hunters and fishers, although

[19] T. D. Kendrick: "The Axe Age," 1925, p. 138.

so bound by customs and traditions that they had ceased to progress without a stimulus from outside, were capable of learning new arts and crafts and ways of improving their condition. We can imagine that rumours of a new method of making stone implements reached these people and that later some of the new polished stone implements themselves came to them after having been passed from tribe to tribe. The next step would be for the expert tool maker to attempt to fashion a similar tool. Thus crude imitations would appear, such, possibly, as the shell heap (Ertebolle) pick (see Fig. 37, (3)) or the early pointed celt. Finally, when the technique was acquired, different, and characteristic types of implements would be made in different places. To these backward peoples this new technique was a revolutionary invention and had a profound effect in stimulating thought and invention. In some regions, the nearly full culture was doubtless introduced rather quickly, and axes of various shapes appear to have been used at the same time. For example, in a carefully excavated site in one of the Swiss Lakes, pointed stone celts and celts with thin, and with thick butts were used at the same time and show no signs of evolution.[20] The form of the celts was determined largely by the form of pebble, and the aperture of the haft they were to fit.

The technique of flint-working in Europe reached its highest degree of excellence in Scandinavia in the last stage of the Neolithic or the very earliest part of the Bronze Age (Copper Age, Chalcolithic or Eneolithic). It has, indeed, been excelled in but few places in the world. The predynastic Egyptian knives, spear and arrowheads are superior in some details, as are the obsidian and crystal masks of Mexico and Yucatan. Moreover, no battle-axes (see Fig. 62, p. 141) comparable in execution and finish to those of the second city of Troy (Bronze Age) were made in the North.

The variety of chipped implements is not very large but the workmanship varies greatly in different places, and in the

[20] T. D. Kendrick: "The Axe Age," 1925.

same place at different times. Many of the flint implements were little more than flakes whose fortuitous shapes when slightly modified were found useful. In this way, piercers, awls, scrapers, small knives, and other tools were made.

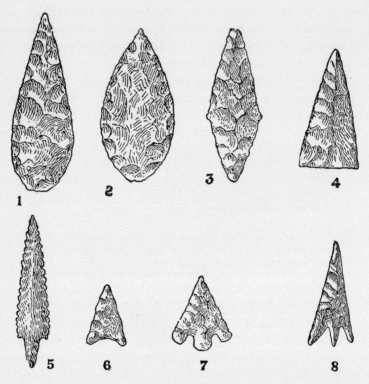

Fig. 41.—Neolithic flint arrowheads. Number 5 is triangular in cross section. After Déchelette.

Arrowheads (Fig. 41) and lanceheads vary greatly in shape and finish. Some arrowheads have a tang (Fig. 41, (5) and (8)), some are nearly lozenge-shaped, and some have two projecting, carefully-made barbs (Fig. 41, (8)), while some of the earliest have transverse ends instead of points. The most skilfully made arrowheads are probably of the Early Bronze

Age. Knives were made from long flakes which were generally carefully chipped along the edge.

Various devices must have been employed to protect the hand, when holding the rough flint tools. Skin and wood were doubtless used for handles. A flint knife found in Ireland (Fig. 42), which still retains the moss which the workman had wound about it to serve as a handle, is an interesting example and is a suggestive discovery, as it indicates that the hand was protected by any suitable material.

Mining. As flint was the most important material used by the Neolithic peoples for making cutting tools and weapons,

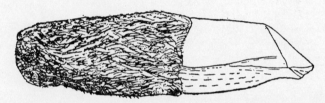

Fig. 42.—The butt of the flint flake shown here was wrapped in a wad of moss so as to protect the hand and at the same time to act as a handle. Prehistoric man probably used many things such as leather, cloth, wood and vegetable fibres for handles and to protect the hands. After Macalister.

and as the intellectual capacity of the Europeans of that time was probably equal to that of the average European of to-day, it is evident that the flint-maker would, in the course of time, learn a great deal about flint and its occurrence. He doubtless early discovered that flint which had been exposed to the action of the weather was not as good for making implements as flint fresh from the earth. He soon learned to distinguish the kind that could be broken into long, thin flakes suitable for knives, from that which was not as good.

The demand for the best material led to mining, and as a result, the people of the New Stone Age became miners. Their shafts and pits are known in various parts of Europe and England. Where the bed of flint nodules lay near the surface, they merely dug a trench down to the bed, just as to-day in the Lake Superior Region, a great deal of ore is mined in open cuts. Such a method, in its early form, required little skill and little knowledge of mining but when the beds containing the best flint were twenty or thirty feet below the surface it was necessary to develop mining methods to reach them.

The Neolithic miners were the first the world has known, if we except the possible crude attempts of Mousterian man to get flint from below the surface. With deer horns for picks (Fig. 43), shoulder blades of the ox for shovels, and a cup

Fig. 43.—(*Left*) The Neolithic miner found the deer antler pick the best tool for mining in chalk for flint. The pick shown here was used in a flint mine at Grime's Graves, England. Much reduced in size.

(*Right*) Lamps made by merely hollowing out a lump of chalk were used to furnish light for the Neolithic flint mines. One such lamp was discovered on a ledge of chalk in just the proper position for throwing light upon the place to be worked. Cissbury, England. Reduced in size.

Courtesy of the Trustees of the British Museum.

hollowed out of the chalk for a lamp, Neolithic man sunk his shafts, in some places thirty feet and more in depth, passing through one or more layers of flint to get to material of the best quality. At Spiennes, Belgium, ten beds of poor flint were passed through before the bed of good flint was reached. The shafts decrease in diameter with depth until they are only some ten feet across at the bottom, although thirty or more feet in diameter at the top. When the layer of superior flint was reached, galleries were driven along the beds, radiating from the shaft somewhat like the spokes of a wheel. Some of the galleries are nearly thirty feet in length, and vary considerably in height. Some are so low that the miner could crawl through them with difficulty, but some were five or six feet high. The miners preferred to sink a large number of shafts rather than to drive galleries long distances. This is seen at Grime's Graves, in England, and Spiennes, near Mons, in Belgium. In the former place there are 346 shafts in twenty-one acres.

The principal tools used in mining were the deerhorn pick (see Fig. 43) made by merely breaking off an inconvenient projection or two from a deer's antler. One specimen in the British Museum still retains in the chalky clay which adheres to the surface the imprint of the miner's hand. Punches and chisels of deerhorn and flint implements made at the mine were also used. In the dark galleries the miner used lamps hollowed from the chalk, with wicks fed by melted grease. Such lamps of chalk have been found in the mines (see Fig. 43).

The flint obtained from Grime's Graves and Cissbury Camp in England was apparently not worked up into finished form at the mines as the implements found there are extremely crude and many of them are not unlike Late Paleolithic artifacts. The Scandinavian miners had skilful flint flakers who fashioned half-made celts which were sold in the unfinished condition to be polished and hafted by the purchaser. A cache of 140 partly-finished flint celts and gouges was found in Sweden where they had been brought from Denmark.

The most noted locality for flint in France is at Grand Pressigny near Tours. Here occur flint nodules of such a nature, size, and shape, that long blades can be struck from them. A considerable traffic was carried on in this flint. Flint from this locality was widely distributed either in the form of nuclei or cores (Fig. 44) ready for flaking, or in a half-finished condition.

That the life of the Neolithic miner was a precarious one, and that the shaft holes were dangerous, is shown by two skeletons which record the tragedies of that distant time. At

Obourg, Belgium, the skeleton of a miner with his deerhorn pick beside him lay in a tunnel where he had met his death while at work. The skeleton of a woman was found near the

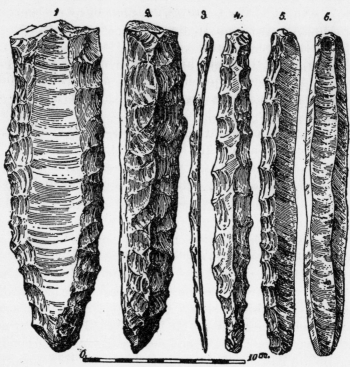

Fig. 44.—A considerable trade in large flint nuclei from Grand Pressigny, France, was carried on. The flint is of fine quality and as it has a characteristic beeswax colour and lustre it is easily recognised. In addition to the nuclei, long flint blades (3) occur. The nuclei were exported to be broken into knives and other tools and implements. After de Morgan.

bottom of a shaft at Grime's Graves in such a position as to indicate that she had fallen headlong down the open shaft.

The shaft holes of these ancient mines are now nearly filled. The miners themselves dumped the débris from tunnels and shafts into old shaft holes where it could most easily be disposed of, and the work of rains, rivulets, and wind have nearly filled all of them.

Pottery. Of the principal contributions of the Neolithic to civilisation—agriculture, the domestication of animals, housebuilding, weaving, and pottery—the art of making pottery was of fundamental importance. With the invention of pottery, man could boil foods more easily and better, and was thus enabled to use vegetables, roots, and grains which previously could not be well-cooked. He thus increased the variety of his food, and also made more palatable and digestible some that had long constituted an important part of his food supply. Because of this increase in the kinds of food famines were less frequent.

It is not known when pottery was invented. No pottery of unquestioned Paleolithic age is known and it seems hardly probable that the wandering Paleolithic hunters could have invented it. As they did not lead a sedentary life, the heavy, poorly-fired pots of the experimental stage could not have been transported from place to place. Pottery attributed to the Epipaleolithic has, however, been reported.[21]

One of the pressing needs of Neolithic man was for vessels in which to store and cook his food and he also wanted dishes and cups. His attention may have been called to the possibility of utilising clay for vessels as a result of placing baskets daubed with clay on his hearth-fire. The clay burned by the hot embers would occasionally retain the rounded shape of the bottom of the basket. This would, in time, attract the attention of some observant and inventive individual who would experiment with the baskets daubed all over or within with clay. Experiments must have been re-

[21] A discovery of what appears to be an Epipaleolithic culture in Germany may prove to be important as it contains fragments of coarse pottery and seems to show how ceramics were first made. As this pottery has impressions of basketwork on the outside, it is suggested that the method was to line the basket with clay and after the clay was dry, to take the air-dried pot from the basket for firing. The possibility that this is merely the work of a backward people who lived when more advanced tribes were making ceramics of a higher grade must not be overlooked.

Max Schneider: Die Binsen Keramik, eine neue Steinzeitliche Gattung. *Praehistorische Zeitschrift*, XV, 1924, p. 75.

peated many times, and with many discouraging failures, for to make a vessel without cracks under primitive conditions is very difficult. It is necessary in manufacturing a clay vessel, first to dry it in the shade, and later in the sun. If the clay contains much water it will crack when subjected to great heat. Unfortunately for the Neolithic experimenter, the thicker the wall of the pot, the more liable it is to crack. Moreover, the first pottery was fired on a hearth in the open air and it is to be noted that it is much more difficult to make a clay vessel by open-air firing than in an oven. It was against these odds that the Neolithic potter worked. Pottery must be considered one of the world's greatest inventions. The shapes of the earlier pottery may have been made in imitation of the leather bottles of Paleolithic times, of gourds which had probably been used for thousands of years as receptacles for liquids, and of baskets.

The potter's wheel was not known in Central and Northern Europe until the Early Iron Age, although it was employed in the Mediterranean basin long before.

The pottery of the earliest Neolithic (see Fig. 39, p. 83) in Northern and Central Europe (Ertebolle or Shell Heap culture) was very thick and was made of very coarse material, namely, of clay and fine gravel. The large size of the pots—eighteen and more inches in height—is unexpected, because of the difficulty of making pots of this size.

Characteristics of Neolithic Pottery. It is not easy to make a general statement about the Neolithic pottery of Europe because, (1) different shapes, designs, and techniques were employed in different places; (2) styles changed from time to time, and (3) the pottery of one region was modified when an alien people conquered or peaceably settled in a country where a distinctive style had been developed.

The pottery of Europe may be roughly classified into: (1) Northern or Megalithic, (2) Cord or String Ceramic, (3) Southern or Pile Dwelling, (4) Eastern or Danubian, and (5) Western or Bell Beaker. These principal types influenced each other, and on the boundary of two regions, mixed styles appear. Moreover, where a people with a characteristic style of pottery migrated or went on conquests, they imposed their pottery shapes and designs, either wholly or in part, on other peoples. If, however, the conquerors did not take their women —the potters of the time—with them, the style probably remained unmodified.

It should also be borne in mind that in every region the designs and technique varied from time to time. For example, in Moravia the decoration first consisted of spirals and meanders (*Bandkeramik*) made of engraved lines but, later, the spirals and meanders became zigzags and the lines were no longer engraved but consisted of punctuations (*stichband*).

The Northern or Megalith pottery is characterised by deeply incised designs (*tiefstich*) usually arranged in horizontal lines around the upper part of the vase, and below this vertical lines in groups (Fig. 45 (1) (3)). In the later vases zigzags occur. The designs were made, for the most part, by means of edged tools and stamps. Pottery of this technique was the work of the Megalith peoples of Scandinavia and Northern Germany who throughout the Neolithic manufactured pottery with designs of essentially the same technique.

A people living in the region of Thuringia, Northern Germany, as a centre decorated their pottery with designs made by pressing twisted cords or strings into the paste before firing. This pottery is therefore called Cord or String Ceramics (*Schnurkeramik*). The decoration is confined to the neck or upper part of the body of the vase and consists of horizontal lines (Fig. 46 (5)) and dog-tooth motives (Fig. 46 (3)). The typical shapes are the beaker (Fig. 46 (5)) and the amphora (Fig. 46 (3)) which generally has two or four straplike lugs at the widest part of the vase.

From their home in Thuringia, the Cord Ceramics folk spread to the south and east. In Germany, they were hunters, fishers, and cattle raisers. They settled on the uplands along the river valleys and, it has been suggested, they made the

FIG. 45.—The three vases 1, 2, 3 are from North Germany, Schleswig-Holstein, and Osnabrück. Figs. 4, 5, and 6 illustrate the typical, deeply-incised ornament of the Megalithic or Northern ceramics. 7, 8, 9, Lake Dwelling ceramics. The first two figures are more typical than the third as most of the pile dwelling pottery was without decoration. The pottery was, however, of good quality.

Photograph by the courtesy of the Berlin Museum of Ethnology.

Spiral Ceramics peoples work for them. Their characteristic weapons were the faceted battle-ax supplemented by flint celts of almond section.

The Southern or Pile Dwelling ceramics (Fig. 45, (7), (8), (9)) is generally thinner and but slightly ornamented but is of many shapes. Many jars were made with handles or lugs for suspension. Pitchers, dishes, spoons, large storage jars for grain, cheese strainers, spindle whorls, loom weights, and other objects were made of clay. Doubtless the reason for the seemingly great variety of Pile Dwelling earthenware objects is due to the fact that practically all of the pottery in daily use has fortunately been preserved in the mud of the lake bottoms. In other regions we know little of the pottery of the people except that which was placed in graves. Toward the close of the Neolithic, designs were made on the Pile Dwelling pottery as a result of the influence of neighbouring peoples.

The Eastern or Danubian pottery (Fig. 46, (1), (2)) is characterised by incised, ribbonlike designs (*Bandkeramik*) generally in spirals or volutes. Later, a pottery painted in spiral ribbons and other curvilinear forms appeared. The pottery with ribbon designs spread westward to the Rhine but, in general, did not wholly displace the indigenous types. The typical shapes are bottles and gourdlike bowls. Other, and possibly later shapes, have rectilinear designs made of short dashes. Clay female idols were manufactured by this same people.

A later form of pottery called the Bell Beaker (*Zonenkeramik*) (Fig. 46, (4)) with the ornament disposed in horizontal bands generally covering the whole of the vessel, came from the southwest through Spain and spread to Britain, Ireland, France, and over a large part of Central Europe. The designs, which in Central Europe were for the most part made by pressing cords (*Schnurkeramik*) into the wet clay before firing, are arranged in horizontal bands or zones (*Zonenkeramik*). In the West, some of the bell beakers have very thin walls and are beautifully engraved.

FIG. 46.—Ribbon ceramics. (1) Note the faintly incised ribbon design (*Bandkeramik*), Czechoslovakia. (2) This vase has painted spirals and volutes (ribbon design). It marks the transition between the Neolithic and Bronze Ages.

(4) Bell beaker (*Zonenkeramik*) ceramics. The makers of this type spread from Spain to Great Britain and Ireland, and through Central Europe to the Danube. The shape of the vase and the arrangement of the designs are characteristic.

(3) and (5) String ceramics. This pottery like the last was decorated with designs made by pressing twisted cords into the wet clay. Fig. 5 is more typical than Fig. 3, which is an exceptionally artistic jar with lugs for suspension. Thuringia, Germany.

One of the more important of the border peoples lived in Thuringia, Germany. Their pottery with string decoration (Fig. 46, (3, 5)) is so widely spread as to indicate that they were a warlike people. Because of the predominance of cord or string designs on their pottery, they are sometimes called the String or Cord Ceramics People. Another example of a composite style is that seen in the Rössen pottery (Fig. 46, (6, 7)) in which the northern influence is strong.

Fig. 47.—The Neolithic pottery of Great Britain was coarse and inferior to that made on the continent. A bowl of the best British workmanship is shown at the left, and at the right the character of some of the ornamentation.

Courtesy of the Trustees of the British Museum.

The Neolithic pottery of Great Britain and Ireland was coarse (Fig. 47) throughout the age and, in general, was much inferior to that of the continent. The ornament was made by pressing a twisted cord or the finger nail into the wet clay. Measurements of the finger-tip impressions on jars show that they are small and indicate that the potters were women.

A false impression of the characteristic pottery of the Neolithic peoples is probably given by illustrations since the

(6) and (7) The Rössen pottery has the characteristic deeply incised decoration (*Tiefstich*) of the Northern ceramics but differs in shape. It is a modified form of the Northern technique.

Photograph by the Berlin Museum of Ethnology.

vessels shown are either the best preserved or the most carefully and artistically made. For example, in each of the four groups discussed above, the pottery of everyday use was crude, and either with no designs or with hastily made ones. The vessels placed in graves with the dead were the best they had and probably show the work of the most skilled workmen (Fig. 47). The common pottery of everyday use in the classical period of Greece was not the thin and artistically embellished ware shown in museums but was as coarse as the common jugs and crocks in use to-day.

The pottery made and used in the Eastern Mediterranean basin in Neolithic times (p. 74) was, in general, much more advanced than that of Central and Northern Europe. In Greece, for example, there were dishes with vertical sides and hollow feet, globular vessels with straplike handles, and vases with small necks. Designs were made with stamps as well as freehand. A common kind of pottery had a white slip on which patterns were drawn in red paint. In other places, black ware was made.

Weaving. Although most of his clothes were probably made of skins, Neolithic man early learned to spin and weave. Little is known of his cloth except from the charred fragments in pile dwellings but the many spindle whorls for making thread, and loom weights for keeping the threads taut in the loom, show that the women were constantly employed in this work. A further discussion of weaving is given in the paragraphs on pile dwellings. It is known that blue, black, yellow, and red dyes were used and doubtless the cloth was dyed not only in these colours but in various shades and tints. Without doubt he made sandals to protect his feet, of leather by preference, but when leather was not available, of vegetable fiber (Fig. 48).

Agriculture. Without agriculture civilisation would have been impossible and man, for all time, would have remained in a state of savagery. Agriculture revolutionised man's life. As soon as he became a farmer he was no longer obliged to depend on a chance kill for food and he was not compelled to change camp frequently in order to find game. With food of his own raising he was not so frequently subject to the famines and hardships of the hunter. A settled agricultural life led to the building of houses and he no longer lived habitually in natural caves and rude shelters. He needed to measure the seasons in order to know when to plant and he invented a crude calendar.

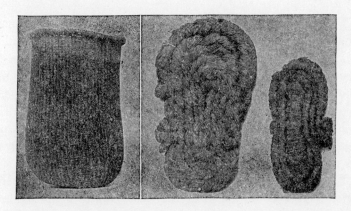

Fig. 48.—At the left a finely woven basket and at the right sandals. The sandals and basket illustrated here were found in a cave in Spain. The similarity of the sandals to those worn by American Indians of South America has raised a question as to their age. Without doubt, Neolithic man in Europe made articles of this kind.

Photographs by courtesy of the National Archæological Museum, Madrid.

It is often assumed that agriculture is an obvious invention. That this is not true is shown by the fact that for thousands upon thousands of years Paleolithic man failed to learn the lesson that if seeds are planted they will germinate and will yield a harvest. Agriculture is, in fact, one of the few truly great inventions of mankind. This being true, we should endeavour to learn how it was acquired. To do so we must search for the places where it has longest been practised, where the most favourable conditions for agriculture exist, and

where originated the ancestral stocks from which the cultivated grains were developed.

The Nile Valley [22] seems to have possessed more favourable conditions than any other region in the world for the
invention of agriculture. Grain has been planted and harvested there for probably 10,000 years, and conditions are
especially favourable for the discovery that grain will grow
when planted. Moreover, it seems likely that barley, probably the earliest of the grains cultivated by man, originated in
Abyssinia [23] as well as in Southeastern Asia where it grows
wild to-day.

The exceptional conditions favourable for the invention of
agriculture in Egypt are the yearly floods of the Nile which
are quiet and come at a propitious time. They begin about
the middle of July, gradually rise to their maximum about
the middle of September, and subside in October. As they
are not turbulent, an elaborate system of irrigation is not
necessary. The great discovery that seeds when planted will
germinate and yield a more abundant harvest than in the wild
state was probably made by some one man, and not by a
number of men in many places. It probably came about in
some such way as this: an observant man noticed that barley

[22] See discussions by W. J. Perry: "The Growth of Civilization," and G.
Elliot Smith: "Essays on the Evolution of Man." A bibliography on this subject is given in each.

[23] According to the work of Prof. N. Vavilov, Director of the Institute of
Applied Botany and New Cultures (*Bulletin of Applied Botany and Plant
Breeding*, 16, 2, 1926, Leningrad) as reviewed in *Nature*, Sept. 11, 1926, pp. 392-
393, two centers of origin for the barleys are indicated: in Abyssinia and in
Southeastern Asia. Cultivated oats are undoubtedly of polygenetic origin, and
five geographical and genetical centers are established. Southwestern Asia is
recognised as the chief center of diversity of rye. Flax is referred to three
groups, of which one is Mediterranean, one Southwestern Asian, and one Abys-
sinian. The mountainous districts of Asia and the Mediterranean region were
the centers of varietal diversity of nearly all the important agricultural crops.

Schweinfurth (Ackerbau. *Reallexikon der Vorgeschichte*) thinks that we
must look for the original home of agriculture in regions where men were
especially advanced and where cattle, goats, sheep, pigs, and farm animals
existed in the wild state and where the oldest grains, barley and wheat,
existed in the wild form. These conditions, he says, are found only in Asia
Minor.

grew where the ground was moist and he observed that water had recently covered the depression where it grew. The idea occurred to him that he could increase his food supply by making a larger depression for the water to gather in. This he did and was rewarded by a large crop. Thus artificial irrigation and agriculture were invented and discovered at the same time.

Another suggestion is that agriculture was discovered by some unusually observant woman who noticed that where she had spilled seeds or bulbs the year before, there were many food plants the following spring. She may have pulled up some of the larger weeds and even cultivated the plants with a stick. Her labour being rewarded, she began to plant other seeds and gradually started a garden.

It is not known what plants or grains were first cultivated but the claim for barley seems well established. Examinations of the contents of the stomachs of the earliest Egyptian mummies show that all of them contained grains of barley, while ten percent of them also contained millet. There were no grains of wheat, oats, or other cereals. Barley was the universal food. Later, wheat and oats were cultivated, but rye was a rather late acquisition. Beans were used very early in man's history.[24]

After the technique of agriculture and irrigation was acquired, this wonderful knowledge spread to other places where irrigation was possible,[25] as in Mesopotamia. By experimenting in different places with different kinds of indigenous seeds the variety of cultivated plants gradually increased. The seed was carried by peoples on their wanderings and conquests, and at last became nearly universally distributed. There is no

---

[24] Although the evidence is conclusive that the predynastic Egyptians ate barley there is no convincing proof that they did not also eat wheat. The use of barley is proved by the presence of barley husks in the stomachs but as the glumes of wheat do not adhere to the grain the evidence would not be so easily obtained, even though the cereal were commonly eaten.

[25] W. J. Perry: "Children of the Sun." "Origin of Magic and Religion." "The Growth of Civilization."

evidence that any of the grains cultivated by Neolithic man in Europe were indigenous to that continent.

The augmentation of the food supply led rapidly to an increase in population, to overcrowding, and to migrations. With a dense population, political problems arose which eventually led to kingships and to complicated religious cults.

The Neolithic peoples who first came to Europe had both agriculture and domesticated animals, but not a great variety of either plants or animals. It was not long, however, before practically all the food plants and animals now used for food were introduced. We owe most of our knowledge of the domesticated plants to the preservation of the seeds in the mud of pile dwelling sites. Such deposits have yielded two species of barley, three of wheat, two of millet, the pea, lentil, poppy, and flax. Besides these, there are some which may or may not have been cultivated: the pigweed, parsnip, carrot, grape, and walnut.

It is generally agreed that agriculture originated either in Egypt or in Central or Western Asia but, wherever its home, it spread from Crete and the Danube basin to all parts of Europe. It has been suggested that it was carried with painted pottery from Turkestan to North China and possibly to Northwestern India.[26]

The Origin of Agriculture in the New World

The question of the origin of agriculture in the Americas has given rise to much discussion. The fact that European and Asiatic food plants were not cultivated in the New World has led one writer [27] to state "that the agriculture of the native peoples of North and South America was not introduced from the Old World but had an independent, indigenous development as is demonstrated by the fact that the American agriculture was based on native American plants." It is held by

---

[26] H. J. E. Peak: *Nature,* June 18, 1927, vol. 119, pp. 894-896.
[27] O. F. Cook, Peru as a Center of Domestication. *Jour. of Heredity,* vol. 16, nos. 2, 3, Feb.-Mar., 1925.

some that Peru was the centre from which agriculture spread. "In Mexico, as in Peru, the chief food product was Indian corn, or maize, and many other plants of the lower Peruvian valleys were cultivated throughout tropical America, including Mexico, as sweet potatoes, cassava, xanthosoma, gourds, squashes, peppers, beans, peanuts, tobacco, and cotton. That the same series of crop plants should attain such a wide distribution shows that many migrations took place and that many contacts were established." There are a great number of native food plants, of which eighty-nine are listed by Cook, and of this about seventy were cultivated. This fact shows that the conditions for the acquisition of agriculture were extraordinarily favourable. Even to-day the United States Department of Agriculture sends its agents to Peru to obtain new varieties of potatoes and other food plants .In addition to the numerous crop plants, at least four kinds of animals were domesticated in Ancient Peru—the llama, the alpaca, the guinea pig, and two or more species of dog. The llama and alpaca furnished wool and served as pack animals—the only beasts of burden in the New World. Guinea pigs were kept in the houses and were generally distributed among the natives. A species of duck was also probably domesticated. In Central America the turkey was tamed.

Not only had the Peruvians learned agriculture but they terraced their hills, they built aqueducts along precipitous slopes and narrow crests of mountains, some of them for many miles. Two examples will suffice to illustrate their engineering skill. A reservoir in the Valley of Nepeña is three-quarters of a mile long by more than a half-mile broad and has a massive stone dam eighty feet thick. At Chimbote was an aqueduct from the Santa River sixteen miles distant.[28] They fertilised their soil with great care and skill using guano from the islands of the coast and small fishes brought from the ocean. They had learned soil conservation and practiced it so successfully

[28] C. W. Meade, "Old Civilization of Inca Land," p. 27.

as to make our present wasteful methods seem those of a primitive and ignorant people.

It is not surprising that such expert agriculturists should have attained great skill in weaving. For their cloth they used three kinds of wool: coarse wool from the llama, fine wool from the alpaca, and very fine wool from the vicuna. Their cotton cloth was made from cotton raised in the lower valleys. They also used fibres from the maguey plant. Their skill in making cloth has been called "the most extraordinary textile development of a prehistoric people." The thread they spun is of such quality as to lead one writer [29] to say "the perfect thread is not to seek; it has been made."

The origin of American agriculture and civilisation raises an old and interesting question. Was agriculture independently invented in different parts of the world or did this great invention originate in one place and was it spread from that centre over the world? It is probably safe to say that most students of Prehistoric America hold that the ancient American civilisation are indigenous. However, the possibility that the impulse which had its fruition in the remarkable civilisations of Mexico, Central and South America came from Southeastern Asia by way of the islands of the Pacific as stepping stones must not lightly be thrown aside. The fact that small islands hundreds of miles apart—the Hawaiian Islands and many others—were populated and that many of them at one time had a relatively high archaic civilisation is evidence that what theoretically seems impossible has been accomplished. It does not seem impossible that natives from an oceanic island, in a starving condition, with not a vestige of seeds or roots of food plants that could be used for propagation, might have drifted to the western shores of South and Central America, having been carried far out of their course while attempting to reach some distant island in their many-oared canoes. Such peoples carrying a knowledge of agricul-

[29] W. S. Murphy, "Textile Industries," vol. 3, p. 83.

ture would immediately utilise any native food plants they found and would quickly learn to cultivate them.[30]

Whether or not agriculture was independently invented in the New World, the food plants which these ancient Americans discovered, cultivated, and improved have played a part in the modern world which cannot easily be overstated. The introduction of the potato from the tablelands of Peru, for example, made possible the great industrial development of Germany. If it had not been for this food the World War could have lasted but a few months, the consolation that tobacco brings would have been lacking, and the soldier would have been without the stimulating and nutritious chocolate which he so highly prized.

Domestication of Animals. It is not impossible that Paleolithic man captured young animals now and then and tamed them. A colt so captured might readily have been reared. However, the only evidence of the domestication of the horse by Paleolithic man consists in an engraving of a horse's head with what appears to be a halter.

It seems certain that all of the domestic animals of the Neolithic in Europe, with the possible exception of the horse and swine, were introduced from the East along with agriculture. The pile dwelling deposits yield remains of two varieties of pig (*Sus scrofa palustris* and *domesticus*), the goat, and sheep, three varieties of cattle (*Bos primigenius, brachyceros,* and *akeratos*), and the dog. No trace of the domestic cat has come to light in Europe. The discovery of a churn dash, and pierced pottery vessels for making curds shows that cows and goats were tractable.

The native home of the domesticated animals is not definitely known, but Western Asia seems to be the most probable place of their origin. Cattle were probably not derived from the wild cattle of Europe, but from an Asiatic species:

[30] For an interesting discussion of this subject by an enthusiastic exponent of the diffusion of cultures, see "The Growth of Civilization," Chap. V, by W. J. Perry.

and the swine, goat, and sheep could not have come from any European wild forms. The swine may be domesticated wild boars (*Sus scrofa*) although the Turbary pig (*Sus palustris*) found in pile dwellings is probably of Asiatic origin. Moreover, the evidence indicates that most of the domestic animals had been under man's control in Asia at least a thousand years before they appeared in Europe. There is some evidence that the Asiatic cow (*Bos nomadicus*) was domesticated as early as 8000 B.C., and the pig not later than 7500 B.C. Man had flocks of sheep and goats in Asia as early as 6000 B.C.[31] The fact that the habits of sheep have been so changed by human contact that they are now more stupid than any other of the domestic animals, points to a long domestication, but the evidence, nevertheless, indicates that they were late in coming under man's control. The camel is thought to have been used at least as early as 6000 B.C., when copper was first smelted, but it may have been domesticated much earlier. When and where the horse was tamed is not known. Wild horses lived in Europe as well as in Asia and it is possible that they were domesticated in the former continent.

There is a difference of opinion among prehistorians as to which came first, agriculture or the domestication of animals. In the writer's opinion it was not until man built houses and had a place of permanent abode that a captured animal could be raised successfully.

Ornaments. Although art is poorly developed in the Neolithic, the ornaments are, nevertheless, of considerable variety. Shells strung for necklaces and bracelets, and even carved into rings, were favourite adornments. Necklaces made of flat pebbles, clay beads, horn, soapstone, and amber, and of the teeth of such animals as the dog, wolf, fox, bear, deer, and wild boar, were worn (Fig. 49). Bracelets were made of marble, serpentine, jadeite, jet, and lignite. In some graves (Rössen) the arms of the skeletons are decorated with heavy,

---

[31] If the recent, more moderate estimates prove to be correct the figures given in this paragraph are too high.

well-polished marble bracelets. Amber was used in Denmark
in profusion during parts of the age, especially in the form of
beads in the shape of a double ax. In the so-called "separate
graves" (see Fig. 60, p. —) of Scandinavia, there are nearly
always two flat disks of amber, some of which are as much

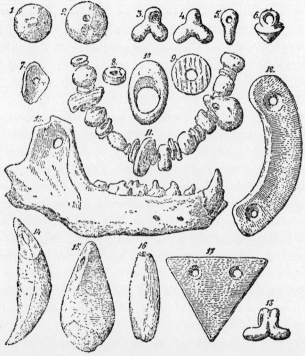

FIG. 49.—Amulets and necklace from Neolithic graves and megalithic tombs.
The materials are (7) soapstone; (9) scallop shell; (11) shell, bone, and
schist; (14) dog's canine tooth; (15) calläis; (17) lignite; (18) alabaster.
After de Morgan. Reduced in size.

as three inches in diameter. Bone pins were used to ornament
the hair or to fasten the clothing. A few breastplates made of
boar's tusks which had been split lengthwise and pierced have
been found. As metal was rarely used, it was difficult to find
any durable material that was really ornamental. Consequently, the use of such ornaments as are known does not

necessarily prove a lack of æsthetic taste. The love of flowers and colours may have been as strong then as now.

The tattooing and painting of the body were probably practiced—a custom which survived in the Balkans within historic times. Instruments for tattooing and stamps for marking the body have been found.[32] The custom of painting the body is further indicated by bits of ochre placed near the head or hands of the dead, and in grave pottery. The materials used for colours are red ochre (hematite), brown ochre (limonite), and vermilion (cinnabar). A prehistoric quarry where ochre was mined was discovered in the Dordogne district of France.

Figures of animals in amber and schist, figurines of women in pottery, and especially the decoration of pottery show the striving of the æsthetic sense.

Habitations. As long as man was in the hunting or food-gathering stage, he frequently moved from place to place and probably did not erect permanent huts, but was content with skin, bark, or branch shelters, and such natural caves and shelters as he could find. With the adoption of agriculture the need of a permanent home made itself felt. In such regions as Western, Central, and Northern France, where fertile valley lands lie close to natural shelters and caves, Neolithic man inhabited these just as did Paleolithic man (Fig. 25, p. 149), and as they are used by some of the present inhabitants of these regions. He was, however, not content with what Nature had done to make a home for him, but enlarged and changed the natural shape of the caves and shelters so as to make them more convenient and comfortable. Many such grottoes have been explored in the Marne region. These Marne caves are generally entered through a small antechamber, and in some of them the actual entrance is round and not unlike a porthole. It is possible that some megalithic graves may have been made in imitation of them (p. 139).

Over the greater part of Europe it was necessary for man

[32] A. Schenck: "La Suisse Prehistorique," 1912.

to construct his own dwelling places, and wood was generally used as a building material. Because of its rapid decay, all remains of the wooden buildings of that time have disappeared except those which have been preserved in marshes and in the mud of lake bottoms. Our knowledge of the homes of Neolithic man, therefore, is obtained from marshes and lake muds, and by carefully excavating the sites where houses once stood. In this way, the size and shape of the houses can be learned. The position of palisades is indicated by the holes where regularly placed posts once stood. The shortness of the life of wooden houses is well shown in parts of Sweden where, even in its ancient capital, little that is old is preserved.

The walls of the huts were generally made of wattle-and-daub which filled the spaces between wooden uprights. The earthen floor was often partly sunk in the ground, and it was not unusual to surround the house with large boulders to support the wall and roof beams. There was commonly a food pit, six or eight feet deep, for each hut or group of huts which was used for the storage of food. A similar device for preserving potatoes, beets, turnips, etc., and preventing them from freezing is employed in Nebraska, the Dakotas, Manitoba and elsewhere in the colder parts of Canada and the United States.

The pile dwellings, which are discussed in another place (p. 153), probably give a fairly accurate picture of most of the land houses. A land village (Michelsberg) in Southern Germany, which has been carefully excavated, was situated on a hill, about 850 feet high, and is probably typical of the region. It was admirably suited for defense and was a favourable site for a settlement because of numerous springs and nearby fertile plains. The settlement was surrounded by a ditch fifteen to twenty feet wide, by an inner earthen rampart, and, still further inside, by a wooden palisade.

Pit dwellings, that is, circular excavations partly or wholly underground and covered with a roof, were inhabited by some people. Such habitations were warm, if not elegant, and were used by the poor.

The Neolithic peoples of Greece lived in regular villages of square or round huts, some with stone foundations. In Sicily some villages had cobbled lanes or squares and were defended by ditches and rude fortifications.

The people of this age were probably comfortable in winter, and were able to raise large families. The wattle-and-daub or log houses were warm and there was an abundance of wood for fuel.

Writing. One cannot do more than hazard a guess as to the origin of writing. A few symbols of unknown meaning associated with the paintings made by Magdalenian man and on some of his bone engravings, may be the signatures of the artists or owners. If so, were these the earliest attempts of man to represent a thing by a sign? If they were, it would seem an easy step to add other symbols for animals, tools, weapons, and utensils, until a large number of ideograms were invented.[33] Although some ideograms may have originated in such a way, it is probable that most of them were the result of the gradual conventionalisation of realistic figures, until, in time, some of them lost all resemblance to the objects they represented and became geometric designs. Evidence from rock paintings in Spain and painted pebbles (Fig. 33, p. 64) from Mas d'Azil in Southern France, seems to bear out this last suggestion. In Obermaier's opinion [34] this change took place gradually and almost imperceptibly. A study of the figures in which Spanish rock paintings are shown on the left and painted Azilian (p. 64) pebbles on the right will make this argument clear.

Ideograms require so many characters that the next step would be the invention of symbols to represent sounds, such as a syllable, and, in this way, reduce the number of symbols.

[33] Common ideograms in use now are: $, %, £, =, +, ÷, ¶.
[34] H. Obermaier: "Fossil Man in Spain," p. 329.

If this supposition is correct, we may be obliged to go back to the Paleolithic for the beginnings of the written language. It is probable that the invention of an alphabet is another product of the Neolithic, that great age of fundamental inventions. It should be noted, however, that the Scandinavians of the Bronze Age made pictographs (Fig. 112, p. 242) but, as far as known, knew nothing of any other form of writing.[35]

Medicine and Surgery. Man has never been free from disease and injuries. From time immemorial, he has tried to find a cure for his ailments. We know nothing of the herbs which Neolithic man collected for medicines, the charms he may have practiced, or the dances which he may have performed to drive away the evil spirit. The equipment of a "medicine man" of the Bronze Age, described on page 256, may give us some insight into the custom of treating disease in the Age of Stone. The two ages merge without a break and, although the introduction of bronze made a great difference in the comfort of the people and in their knowledge of the world, it probably did not greatly affect their household beliefs and superstitions. Note, for example, how many of the natives of Haiti and San Domingo cling to the beliefs of their African ancestors although they have been under European influences for many years.

The most important surgical operation practiced in Neolithic times was trepanning. By means of a flint knife, a circular opening was made in the skull. In the Berlin Museum,

[35] A striking example of the rapidity with which the idea of a written language may be translated into action when once its value is recognised is afforded by the life of a remarkable Indian, Sequoya, who invented a written language for the Cherokees. Impressed by the ability of the whites to communicate thought by writing, he set to work to devise a similar system for his own people. Using an old spelling book, taking capitals, lower case letters, italics, and figures, and placing them right-side up and inverted, without any idea of their English sound, he utilised about thirty-five characters. He made fifty additional characters by modifying English letters and by inventing others. His final alphabet was capable of expressing every sound in the Cherokee language. Its value was soon recognised and thousands of Cherokees within a short time were able to read their own language.

there is a skull with an opening equal to about one-quarter of the area of the top of the skull (Fig. 50). When one considers that these operations were performed without anæsthetics and with no knowledge of the dangers of infection, it is remarkable that every patient did not succumb to the

treatment. That not all of the operations were fatal is proved by the healed edges of the bone of the openings on many skulls. Not only was one operation performed but some individuals submitted to the operation two or more times as is shown by some skulls with several openings, all of which had healed perfectly. One investigator, in order to determine the value of a flint knife in such an operation, trepanned the skull of a two months' old dog. The operation took eight minutes and was wholly successful: the wound healed quickly and the

FIG. 50.—Top view of a skull from which a very large piece has been trepanned. The healed edges show that the operation was not fatal.

Photograph by the courtesy of the Berlin Museum of Ethnology.

dog was none the worse for the experience. The trepanning was done by scraping.

What gave rise to such an unnatural and painful practice? It is possible that a man suffering from a depressed cranial fracture was relieved when the broken bits of skull were removed. After the splintered bone had been taken out, it was observed that he no longer suffered from convulsions and from this it was deduced that the imprisoned demon, who had caused the convulsions and who had given the patient such superhuman strength had escaped through the opening. From such experiences as this would grow the practice of relieving persons suffering from epilepsy, convulsions of all kinds, and, possibly, severe headaches, by taking out a part of the skull to permit the demon who caused the trouble to leave the body.

Strange examples of partial trepannation have been observed in female skulls from France. The scars are T-shaped and, in making them, only the outer layer of bone of the skull was removed. Their meaning is not clear. Possibly, the surgeon knew his limitations and, after scraping off the upper layer of bone, deceived his ·patient into believing he had reached the brain. However, this explanation does not account for the peculiar shape of the scars and the fact they are found on female skulls only. Were these the skulls of priestesses, and the scars the symbols of their high office or the marks of an initiation?

FIG. 51.—A female Neolithic skull with a T-shaped scar made by scraping the bone. France. After Manouvrier.

The illustration shows the curious shape of such trepannations (Fig. 51).

The practice of trepannation seems to have been more common in the Neolthic than in subsequent times. Few examples of trepanned skulls are known from the Bronze and Hallstatt Ages, possibly because of the incineration burials, but a large number of such skulls of La Tene Age have been found.

FIG. 52.—Bones pierced by Neolithic arrows. After Déchelette.

The need of surgical care is proved by skeletons with arrow heads embedded in them (Fig. 52). Skulls from Neolithic stations in France have been found which bear the marks of cauterisation. It is probable that such cauterisation was a treatment for melancholia and epilepsy as it was in classical and medieval times.[36]

Trade. The needs of Neolithic man were few and simple and he was able to satisfy most of them without the aid of the trader. He raised his own grain and vegetables, reared his own sheep, goats, and cattle, and wove his own cloth from flax and wool from his own farm. As clay suitable for coarse pottery is found almost everywhere, he could make his own pottery. His ware may not have been as fine or artistic as that of some of the neighbouring tribes who had either better clay or more skill, but it served his purpose. Generally he found some material from which to make his stone and flint tools. If he had none or poor material, he either had to go elsewhere for it or he had to barter something for it. In the Eastern Mediterranean, the best material for knives was obsidian, and as volcanic glass of good quality occurs on Melos and other islands, it was obtained from them either by trade or, more probably, by expeditions sent to get it.

One of the best examples of Neolithic trade (see map 117, p. 258) is seen in the widely distributed flint of Grand Pressigny (France). As this flint has a peculiar beeswax lustre, and as it occurs in large nodules from which long flakes can be struck, it is easily recognised. At the outcrop of the chalk in which nodules occur, the raw material was worked up into carefully prepared cores from which long flakes could be struck, and when broken off were ready for use with little retouching (see Fig. 44, p. —). Such flakes were used for knives and saws. There seems to have been a division of labour, some workmen carrying the manufacture to a certain point and more skilled men then finishing the work.

Caches or hoards in Sweden, the hidden stocks of Danish merchants who brought half-finished celts for exchange, have been found. It is not known what was given in exchange, but

[36] Walter Hough: "Fire as an Agent in Human Culture," *U. S. National Museum, Bulletin* 139, 1926.

it is possible that furs were needed for the large Neolithic population of Denmark and flint tools were bartered for them.

Shells of the Mediterranean and Red Sea are not uncommon in Southern Germany, Switzerland, and France, and amber was worn, though sparingly, by the pile dwellers. Either these objects were passed from person to person or they were carried by traders.

There seems to have been a brisk local trade on the Swiss lakes. This is indicated by the difference in the character of the products of different settlements. Some were largely agricultural, some made more pottery than they could use themselves, and some made finer cloth than others. Under such conditions trade would be inevitable.

It has been urged that the megalithic monuments of Scandinavia were erected to honour the dead leaders of expeditions who had come to these shores for amber.[37]

In the discussion of the Bronze Age it will be shown that the trade of Neolithic times was not widespread and had little effect on the life and thoughts of the people as it was largely confined to cultural circles. The Neolithic in Northern Europe was gradually brought to a close when trade routes were established to exchange amber and other commodities from the North for the much desired bronze from the South and West.

Neolithic Peoples. One cannot properly speak of the Neolithic peoples of Europe in the sense that there was but one race or type, any more than one can now speak of a European type or of a typical European or a typical American. The Neolithic lasted a long time and it is inconceivable that the population should have remained unchanged. At times, there were peaceful penetrations of unoccupied lands; at others, conquering tribes came, murdered the men, and carried off or killed the women and children, and either destroyed or took as their own the fruit of the labour of the conquered people.

[37] W. J. Perry: "The Growth of Civilization," p. 75.

The shifting of populations and of cultures can best be understood by considering a limited area of a part of the New Stone Age which has been carefully studied and where one can depend more on fact than on theory. Such a region is to be found in Germany where the careful work of archæologists has unravelled a most interesting history. This history begins at a time when the people who erected megaliths (p. 169) lived in the North and the lake dwellers and their land-living relatives (the Michelsberg people) lived in the South. After these people were well established, a people who made a distinctive type of pottery with ribbon designs (*Bandkeramik*) (Fig. 46, (1), (2), p. 98) began to move westward from their home on the middle Danube. As they were farmers who brought with them most of the grains now used in this region as well as domesticated animals, they followed the fertile plains and established colonies in favourable places. Here they remained for a time as their graves and pottery show, but not for long. They spread westward on the Rhine and, at the time of greatest extent, were in Northern Germany. These first invaders, the Band or Ribbon Ceramics people, at one time occupied a large territory but the megalith builders of the North and the lake dwellers of the South gradually encroached on them.

In the meantime, a people who made vessels ornamented in horizontal bands, called the Bell Beaker (*Zonenkeramik*) people, were spreading northward and eastward along the great water courses from Spain and France and penetrated as far east as the Hungarian plains.

Such movements made a homogeneous type impossible except in isolated islands such as Great Britain and Ireland, and regions such as Scandinavia. Although one type usually predominated in each region, other types were also there.

Because of such movements as those described, every country in Europe had varied physical types: long heads (*dolichocephalic*), short heads (*brachycephalic*), and intermediate (*mesaticephalic*) heads. In France, for example, 58 percent of six hundred and eighty-eight Neolithic skulls studied are long-headed, 21 percent short-headed, and 21 percent intermediate. The long heads predominated at the beginning of the age in France, but the short heads increased until at the close the latter were established. The short heads are similar to the Alpine type found at Ofnet.

In out-of-the-way places, such as the Cévennes, the old Upper Paleolithic, long-headed type persisted. Their contemporaneity with the Neolithic peoples is proved by several of their skeletons which still bear the Neolithic arrows which pierced them (see Fig. 52, p. 115). Before the close of the Bronze Age, the short heads seem to have largely ousted the aborigines even in such isolated regions as this.

Before the close of the Neolithic there were in existence in Europe the same three regional types of man which prevail now. In Spain and Portugal, the long-headed Mediterranean type appears to have predominated. This type is characterised by a long (*dolichocephalic*) skull, and a long narrow face. The stature is small or medium, the body slender, the nose rather large, the eyes dark, the hair brown or black, and the skin swarthy. At present, this race holds sway in the countries bordering the Mediterranean. It has been explained as the product of an easy life in a warm climate and bright sunshine.

The second or Nordic type has a long skull, long narrow face, straight fine aquiline nose, large stature, blue eyes, fair hair, and rosy skin. It is now widespread in the North of Europe, in Scotland, in the North and East of England, and especially in Norway and Sweden.

The third or Alpine type is of small or medium stature, but thick set, and round-headed. The face is broad and round, the nose is rather large, the eyes are light or dark brown and the hair black. This type first appeared, as far as is known, in the Epipaleolithic period. The Alpine type is said to be the result of an age-long adaptation to mountains and barren regions. It seems to have entered Europe during Epipaleolithic times and occupied a region between the Nordics on the North and the Mediterraneans on the South. It is a successful type, for it has gradually spread until it is now dominant in France, Switzerland, the Balkan States, Hungary, Czechoslovakia, Russia, and Asia Minor.

"Nevertheless, the fact remains that even in the Neolithic period, or rather near the end of the Neolithic, the anthropological complexity which now exists in Switzerland becomes clearly noticeable. Here, for the first time, we recognise the presence of representatives of the big, dolichocephalic people of the North. These become more and more numerous as we pass towards Central and Northern Europe.

"In Germany, Neolithic human remains are generally dolichocephalic. In the southwest, according to Schliz, the dominant type is at first the long-faced, Nordic type, but later we see the arrival of brachycephalics, and dolichocephalics of Mediterranean type. In Bohemia and Silesia, the men of the Polished Stone Age usually belong to the Nordic race. So it is also in Hungary. According to Giuffrida-Ruggeri, in the Illyrian and Danube regions, dolichocephalic skulls are very numerous in the most remote periods; they gradually decrease in number and almost entirely disappear in many regions on the descent of the Alpine peoples from the mountains to the plains.

"If we penetrate into Russia, we see that in the southwest, in Ukraine, Volhynia, and also in Poland, dolichocephalics of great stature are more or less dominant in the Neolithic "kourganes" or tumuli; and farther north and east, we find only dolichocephalics. Bogdanov has shown that the most ancient race of Central Russia (inhabitants of settlements on the shores of Lake Ladoga described by Inostranzeff) had long heads and faces like the modern inhabitants of Sweden.

"Finally, in Scandinavia and Denmark, the phenomenon is still more marked. According to Montelius some skulls from Neolithic burials are brachycephalic and resemble in form the skulls of Laplanders, but the majority resemble those of

modern Swedes. The skeletons indicate a high stature and ro-
bust frame. Scandinavia at this period was already populated
by the direct forebears of the modern populations who best
represent the ideal type of *Homo nordicus.*" [38]

Thus, even at the end of the Neolithic period, it is possible
to recognise, in its broad outlines, the geographical distribution of the three principal types which anthropologists have
been able to distinguish as the result of their studies of the
numerous varieties or sub-races, the amalgamation of which
forms the ethnographical constitution of present-day Europe.

Great Britain and Ireland seem to have been populated by
a race of long-headed people of less than average stature with
well-shaped heads of rather more than average size. The discovery of a Neolithic skeleton on the coast of Essex, England,
in a cliff, two feet below the prehistoric level and twelve feet
below the present land surface, is interesting. It lay on its left
side with arms folded on the breast, knees bent and thighs
flexed close against the body. "An examination of the
state of the bones and its position in the bank showed
that this 'crouched' burial had been made by the people
who lived on the old land surface and worked the Neolithic
flints. The skeleton proved to be that of a young, well-built
woman, five feet four inches in height, with a rather small
but finely proportioned head, a face with regular features, a
somewhat prominent nose and well-formed chin. All her teeth
were sound and regular, being set on a well-spread palate.
Her cranial dimensions are those which are still prevalent
among English women. Amongst her ribs was found a heap—
nearly a pint—of the seeds of the wild blackberry and dog-
rose, but whether these represented a last meal, or a store
provided by relatives for her journey after death, one cannot
tell. Clearly she died in the autumn of the year. As to
the period at which she lived there can be little doubt.
The kind of flint tools and the fragments of pottery—of

[38] M. Boule: "Fossil Men," 1923, pp. 340-341.

FIG. 53.—Restoration to show the activities of a Neolithic farmer in a part of Germany. Note the jar with the ribbon design (Fig. 46, (1), p. 98) on the woman's head, the plows and hoes with stone points, the form of the houses, and the herds of domesticated animals. There is little evidence for the dress. *After Karl Schumacher.*

an early 'beaker type'—are those common in England about 2000 B.C." [39]

It has been urged, with much reason, that the dominant stock of Ireland is not Keltic but Neolithic and is characterised by people with rather long heads, dark hair and a short, though well-proportioned, body. The apparent increase of dark-haired, long-headed, rather short people in the slums of London and in British manufacturing centres has led to the assumption that these people are the descendants of British

Fig. 54.—Clay figures. These figurines covered with designs which probably represent tattooing were found at Cucuteni, Roumania. They may be female idols. After H. Schmidt. Reduced in size.

Neolithic ancestors, who, having survived because of their ability to withstand hardships, are now increasing because they are better able than others to live under slum conditions.

Personal Appearance. It is evident from the above that it would be idle to attempt to describe the appearance of Neolithic man except in a general way. The illustration (Fig. 53) gives as true a picture as is possible with the fragmentary material at hand. Their clothing was made of skins, and linen and woolen cloth. They wore sandals (Fig. 48) and wove

[39] Sir Arthur Keith: "The Antiquity of Man." London, 1925, pp. 47-48.

baskets. They were in no sense savages, and their standard of living was probably as high as that of some millions of the civilised people of Europe to-day.

Religion. Our knowledge of the religious beliefs and customs of the Neolithic is obtained (1) from the kind of burial, whether inhumation or incineration, (2) from the posture

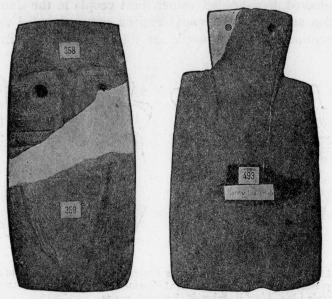

Fig. 55.—Pendants probably with religious significance. Reduced in size.
Photographs by the courtesy of the National Archæological Museum, Madrid.

of inhumation skeletons, whether contracted or outstretched, (3) from the contents of graves, (4) from the kind of monuments, such as dolmens, and flat burials, (5) from objects of supposed religious significance, as, for example, clay figurines (Fig. 54), carved pendants (Fig. 55), and other idols (Fig. 56), (6) from the religious beliefs of the Eastern Mediterranean peoples and Mesopotamia, (7) from rock engravings, (8) from the religious beliefs of primitive peoples of the present era, and (9) from theoretical considerations. Of these, perhaps the greatest dependence can be placed on the grave furniture, figurines, and the beliefs of Early Mediterranean, and primitive peoples.

Without doubt, the Neolithic folk were full of superstitions just as are all primitive peoples. Civilised man to-day has

Fig. 56.—Female idol. After Kendrick.

fewer superstitions but he has some as senseless as ever had Neolithic man. Nothing that Neolithic man believed, for example, could have been more unreasonable and senseless than the modern belief in the evil influence of the number thirteen. Could anything be more absurd than this belief that the Supreme Being would cause or permit the death of one of His children if, perchance, thirteen instead of twelve or fourteen sat at a table?

The law of taboo was doubtless rigidly enforced, because if disaster came to a community, it would be thought to have been brought about because someone had broken the law of taboo. Ornaments, such as miniature axes and pointed objects, may have been amulets to ward off the "evil eye."

The dead may have been buried with the knees bent and bound to the body in order to keep the spirit of the dead man in the grave. The placing with the skeleton of the most skilfully made vessels, weapons, ornaments, and tools, may not prove a belief in a future existence, but it is difficult to explain the practice in any other way.

During the Neolithic, images of a primitive deity in the form of a female idol appeared, which in the Danube and Aegean basins are of clay and are generally steatopygous, and in France are engraved on stone. From these it would appear that "there was a gradual development in prehistoric times of the conception of a creator, the giver of life, health, and good luck." This "great mother," at first with only vaguely defined traits, was probably the first deity that the wit of man devised to console him with her watchful care over his welfare in this life and to give him assurance as to his fate in the future.[40] It has been maintained that in the megalith regions of Western France, the female goddess acts as the guardian of the megalithic tomb.[41] This female goddess, called the Great Mother, was in later times, at least, the incarnation of the principle of fertility, and, as such, collected around herself all sorts of qualities associated with the welfare of mankind.[42]

A change in religious beliefs which swept over Europe in the Bronze Age began near the close of the Neolithic. This

[40] G. Elliot Smith: "The Evolution of the Dragon," 1919, p. 151, W. J. Perry: "Children of the Sun," p. 216.
[41] J. Déchelette: "Manuel d'Archéologie," pp. 217, 428-429, 584, 594.
[42] W. J. Perry: "The Children of the Sun."

is shown in the adoption of incineration. Does this mean that it was believed that unless the body is destroyed, the soul cannot escape? With incineration probably came the worship of the sun, of which there is abundant evidence (p. 253) and which was widespread in Great Britain and Ireland and on the Continent during the Bronze Age.

Agriculture gave rise to religious ceremonies of many kinds. It became a sacred thing throughout the world and the festivals of planting and harvest led to elaborate religious rites. The more uncertain the harvests, the more sacred the religious rites. Perhaps nowhere in the world to-day is this better seen than in the ceremonial dances of the desert Indians of New Mexico and Arizona.

Burials. The Neolithic peoples buried their dead as carefully and as reverently as the people of our generation. Whether this was done wholly because of affection for the dead, or because of fear that the spirit of the deceased might do harm to the living if his body were not properly cared for, is not known. But it is probable that family affection was as strong then as now and that, although both motives may have impelled them, nevertheless, the love of the living for the dead was the stronger.

Along the Atlantic and Baltic coasts, in Great Britain and Ireland and from Palestine to India, megalithic monuments were erected to honour the dead. These tombs were constructed of monoliths, the earlier ones, called dolmens, of four to six upright slabs and a large covering slab; later ones, called passage graves, had a covered passage leading to the burial chamber and, still later, the hallcists (see Fig. 83, p. 179) had covered passages for the reception of the dead made of large upright slabs with several covering slabs. Megaliths are discussed in Chapter VI.

In the Marne region, where the underlying chalky limestone is easily excavated, artificial caves were made. A trench led to the cave entrance which was generally a small rounded hole closed by a stone slab. Some of the caves had an antechamber. The smallest of the caves is a little more than six feet square and the largest about twelve feet on each side. The height varies from three and one-half to five and one-half feet. Each of these artificial tombs had a number of skeletons but some of the largest contain the smallest number of burials, suggesting that the latter may have been mortuary chapels or possibly the burial places of chiefs. On the walls of some of these tombs are rudely carved images of female figures, probably a deity, and drawings of hafted axes. Buried with the bodies were fine flint and jadeite celts, flint knives, scrapers, arrowheads and flakes. Some amber and "calläis" objects were found. No metal was discovered. In parts of France and Belgium, some of the caves in which Paleolithic man had lived were used by Neolithic man as communal burial places. In one such cave the remains of not fewer than fifty skeletons were interred.

In several places in France, Neolithic skeletons were buried under huge glacial boulders. In the Seine-et-Marne district, for example, more than fifty skeletons with flint celts, serpentine amulets, bone awls, and flint implements, were buried at three different levels beneath a large boulder. In the same province, a skeleton with fragments of pottery and beads was discovered under a boulder surrounded by flagstones.

Most of the Neolithic burials were not made in caves, or under boulders, or in megalithic tombs, but were, as now, in graves in the earth. Over the most populous parts of Europe —the Danube and Rhine valleys, in Switzerland, Italy, and elsewhere—interment was in the ground, and even in the regions of caves and megaliths most of the people were probably buried in the ground. Consequently the striking burials just discussed should be considered as exceptional. A great deal is known about flat burials, in graves without mounds, in Germany. One Neolithic people (Hinkelstein) buried their dead in an outstretched position, that is, they were laid on their backs with their arms at the sides. The men's skeletons were each accompanied by a pottery jar of the best workmanship, and some of the following objects: polished celts, shoe-last celts, arrows, small flint knives, and scrapers, whetstones, punches, awls of bone and horn, ornaments made from stone, shells, horn, and teeth, flint and pyrites for making fire, and ochre for painting. The grave furniture of the women's burials was somewhat different. It consisted of a pottery jar, a hand mill for grinding grain, and many ornaments. The graves were flat and none had a mound of earth over it.

Another Neolithic people (Rössen) laid the body on its side with the knees drawn up to the chest, that is, in a contracted position. The graves were in rows. Still other tribes (Thuringian or String Ceramics peoples) used small cists or shaft graves, and mounds. In these graves some of the skeletons were in a contracted and some in an outstretched position. The latest bodies were cremated.

In Scandinavia, there lived at the same time as the builders of the megalithic tombs a race that had battle-axes with one hammer end, and wore large disk-shaped buttons of amber. Whether this was a warrior race who exacted tribute from the megalith builders or who served as the latter's warriors is not known. They interred their dead in artificial mounds or barrows, and the same barrow not infrequently is found to cover a number of successive burials.

In parts of England, the dead were buried in long barrows or mounds, all of which are collective burials. Generally, inhumation was practiced. These "long barrow" men were long-headed. The objects buried with them are perforated animals' teeth, jet beads, and beautifully-worked, leaf-shaped arrowheads. The Neolithic pottery of the British graves is, as has been stated, in general, much inferior to that of the Continent.

The weapons and ornaments of the dead were buried with him, just as they were in the Paleolithic graves of Le Moustier and Combe Capelle (p. 21) and just as in parts of Sweden to-day, the dead man is buried with his pipe, knife, and a flask of wine. In inhumation burials, the body was clothed as in life with its ornaments and weapons. In some graves, food was placed conveniently at hand for the journey to the other world.

Toward the close of the Neolithic, incineration began to be practiced. When first adopted, the grave objects were placed entire in the graves without first having been burned on the funeral pile. The burning of the possessions of the dead along with the corpse came later when the religious beliefs were more fully developed and it was believed that the weapons and other possessions had to be "killed" so that their spirits might be useful to the spirit of the dead man in the other world.

Summary. The Neolithic period was the most important chapter in the whole history of man. Compared with it, the history since the beginning of the Christian Era seems trivial. Compare the achievements of that distant time with the greatest inventions and discoveries of modern times: the inventions of the steam, and of the internal combustion engines, of the aeroplane, of the radio, the many applications of electricity, and the hundreds of other inventions and discoveries of which we are so proud. Man's greatest needs are for food, clothing, shelter, transportation, government, and religion. He can get along without books, without rapid transit, and without great cities. His most complete rest and recreation is in the woods and mountains where he lives the life of Neolithic man.

The Neolithic is the greatest of all chapters in human history because the inventions and discoveries of that time are the broad foundations upon which the whole structure of modern civilisation is built. Neolithic man invented agriculture. He domesticated animals. By these means, he made himself more independent of the caprices of Nature and was better able to cope with famine. He invented pottery and the baking oven and could cook his food nearly or quite as well as it is cooked to-day. He learned the art of spinning and weaving and, although the cloth commonly was coarse, it was probably as warm as that made now. He learned to dye his cloth and thus satisfy his æsthetic taste. He learned to construct well-made, comfortable houses, and to lay out villages. As a result of living in organised communities, he invented the fundamentals of government. The only means of transportation, as far as known, was by foot and by boat. But this was sufficient to enable him to spread over nearly the whole world: over Asia, Africa, Europe, the Americas, and the islands of the sea. Then, progress was slow; now, it is rapid. It is merely a matter of degree.

Not only did man invent means of improving his condition but he learned the fundamentals of war: he fortified his house and his village, and sometimes he warred with his neighbours. Warfare, however, in the modern sense, did not arise until the Age of Metals.

Even in that distant time, man was not content to spend all of his thought on material things but reflected on death and life after death. His philosophy finally led him to think of the body as a clog to the soul and he arrived at the conclusion that only by destroying the body by fire could the soul escape.

His inheritance from his Paleolithic and Epipaleolithic ancestors consisted of the technique of making flint, horn, and bone implements, of hunting, of the knowledge of edible fruits, vegetables, nuts, and roots, of the way to make fire, possibly of tanning, but of little else. By persistent effort, he added to this meagre equipment until he had acquired the elements of which our modern civilisation is merely an elaboration. When he discovered how to smelt copper and tin, and to make bronze, he entered the Bronze Age.

CHAPTER IV

THE REMARKABLE NEOLITHIC CIVILISATION OF SCANDINAVIA

THE peoples of Scandinavia developed a Neolithic civilisation so unique and unexpected that it cannot be discussed with that of the rest of Europe without confusion. Even the casual observer who visits the larger museums of Scandinavia, at Copenhagen, Stockholm, Gothenburg, Oslo, and those of Germany, France, Spain, and Great Britain, is struck with the wonderful flint- and stone-work of the North as compared with the relatively few and uninteresting Neolithic stone and flint objects in the museums to the South. The thousands of beautifully and skilfully wrought tools and weapons indicate a numerous, intelligent, and inventive people. In no other region in Europe did flint-working reach such a high degree of perfection.

This peculiar and high civilisation was the result of a number of causes, of which the following seem to have been the most important. (1) There was a supply of flint of unusually fine quality. As this had been brought by the Great Ice Sheet and left on and near the surface with other glacial débris over a wide area it could easily be obtained. Some glacial deposits were mined for it. (2) The lands of Denmark and Southern Sweden were fertile and were doubtless covered with fields of wheat, millet, flax, and barley, and with pastures with cattle, horses, and sheep. The pig may have run wild or have been kept as now. It is possible that Denmark was even then noted for its cattle. With a large population and a constant supply of food from their flocks and herds, their fields, and fisheries, the leaders of the region acquired wealth, and had the leisure and means to employ men to do their bidding. As a result, the more skilled flint- and stone-workers were employed to make and invent tools and weapons, and ornaments to satisfy the vanity, the artistic taste or purposes of their masters. This can be surmised since progress is retarded or stopped when the clutch of poverty compels man to expend his energies for a mere existence. (3) Ideas may have been brought in by traders who had come north for amber. (4) The isolation of the region enabled the people to develop a characteristic civilisation. (5) Finally, the Neolithic lasted longer in Scandinavia than elsewhere in Europe and more time was given for the acquisition of a superior technique, the invention of different implements and weapons and the development of social customs which reacted on the kinds of objects employed. Some of the reasons, then, for the uniqueness of the Scandinavian civilisation were an abundant supply of high-grade flint, a constant supply of food, leaders with leisure, the isolation of the region, and a longer time in which to perfect the technique of flint-working and to invent artifacts. It is probable that the Neolithic Scandinavians were skilled navigators and, as will be shown later, there is evidence that they reached North America some thousands of years before the Norsemen touched the shores of New England.

Scandinavian Geography. Scandinavia was the last region in Europe to be occupied by man. During the Paleolithic it was almost completely covered by the Great Ice Sheet, except during the Interglacial stages.

Yoldia Epoch. When the ice sheet withdrew to the mountains of Norway and Sweden, it left the northwestern part of Europe under very different conditions from those of the present. The low-lying parts of Denmark, Sweden,[1] and Norway, and most of the coastal lands of the Baltic were then under the water of a great arm of the sea which extended from the Atlantic over the Russian plain to the Arctic Ocean. The

[1] A good summary of the Neolithic climates and geography is to be found in C. E. P. Brooks: "The Evolution of Climate," 1922.

shells which were buried in the muds of this great strait are not of the same species as now live in the Baltic but are more like those of the colder parts of the Arctic Ocean. One of these shells, *Yoldia arctica,* now lives only in water whose temperature is below 32° Fahrenheit, and thrives in the mud of thaw water discharged by glacial streams. These shells are so abundant in the deposits of this enlarged Baltic that the sea is called the Yoldia Sea.

The vegetation of the land was that of the cold tundra, such as now thrives in Spitzbergen and Lapland. This is indicated by fossil plants which include an Arctic willow (*Salix polaris*) and *Dryas octopetala.* All the evidence points to a climate much colder than that of the present and to a sea in which icebergs floated.

Ancylus Epoch. The Yoldia epoch closed with an elevation of the land which closed the straits and converted the Baltic into a fresh-water lake, called *Ancylus Lake* from a characteristic mollusk (*Ancylus fluviatilis*). A warmer climate succeeded the cold Yoldia climate and the birch, aspen, and pine replaced the tundra flora. It was at this time that man first set foot in Scandinavia, for it was then that the Epipaleolithic folk (*Maglemose*) lived on the west coast of Denmark and in Southern Sweden. As the present fertile and populous districts of Sweden were then covered with water, the shores on which these earliest people lived are now well above the sea. The Ancylus stage, therefore, marks the beginning of man's occupancy of Scandinavia and is in the Epipaleolithic period. The date of this lake is placed at 6000-4000 B.C. by Brooks, and 10,000-4000 B.C. by Kossina.

Littorina Epoch. In the next stage the land was again depressed. The southern part of Scandinavia sank and a broad opening to the Atlantic converted the fresh Ancylus Lake into a sea in which the water was nearly or quite as salty as that of the ocean. This is called the Littorina Sea because of the presence in it of the mollusk *Littorina littorea.* The climate was warmer than in that region now. Oysters were abundant and the lands were clothed with forests of oak. With the appearance of this flora, the pines and birches became unimportant. The fir and beech had not yet arrived. This is the period of the shell heaps, or Ertebolle stage, in Northern Europe. During this epoch, the Kitchen Midden folk (p. 80) found an abundance of oysters and other shellfish and lived throughout the year on the shores of the sea.

Following the Kitchen Middens comes the Full Neolithic. The geography and climate of the Full Neolithic was so nearly like that of the present that it may, for convenience, be regarded as identical.

SUMMARY OF SCANDINAVIAN CHRONOLOGY

1. Retreat of the last Ice Sheet which covered the Baltic and surrounding lands.

2. *Yoldia Sea.* Land depressed; Scandinavia an island; Climate cold; Vegetation that of the cold tundra; Probably no human beings.

3. *Ancylus Lake.* (Maglemose Stage, p. 63.) Land higher than in last stage; The Baltic a fresh-water lake; Climate warmer; Man enters Scandinavia; Maglemose culture.

4. *Littorina Sea.* (Ertebolle or Kitchen Midden Stage, p. 80.) Land lowered; Baltic sea enlarged; Water, normal sea water; Climate warmer than now.

5. *Full Neolithic.* Climate and geography nearly as now.

Development of the Scandinavian Cultures. There seems to have been an orderly development of flint and stone implements in Sweden with little influence from without. Some of the Scandinavian axes and pottery, for example, were carried to the south or were copied by their southern neighbours and some things from the south were brought north but, in general, the culture of these Neolithic tribes does not seem to have been greatly influenced from the outside. This is rather unexpected because the Scandinavians of that time, with little doubt, were skilful navigators, as is shown by the similar cultures of Denmark, Sweden, and Norway, which indicate frequent visits across the Baltic.

It is possible to divide this Northern Neolithic into four fairly well-defined periods which are based largely upon the kinds of flint and stone implements and weapons, which were somewhat gradually evolved, and upon the kinds of megalithic tombs which were erected.

Period I:[2] In this earliest stage of the Full Neolithic the characteristic flint celt has a pointed butt and is elliptical

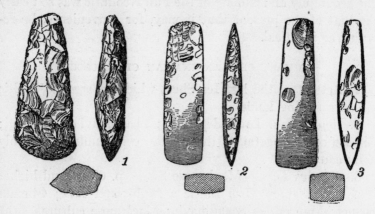

Fig. 57.—The evolution of Scandinavian stone celts, with cross sections: (1) is of the first period, (2) of the second, and (3) of the third. In the fourth period, the celts were like those of the third period but flared more toward the cutting edge.

in cross section (Fig. 57 (1)). Some of these celts are polished. The reasons for believing them to be the oldest of the flint celts are: their rarity, their shape, which is one from which the subsequent celts could, by modification, be derived; and because they have not been found in megalithic graves, and, consequently, probably preceded them in time.

Period II: In the second period, the flint celt has a thin butt with squared sides, and flattened convex surfaces (Figs.

[2] O. Montelius: "Chronologie der jüngeren Steinzeit in Skandinavien" (*Korr.-bl. d. d. Ges.*), XXII, 1891, pp. 99-105.

Fig. 58.—(1) A roughly shaped celt of Period II ready for polishing; (2) a celt of Period II polished and ready for use; (3) a sandstone whetstone for polishing flint implements. Williams College Museum. Reduced.

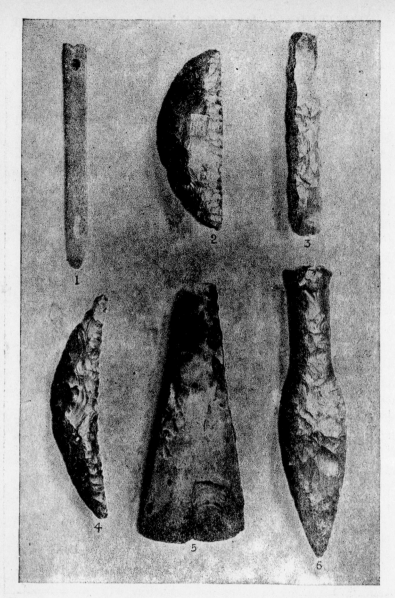

Fig. 59.—(1) A slate pendant. Such pendants are common but their significance is unknown. (2) and (4) Crescent-shaped cutting tool common near the close of Period IV; (3) a flint chisel; (5) a polished celt with a square butt and wide cutting edge, probably of the last period; (6) a flint dagger, probably made in imitation of bronze daggers, Period IV. All of these objects are from Sweden. Williams College Museum.

138

57 (2) and 58 (1), (2)). These are found in dolmens, the oldest and simplest of the megalithic graves.

Period III: The flint celt of this period has a thick butt with nearly square cross section (Fig. 57 (3)). Skill in making battle-axes (Fig. 62) of exquisite shapes and workmanship reached its climax in this period. Flint daggers were skilfully made but the technique of flaking did not reach perfection until the following period. Arrowheads with triangular cross section, and amber beads were in abundance. In this period, the dead were buried in passage graves (see Figs. 78, 79, p 174).

Period IV: The celt is nearly like that of the preceding period but is wider at the edge (Fig. 59 (5)). The typical weapon is the beautiful, flaked, flint dagger of wonderful workmanship with blade and handle in one piece (Fig. 59 (6)). Rough hammer axes are common but battle-axes, as a rule, are no longer of graceful shape. Crescent-shaped knives (Fig. 59 (2) and (4)) of the dagger technique are characteristic. The graves are long megalithic galleries (Fig. 83, p. 179) or "hallcists." Amber is rare in graves.

FIG. 60.—The contents of a "separate grave." Note the (1) "battle-ax," (2) the fragment of pottery with characteristic ornamentation, and (3) flint gouge. Sweden.

Photograph by courtesy of the National Historical Museum, Stockholm.

There seems to have been three cultural groups in Scandinavia during a large part of the Neolithic: (1) the descendants of the Epipaleolithic peoples who lived on the less favourable lands of Norway and Sweden, back from the coast, who were probably not agriculturists but hunters and fishers; (2) the megalith builders, and (3) a people of rather high culture who buried their dead in low mounds (separate graves) (Fig. 60) and not in megalithic tombs. This last cultural group used battle-axes (see Fig. 60 (1)) and a favourite ornament was large amber buttons or disks usually worn in pairs.

Polished Flint Implements. The long, thin, polished stone celts (see Fig. 58 (1), (2)) of Period II were made in great

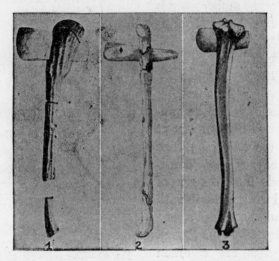

FIG. 61—(1) A flint celt with wooden haft. Denmark. After Blinkenberg. (2) Stone celt in its original haft. England. Courtesy of the Trustees of the British Museum. (3) Celt hafted in bone. Sweden. After Montelius.

numbers, as the hundreds of specimens in museums show. Such tools would not have been possible had not the flint nodules been in large masses and of unusual quality. The celts were first roughly shaped (Fig. 58 (1))—much as early Paleolithic man flaked his hand-axes, but of different shape —and were then laboriously and carefully polished on slabs of sandstone or quartzite (Fig. 58 (3)). The final product was a long, thin celt with slightly convex sides (Fig. 58 (2)) which was usually hafted (Fig. 61) in a wooden handle. A specimen in the Stockholm Museum has a bone handle (Fig. 61 (3)), probably an unusual method of hafting.

Chisels and Gouges. Flint chisels, some with the edge ground, were common tools. Flint gouges (Fig. 60 (3)), probably used for hollowing out logs for boats and for other purposes, have been found in great numbers, especially toward the close of the period. In parts of Sweden, where there is no flint, gouges were made of slate.

Axes. About the middle of the Neolithic, perforated axes came into fashion. As flint is too hard to be easily bored with

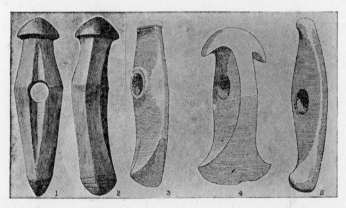

Fig. 62.—Battle-axes of graceful shapes such as those shown here may also have been used for ceremonial purposes. (3), (4), and (5) are from Denmark. Courtesy of the British Museum. (1) and (2) are from Norway. After Gustafson.

the abrasives at hand the axes were generally made of fine-grained igneous rocks, such as greenstones, but where these rocks were not available inferior rocks, such as sandstone, were employed. The most striking polished stone objects of the time are the so-called battle-axes (Fig. 62 and see also Fig. 60) which were probably weapons, symbols of rank, and ceremonial objects. Many of these axes were made with the greatest care and are of beautiful design and finish. Few of them were ever resharpened, which shows that they were not for rough use. The resemblance of some of them to bronze axes from Troy may furnish a means of dating the objects with which they occur. The battle-ax seems to have originated in Scandinavia and to have spread from there to other parts of Europe. There is a possibility, however, that they had their origin elsewhere. Axes almost identical in shape have been found in the Swiss and German pile dwellings, in the Danube Valley, Russia, and elsewhere in Europe and Asia. The shape and finish of the axes varied in time as is shown in the contents of the so-called "separate graves" of different

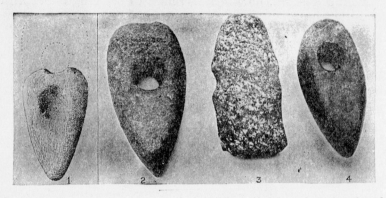

Fig. 63.—(1) A stone hammer ax which had been broken and partly rebored. The drill used here was solid. After Gustafson. (2) and (4) are hammer axes of the late Neolithic or early Bronze Age. (3) is a maul which was attached to a handle by thongs, as was a custom of the American Indians. (2), (3), and (4) are from the Williams College Museum. One-third actual size.

ages, and the style and workmanship of the axes of different tribes living at the same time had individual characteristics. The manufacture of these objects reached its artistic climax in Period III. Toward the close of the Neolithic (Period IV), hammer axes were used for domestic purposes (Fig. 63).such as driving stakes and posts and were made with little care and expenditure of labour. Some of the cruder hammer axes weigh several pounds. The holes for the handles were drilled by means of hollow and solid cylinders of bone or wood. The work was probably accomplished by a bow-drill. Many re-bored axes (Fig. 63 (1)) have been found, as well as the cores left when the holes were bored by hollow cylinders. Mauls (Fig. 63, (3) with grooves for attachment to handles by leather thongs were common. When fine flaking was at its best (see p. 139) the polishing of flint declined and the axes were clumsy and poorly finished. Stone plowshares which resemble perforated axes in shape, were doubtless used for the points of wooden plows.

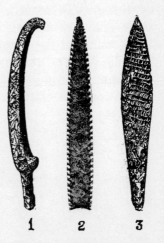

Flaked Flints. The Scandinavian tribes developed a technique in flaking flint which has few equals in the world. Some of their arrowheads are beautifully flaked and have finely serrated edges. A remarkable example of this high technique in flaking is seen in a dagger or small sword, in the National Museum of Copenhagen, which is made of wood with the cutting edges and point inlaid with thin, perfectly-shaped and fitted flint strips. Crescent-shaped tools (see Fig. 59 (2) and (4)), probably sickles, and saws are of fine workmanship. Another example of this marvellous skill is seen in the narrow, curved implement of Figure 64 (1), the spearhead of Figure 64 (2), and the dagger (Fig. 64, (3)) with "ripple flaking" similar in technique to the flint knives of Egyptian workmanship.

FIG. 64.—(1) This long, narrow, curved blade of unknown use from Denmark is an example of the skill of the northern workmen. (2) A spearhead with serrated edges. (3) Dagger with ripple flaking, somewhat like those of Egyptian workmanship. (1) and (2) after National Museum, Copenhagen. (3) Courtesy of the Trustees of the British Museum. The objects are not all of the same size and all are greatly reduced in size.

One of the finest and most characteristic implements of the Late Neolithic of Scandinavia is the flint dagger which reached the climax of its perfection toward the close of the age. The earliest daggers did not have flint handles but handles were doubtless made of leather. In the later forms (see

Fig. 59 (6)) the butt end of the dagger was fashioned into a handle which could have been used without a cover to protect the palm of the hand and to give a better grip. Some examples show a "seam" down the middle of the handle which resembles the stitches of a leather cover and may have been made in imitation of such a seam. Some of the daggers have been broken and resharpened more than once, with the result that the blades of some of them are shorter than the handles. Daggers are so numerous as to suggest that it was the custom for every man to carry one in his belt.

Ornaments. For a large part of the Full Neolithic amber was prized for ornaments. Thousands of amber beads and

pendants have been found in Denmark, most of which were discovered in bogs and damp places, for amber disintegrates when long exposed to the air. Much of it was in earthen jars. One such vessel, uncovered in cutting peat, had 5500 amber beads. A number of pieces of amber crudely carved in the shape of animals have been found, but pendants in the form of the ax (Fig. 65) are the common-

FIG. 65.—Amber models of double axes, Denmark. One-third natural size.

est of the worked objects. The ax was the symbol of the sun god who with his hammer destroyed his enemies. Small perforated stone axes were also worn as pendants. A peculiar, and, for a time, popular pendant has the shape of a chisel (Fig. 59 (1)). What may have been its significance is not known.

Pottery. The pottery of Scandinavia had a number of distinctive characteristics and is termed megalith pottery (Fig. 45 (1), (2), (3), p. 96).

Origin of the Scandinavian Civilisation

Once begun, the Scandinavian civilisation advanced with little apparent help from without. Its influence was felt by the nearby peoples immediately to the south and in Britain, but it did not impress itself on Europe to the degree one would have expected. The similarity of the tanged arrow-head, with triangular cross section, daggers with "ripple flaking," spearheads with serrated edges, and crescent sickles has suggested some influence from Egypt but, if so, it could have been little more than the result of the importation of a few examples of Egyptian workmanship which inspired the Scandinavian workers to modify what they already knew.

Efficiency of Neolithic Tools

The efficiency of the Neolithic stone tools was tested by a Danish archæologist (Sechested), who built a house with tools used by the Neolithic peoples of his country. With but one flint celt he cut down and topped twenty-six pine trees with an average diameter of eight inches—all in ten hours—and the celt was not resharpened during the work. The house, with window, door, and roof, was completed in sixty-six days. He found that a polished celt was much better than an unpolished one for felling trees. Besides the celt, flint saws, flakes, scrapers, and other flint implements were used in constructing the house.

Close of the Neolithic in Scandinavia. Because of the efficiency of these stone and flint tools, because no copper or tin deposits were known, because of the high cost of copper and bronze, and possibly because of the isolation of the region, the introduction of metal was late and did not quickly replace the stone tools. Toward the close of the age, stone tools made in imitation of bronze ones and copper and bronze tools made in imitation of Neolithic polished and flaked implements and weapons, began to make their appearance. The evidence of such imitation is well shown in Figure 66. The stone and copper celts (1) and (2), and the long stone and bronze axes (3) and (4) are almost identical in shape, as are also the stone and bronze axes (5) and (6). The similarity of stone and bronze spearheads (7) and (8) and daggers

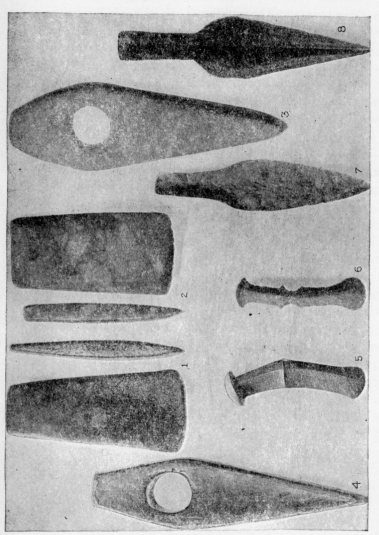

Fig. 66.—Implements made at the close of the Neolithic in Scandinavia showing the influence of bronze models from the South on the shapes of stone tools, and the influence of traditional stone tools on the shapes of bronze implements. (1) and (2) Thin bladed celts of copper, and of flint. Sections are also shown. (3) and (4) Stone, and bronze perforated axes. (5) and (6) Stone and bronze ceremonial or battle-axes. (7) and (8) Flint and bronze spearheads.

Photograph by courtesy of the National Historical Museum, Stockholm.

may be the result of imitation but the evidence is not so strong. Another reason for the slow introduction of bronze in Scandinavia was the great value of the early bronze implements which made their use, by any except the rich, well-nigh impossible. Later in the Bronze Age, when bronze was in general use, as little metal as possible was used in making a tool, and all waste was eliminated.

It is evident from the above that the Neolithic civilisation merged into that of the Bronze Age without a break. There is no evidence of an influx of new peoples. The customs of the peoples, their houses, their agriculture and stock-raising, and their religion probably continued unchanged or but slightly modified.

The reason for the failure of this civilisation to exert a great influence on the rest of Europe was twofold: its self-sufficient isolation, and the fact that until the Bronze Age, the peoples of the South had little that the people of the North desired. The South wanted amber but as it had almost nothing to offer in exchange little of it was exported and, as far as known, no well-marked trade routes were established. Amber, probably from Denmark, has been found in the pile dwelling deposits of the Swiss lakes, and in Germany, but it is in small quantities and could not have brought much intercourse.

CHAPTER V

THE PILE DWELLERS

THE SURPRISING CUSTOMS OF A NEOLITHIC PEOPLE

Not only did the peoples of the Neolithic build houses on land but very early in their career in Europe they learned how to build them on piles. The discovery that Neolithic tribes built pile dwellings was as unexpected as it was important in giving us a knowledge of the life of Neolithic peoples. As a result of a careful study of the tools, weapons, household utensils, pottery, wooden objects, cloth, and grains found in the mud between the foundation piles, more is known of the life and habits of Neolithic man from this source than from any other. Because of the insight they give of the habits and customs of Neolithic peoples, it will be necessary to give more space to their discussion than their relative importance would otherwise warrant. Fortunately, too, a people called the Michelsberg people (p. 118) who lived on neighbouring lands, had much the same culture and were closely related to the pile dwellers. They doubtless had similar habits and customs.

The discovery of the pile dwellings was made in 1853-54 when the waters of the Swiss lakes were very low. The people living on the shores of Lake Zurich took advantage of this condition to increase their lands by throwing up the mud from the temporarily dry shore. While doing this, they discovered many piles, pottery, and stone, and bone artifacts. The discoveries were reported to Ferdinand Keller of Zurich who appreciated their importance and who immediately began an investigation. As a result of careful dredging, scores of villages have been located, more than two hundred in Switzerland alone (Fig. 67). The best known lake villages are in a narrow belt of country forming the foothills of the Alps. The importance of the pile dwelling discoveries is due to the preservation by the water of objects which on land soon disintegrate and disappear, such as wooden utensils and tools of all sorts, cloth, seeds, baskets, and the walls and wooden parts of houses.

It is impossible to say how large a population lived in the pile villages but, if one can judge by the number of piles and the floor space of the houses which rested on them, it is

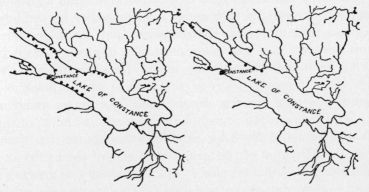

Fig. 67.—(*Left*) Map of Lake Constance, Switzerland, showing the location of Neolithic pile villages.
(*Right*) Map of Lake Constance, Switzerland, showing the location of Bronze Age pile dwellings. The villages were farther from the present shores and were larger than those of the Neolithic, though fewer.

certain that the larger villages contained several hundred people. For example, the first village investigated on Lake Constance was 700 by 120 paces in area and was supported by 30,000 to 40,000 piles. Other villages were 400 to 800 meters long and 30 to 75 meters wide. It should be noted, however, that the piles were not all driven down at the same time but some of them date from the beginning of the Neolithic and some are as late as the Early Bronze Age. It is an interesting fact that the settlements are more numerous where streams flow into the lakes; that is, they were on nearly the same sites as the villages of the present day. The lake shores and bottoms in such places were clay or sand and because of this piles could easily be driven. On other parts of the shore the bottom was either too hard, the water too deep, or the neighbouring land too steep or infertile to support a village.

The conditions were most suitable in lakes with shallow margins and soft bottoms. Such ideal conditions existed at Loubliana (Laibach) in the Julian Alps where at one time a large shallow lake existed. On the shores of this lake many pile dwellings were erected. As a result of the deposition of sediments brought by inflowing streams the lake has since disappeared. Pile dwellings have been discovered in the plain thus formed and probably many more will be unearthed when further excavations are made.

To cut down trees for piles with stone celts, and to drive 30,000 to 40,000, and even 60,000 piles was no small task, for the piles were about ten feet long and four to eight inches in diameter, and were driven three or more feet into the sand or clay. The labour of driving the piles was much less in very shallow water or on a muddy shore than in water three or four feet deep.

If, as seems to have been proved,[1] a dry period, whose duration was not less than 1000 years, coincided with that of the pile dwellings, these settlements were not lake but shore ones. The dry period is believed to have reached its maximum in the Bronze Age when the level of Lake Constance, for example, was two to three meters lower than now. This would explain the distribution of Bronze Age pile dwellings, which are now in deeper water than are those of the Neolithic.

Did Neolithic man settle on the shores of lakes, in moors and in swamps because there was more land free of forest in such places than elsewhere? To man, with nothing but the stone celt and fire, the forest was a formidable obstacle to agriculture and he was obliged to take what Nature offered.

[1] H. Reinerth: "Pfahlbauten am Bodensee." C. E. P. Brooks: "Climate Through the Ages."

FIG. 68.—Restoration of a pile dwelling village of Lake Constance, Switzerland. In this restoration, the village is correctly shown on the shore and in shallow water rather than in deep water. After H. Reinerth.

Fig. 69.—Restoration of the platform and front of a pile dwelling. This shows also some of the activities of the people: one woman is weaving on a primitive loom. Note, too, the method of attaching the floor beams to the piles and the roof to the walls. After R. R. Schmidt.

The typical pile dwelling (Figs. 68 and 69) consisted of two parts: a small workroom which opened on an uncovered platform or porch and an inner room for sleeping and living purposes. In building the house, piles were first driven for a foundation. When possible, the pile was so cut that the stump of a projecting branch would form a notch for the floor beams. The floor beams were then bound to the piles with ropes or withes or were mortised. The floor was made of split saplings four to six inches in diameter (much like the floors of the second story rooms in the cliff dwellings of Arizona). After the floor was laid it was covered with a layer of clay four to six inches thick. Such a floor could be made smooth and, at the same time, it would give warmth and keep out the air. The walls were made of wattle or upright saplings thickly plastered with clay. The gabled roof was covered with thick thatch, and the roof timbers were held together by roots and withes.

The front room had a domed baking oven on one side and, as hand mills for grinding cereals, pottery, and woven mats have been found in such rooms, it may properly be called a workroom. The inner or back room was without windows and had sleeping benches about four feet wide and sixteen inches high on three sides. In one corner was a hearth where the meals were prepared. The earthen floor was partly covered with birch bark mats. To form a true conception of the interior of the houses we must think of the arrangement of the pottery on the floor, of the stone and wooden tools and weapons, and the appearance of the walls hung with garments, dried herbs, and fruits and other possessions of the householder.

Whether there was a platform for the entire village or whether each house had its own platform and was connected with other houses by bridges, it is not possible to say. The description of a pile dwelling in Thrace, as given by Herodotus (early Fifth Century B.C.) is interesting because it may give us something of a picture of the Neolithic pile dwellings. He says (V. 14): "There is set in the midst of a lake, a platform made fast on tall piles, whereto one bridge gives a narrow passage from the land. The piles which support the platform were set there in old times by all the people working together but by a later custom this is the manner of their setting: the piles are brought from a mountain . . . and every man plants three for each woman that he weds, and each has many wives. For the manner of their dwelling, each man on the platform owns the hut wherein he lives and a trap door in the platform leading down into the lake. They make a cord fast to the feet of their little children lest the children fall into the water. They give fish for fodder to their horses and beasts of burden: and of fish there is such an abundance that a man opens his trap door and lets an empty basket down by a line into the lake, and it is no long time before he draws it up full of fishes."

Bronze Age Pile Dwellings. When the bronze celt was introduced it was possible to cut down larger trees and to use hard woods as well as pine. With the experience gained from their ancestors, the Bronze Age pile dwellers were able to build further out in the water, to prop their piles with stones or other piles, and to erect others to break the waves. Judging from the number of fishhooks (Fig. 73) fish was an important article of food. As the Bronze Age dwellings coincide with the period of maximum dryness (see table, p. 165), it would seem that they followed the shore as the water receded. This would account for their greater distance from the present shores. The exposed and dried-up shores were used for agriculture. They had better dwellings and a somewhat easier life than before the introduction of the bronze celt, but instead of villages in almost every favourable situation, the villages were fewer and more compact. With the clearing of the land which must have proceeded rapidly when the bronze celt came into use, it would seem that the necessity for pile dwellings would have ceased. Nevertheless, their existence over a wide area in Europe in the Iron Age has been proved. The

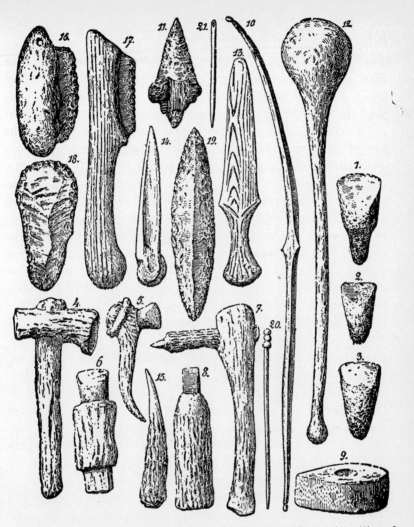

Fig. 70.—Neolithic implements of Swiss pile dwelling villages. (1), (2) and
(3) celts. The methods of hafting such celts are shown in (5), (6), and (7)
of this figure and in figure 71 (1). (4) shows a deerhorn ax with a
wooden handle; (5) a celt mounted in deerhorn; (6) a celt mounted in
deerhorn which in turn was inserted in a wooden handle (see Fig. 71);
(7) a stone adze mounted as is the celt in (6) but with an unusually long
deerhorn socket; (8) a stone chisel mounted in a deerhorn socket; (9) a
stone hammer ax (see also Fig. 63, p. 142). (10) a wooden bow; (11)
arrowhead; (12) a club of yew wood; (13) dagger of yew wood; (14)
bone awl; (15) awl of deerhorn; (16) and (17) flint saws mounted in
wood; (18) flint scraper; (19) flint spear- or javelin-head; (20) bone pin,
and (21) bone needle. After DeMorgan. Reduced in size.

complete abandonment probably coincided with a rise in lake level as the dry climate gave way to a moister one.

Industries of the Pile Dwellers. Flint was the best material for making cutting instruments such as knives, scrapers (Fig. 70), saws, and piercers. Some of the scrapers look very much like those made by Mousterian man and some of the lanceheads might easily be mistaken for inferior weapons of Solutrean workmanship. Flint arrowheads were generally rather crudely made. They even made fishhooks of flint but,

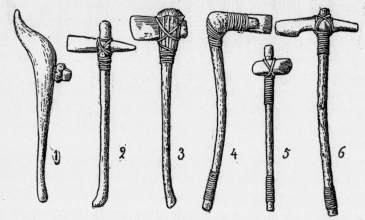

Fɪɢ. 71.—The most important methods of attaching celts and ax heads to handles are shown. (1) shows a common method of the pile dwellers: the stone celt was first inserted in a piece of deerhorn, which, in turn, was inserted in a wooden handle. After Karl Schumacher.

probably because of the difficulty of manufacture, these are rare. Flint daggers, knives, and saws were inserted in wood or staghorn and without doubt the hand was also protected by more perishable materials such as skin and moss (Fig. 42, p. 89).

Nephrite and Jade. Every stone and mineral that could be worked and would make a cutting edge was used, such as hard igneous rocks, quartzite, hard sandstones, and quartz crystal. The tough, hard, and beautiful jade, nephrite and jadeite were especially prized. So thoroughly did they search the stream and lake gravels for nephrite that they so nearly exhausted the supply that until recently it was thought that the mineral was imported. The pile dweller loved the small, polished nephrite celts which he mounted in a deerhorn socket, which, in turn, was inserted in a wooden handle (Fig. 71, (1)). Stone celts were variously mounted; some were inserted in a hole in a deerhorn or wooden handle but the favourite method was the one mentioned above, that is, to insert the small celt in a horn socket first. This was done because of the greater elasticity of the horn which diminished the shock along the line of the blow and so reduced the danger of splitting the shaft. Some of the celts were mounted in the end of a staghorn ax (Fig. 71, (4)) to form an edge and the ax handle was inserted in a hole in the deerhorn. Small celts have been found by the hundreds in Swiss lakes. Their importance is seen in the thousands of piles, as well as platforms and superstructures which were cut and prepared by means of them.

Bone and Horn. As in Epipaleolithic times, many tools were made of bone and deerhorn. Of bone they made knives, tools for smoothing pottery, awls (Fig. 70) skates, and pendants. Needles are not as common nor are they as well-made as in Upper Paleolithic times. Daggers were made from the leg bones of deer and other animals. Leaf-shaped arrow and javelin points were bound to wooden shafts in much the same manner as those made by natives of New Zealand. Bone fishhooks were also used (see Fig. 73). Deerhorn was especially valuable for celt sockets and when ground at the edge and furnished with a long handle it was the material used in their principal agricultural implement, a kind of pick or hoe (Fig. 74, (2)). It was also used for harpoons and picks, and sharpened tines were early made into daggers. Some simple ornaments, such as cylinders perforated or grooved for suspension and either embellished with simple designs or plain, were made of the same substance. Cups, boxes, spoons, buttons, and combs were also fashioned from horn.

Wood. Without doubt, wood was one of the most important materials used by Neolithic man just as it was in the homes of the peasants in Scandinavia and elsewhere less than a hundred years ago, but had it not been for the preservative properties of the water of lakes and moors, one could

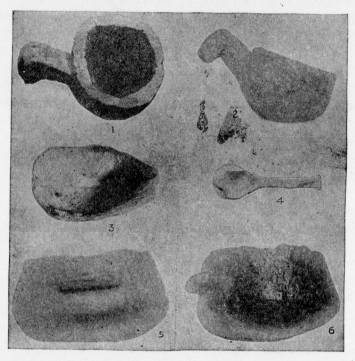

FIG. 72.—Wooden objects from Swiss pile dwellings. (1) and (2) a ladlelike cup; (3) bowl of a spoon without the handle; (4) small spoon; (5) and (6) wooden bowl. (1) to (4) are Neolithic, and (5) and (6) are early Bronze Age.

Photographs by courtesy of Paul Vouga.

have done little more than theorise as to its use. As it is, we know how celts and knives were hafted and we probably have a knowledge of most of the wooden implements. Wood was used for the handles of tools; for paddles much like those of to-day; for clubs (Fig. 70); for daggers and knives; for spoons (Fig. 72); for ladles, some more than a foot long; for large and small bowls, and tubs, and bows and arrows. A plowshare (Fig. 74) made of oak, which was used for scratching the ground much as harrows are to-day, was found in one of the Swiss lakes. Thin strips of wood were bound into bundles for carding linen and wool. Boats, some of which were twenty and more feet long, were hollowed out of large tree trunks with fire and by the aid of stone tools.

Pitch was used to fasten implements to their handles, arrowheads to their shafts, and for other purposes. A specimen in the Neuchatel Museum has two broken arrowheads embedded in pitch evidently for repair. As there is no pitch in Switzerland, it has been suggested that it was obtained from birch bark.

It is evident from the above that wood was probably the most important material utilised by Neolithic man.

Pottery. The earliest pile dwelling pottery is not crude but is, in some respects, of a higher type than that which came later. It seems certain, therefore, that skill in ceramics was an ancient craft even when the first pile dwellings were made.

As has been stated, pottery was of great use to a people who employed no metal. In it they cooked their food, and from it they ate and drank. It was used for cheese making, for fermenting liquor, for holding water, and large jars were made for storing grain, nuts, and dried fruits. Some of the storage jars were three feet high. As the making of pottery required great labour and as the loss in firing must have been heavy, it is not surprising to find broken pots mended with pitch and clay.

The pottery was graceful in form and compares favourably, in this respect, with the pottery made to-day. For some reason that is not clear, the pile dwellers did not seem to care to ornament their pottery as did other peoples (see *Pottery,* Fig. 45, p. 96). Occasionally a piece was made with some simple design on the rim, and toward the close of the age, some jars ornamented like those of their neighbours appear. Perhaps such ornamented jars were made by women who had been stolen from distant tribes. Nothing, perhaps, shows better how self-sustaining the communities were than that their pottery was so little influenced by that of their neighbours. As most of the earthen vessels had rounded bottoms it was necessary to set them in sand, in depressions in the clay floor or on clay rings made for the purpose. In the absence of metal, pottery was used for spoons and ladles. Pitchers, "tea-cups," plates, and jars are similar in shape to those of to-day. Earthenware nursing bottles and perforated jars for making curds, loom weights, spindle whorls, and other clay objects were manufactured. The potter's wheel was not used.

Hunting. The bones of animals in pile dwelling sites show that hunting was an important occupation of the earlier pile dwellers. They killed the elk, wild cattle, and the stag, but especially the latter two. The bear and wild pig were also successfully hunted. In the chase they used bows (Fig. 73, (1)) and arrows, and spears to bring down their game, but they must also have made pitfalls to trap the larger animals, such as the aurochs. When a large animal was killed it was quickly skinned with sharp flint knives and scrapers. Although no skins have been preserved, we can confidently assume that they formed an important part of the clothing of the time. To make garments of skins, scrapers, bone piercers, and needles were needed and many implements of this kind have been found. Hunting was one of the most important occupations not only of the Neolithic pile dwellers but of Neolithic man everywhere.

Fishing. Fishing was next to hunting in importance. The Paleolithic and Epipaleolithic tribes shot fish with their arrows or speared them with their harpoons and the latter people learned to use the hook and line. The first fishhooks (Fig. 73) were straight bits of bone sharpened at the two ends, with a groove around the centre to which the line was fastened. This hook was probably entirely covered with bait.

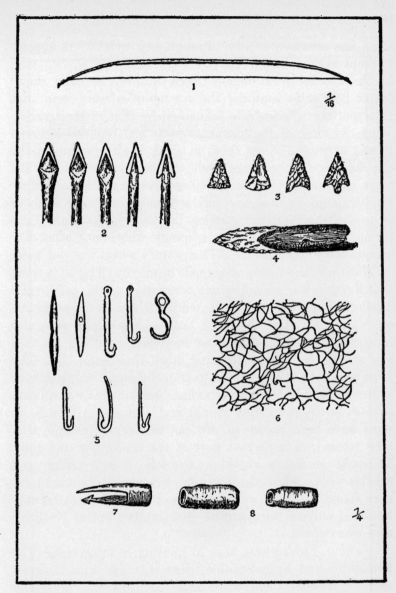

Fig. 73.—(1) A bow from Lake Constance; (2) a series of arrowheads showing the evolution and the method of attachment to the shaft; (3) arrowheads (compare with (2)); (4) a flint spearhead in its wooden shaft; (5) the development of the fishhook from a double-pointed bit of bone to the barbed hook; (6) pile dweller's fish net; (7) a hook; (8) net sinkers. After H. Reinerth.

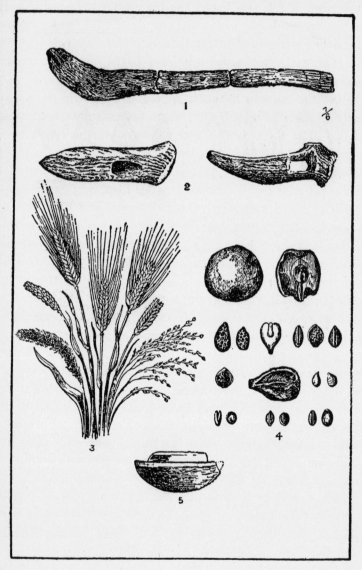

FIG. 74.—(1) A wooden plow; (2) deerhorn hoes; (3) grains cultivated by the pile dwellers; (4) fruit; (5) a hand mill. After H. Reinerth.

Only when a fish swallowed the bait could it be caught. Later the curved hook, made of bone or of flint, was invented. The hooks were notched for fastening the string or had eyelets. The early hooks did not have barbs but the inventive fisherman soon learned their advantage. When bronze came into use the modern fishhook appeared. Not only were hooks used but nets (Fig. 73, (6)) were also employed. Man has learned little about fresh-water fishing since the Neolithic.

Agriculture. The pile dweller gathered wild fruits and nuts in large quantities. Although such foods constituted an important part of his food, it was his farm and garden products that raised him above the Paleolithic and Epipaleolithic savage and led to progress. He planted barley, wheat, bearded wheat, large-kerneled and six-rowed barley, common millet, and the eared millet. He cultivated his fields with the deerhorn hoe (Fig. 74, (2)) and broke the clods with stone mauls, and even used a crude form of a wooden plow. After his grain was harvested and threshed, he stored it in large storage jars in his granary or in his house. The women ground the meal on heavy sandstone blocks with broad smooth upper surfaces by the use of long smooth stones. Although bread was doubtless made, none has been found. Masses of burned meal with partly ground kernels have been dredged from pile dwelling sites but these were probably charred when the huts which contained them burned. The fact that ovens were used indicated that bread was baked, and we can say with confidence, that bread was an important Neolithic food.

Fruits and Seeds. The pile dwellers gathered all varieties of edible wild fruits and nuts. Layers of pressed apple skins, jars full of raspberry seeds, seeds of strawberries, blackberries, elderberries, cherries, plums, wild grapes, crabapples, and carroway and poppy seeds show that no palatable fruit or seed was overlooked. A layer of hazelnut shells sixteen inches thick as well as the presence of many acorns and beechnuts show that these nutritious foods were kept for use. No doubt they gathered wild honey and used it for sweetening their food.

Weaving. The cultivation and preparation of flax was an important industry. Thread, pieces of cloth, knotted and woven matting, and fish nets, both knotted and woven, show that the essential principles of weaving had been mastered. The abundance of spindle whorls and loom weights shows that almost every house must have been supplied with a loom.

Duration of the Custom of Building Pile Dwellings. Pile dwellings were built in the Swiss and neighbouring lakes for perhaps a thousand years. They were first built by the earliest settlers of the Full Neolithic who brought with them a knowledge of agriculture and domestic animals, and they continued to be erected in the Bronze Age. It seems to be proved that during most, or all, of this time the climate of Switzerland was drier than now and that this condition reached its maximum in the Early Bronze Age (p. 165). If the level of the lakes had been the same then as now, the dwellings would have stood in deep water. If such were the conditions, the piles of the Neolithic buildings would have needed to project six to ten feet above the bottom of the lake, while those of the Bronze Age would have had to be twenty to twenty-five feet long. This does not seem probable. We must, therefore, suppose that the houses were built on muddy shores or in shallow water when the level of the lakes was lower than now.

Climate as determined by the Study of Central European Lakes. The earliest Neolithic seems to have been moist but during the greater part of the Age, the climate was warm and dry and the water of the lakes of Central Europe was low. The evidence indicates a dry period which culminated about 2200-2000 B.C. Then followed a period of greater rainfall, but less than that of the present, in which the level of the lakes rose and destroyed many lake dwellings. This "high-water catastrophy" probably occurred about 1300 B. C. After

NEOLITHIC AND LATER CLIMATES [2]

CULTURE	GENERAL CLIMATE
Neolithic.	
Kitchen Midden, Ertebolle or Shell Heap Time........	}Moist and warm.
Beginning of Alpine Pile Dwellings	}Cool.
Early Pile Dwellings Middle Pile Dwellings Late Pile Dwellings	}Dry and warm.
First copper..............	Short period of floods.
Bronze Age................	Very dry; water low.
	Cool and moist, Lake levels.
Hallstatt...................	High, most of the lake villages destroyed.
La Tene Early Middle.................. Late	Maximum moisture.
Gallo-Roman.	Climate as to-day.

this moist period, the lakes again shrank rapidly to a second minimum, about 1000 B. C., that is, near the close of the Bronze Age. During this dry period, the chief settlements were in moist lands and agriculture was carried on in places which are now above the forest level and even above the passes which are now glaciated.

About 850 B.C., in the Hallstatt epoch, the lake level again rose to a height of as much as 30 feet in Lake Constance. Because of this flooding, most of the lake dwellings were destroyed and the population of the Alpine region declined to a minimum. Almost the only settlements were in the warmest valleys. The Alpine mountain settlements, in-

[2] H. Gams and R. Nordhagen.

cluding those where mining for metalliferous ores and salt
was carried on, were abandoned. This wet period, after a
short interval, reached a second maximum between 500-
350 B. C., but, by the Roman period, the rainfall was very
little above that of the present.[3]

Origin. Why did some of the Neolithic peoples build
houses on piles and why did the custom last so long? Were
they built as a protection against wild beasts and human
enemies? It is possible that they afforded some protection
but if they were built in very shallow water on the shores of
lakes, this could hardly have been an important consideration. The suggestion that they were built on piles for sani-
tary reasons has little to commend it as primitive peoples
know and care little about sanitation. Moreover, when the
pile dwellings were in swamps, the accumulation of kitchen
refuse under the house would have been unsanitary in the
extreme. Two other suggestions should be considered. The
first is that people living on some broad, fertile valley subject to inundations, learned to build their houses on piles in
order to bring the floors above the flood waters of the river.
Such conditions have long prevailed in the Danube valley.
When people with this custom migrated to a densely forested
region where the best land for cultivation was near the shores
of lakes they would naturally have built their houses above
the ground in order to have the floors out of reach of spring
floods. It has been suggested that the Maglemose peoples
(p. 63), who lived on rafts may have invented pile dwellings. These structures may have "begun in a simple raft
float on the edge of a lake, moored by posts at the sides. As
the structure became waterlogged, another layer of logs would
be laid upon it, and then another, as occasion arose, until
a regular platform, resting on the lake bottom, was created.
In this way, a pile structure might have been evolved from

[3] C. E. P. Brooks: "Climate Through the Ages," pp. 338-340, from H. Gams,
and R. Nordhagen: "Postglaziale Klimaänderungen und Erdkrustenbewe-
gungen in Mitteleuropa." *Geogr. Gesellsch. Landesk. Forschungen.* H. 25, 1923.

the primitive raft."[4] The reason for the construction of rafts was that they gave a dry floor in a densely wooded and marshy region. As no pile dwellings are known to have been erected in Denmark, the explanation is not convincing.

The available evidence indicates the sudden appearance of the pile dwellers with agriculture, domestic animals, and pottery. Moreover the pottery of the oldest lake dwellings of Switzerland is thin, well smoothed and somewhat better than that which they made later. The fact that the ceramic technique of the Swiss lake dwellers is much like that of the Danube valley, and that the characteristic "shoe-last celts" are found in lake dwelling sites indicates close cultural connections with the Danube region.

A study of the skulls of the pile dwellers gives little aid in determining relationships. The pile dwelling civilisation which lasted so long seems to have had little influence on the neighbouring peoples and was rather slow in adopting new ideas. However, when bronze became known the pile dwellers found a means of getting it and soon became expert metal workers. How this was accomplished it is impossible to say as they had little to offer in exchange for this precious metal.

Life of the Pile Dweller. The life of the pile dweller could not have been especially unpleasant. As he was no longer wholly dependent on the chase for food but had his own fields of grain and vegetables, he was usually well supplied with nourishing food. Wild fruits, nuts, and edible roots gave variety to his diet. He had small, half-wild pigs, goats, sheep, and small cattle which he could kill and eat when the supply of game ran low. As he had pottery, and the oven, his food could be prepared much as it is to-day.

The principal material for clothing was probably skilfully tanned skins, but in addition we know he had linen cloth and probably woolen cloth as well. As the floors and walls

[4] V. Gordon Childe: "The Dawn of European Civilization." 1925. p. 244. See bibliography p. 259.

of his house were covered with thick layers of clay and probably with mats and skins, it would be possible to keep warm even on the coldest days of winter. As he paid no attention to ventilation and did not have windows in his house, his hearth-fire would keep him warm although the odor at times must have been unpleasant. However, he was used to smells.

On fine summer days, the women and children could probably be seen on the platforms of the houses, all busily employed: the women weaving cloth, making baskets or pottery, drying fruit, preparing skins for clothing, and doing the many other tasks necessary for comfort and happiness. The women cooked the food and tended the little fields of grain while the children herded the sheep, goats, and pigs. It was probably the man's place to get the game and fish, and to protect the family. They were able to visit other settlements in the same and other lakes by boat and to exchange surplus articles or products for things they did not have. Such local trade must have been brisk.

CHAPTER VI

MEGALITHIC MONUMENTS

THE RECORD OF AN UNKNOWN RELIGION

THERE is nothing in architecture more imposing than a monolith. A column made of a single piece of stone is much more impressive than one of the same dimensions made of several blocks. It is not surprising, therefore, that the prehistoric megalithic (Greek, *megas* large, and *lithos* a stone) structures of Europe, built some thousands of years ago, should have excited the wonder of all observers and should have given rise to many legends and to much speculation as to their origin. They are remarkable works which were inspired by some great religion which glorified the dead at the expense of the living.

Such works were for the first time possible in the Neolithic period because the density of the population had increased, the social life was organised, and humanity conscious of its strength was able to undertake under the impulse of powerful religious conceptions these funerary works. The custom of erecting huge stones became in time a passion with the people of Western Europe. The great labour involved, their permanence as compared with the log (or wattle and daub) houses in which the people lived, and their imposing appearance made an appeal which we, with our modern buildings and monuments, can but inadequately comprehend.

The practice seems to have spread along the coasts of Western Europe but did not penetrate far inland. Megaliths occur in Spain and Portugal, in southern and western France, in the Channel Islands, Great Britain, and Ireland, in Holland, in Scandinavia, and Northern Germany. They were also built on the islands of the western Mediterranean, and along the coasts of the Black Sea. Other areas are in Northern Africa, India, Madagascar, and Japan. The age of the monuments is not the same in all places, but, in Europe, they were built in the latter part of the Neolithic and in the early part of the Bronze Age.

These prehistoric megalithic tombs have given rise to many local names such as cromlech, quoit, and Druid altars, and to individual names such as Devil's Den, Kits Coty House, Devil's Seat, Maisons des Fées (Houses of the Fairies), and Liag an Eanaigh. The term dolmen has been used to include all megalithic tombs but it is much better to separate the prehistoric megalithic tombs of Europe into three groups: I, Dolmens, II, Passage Graves, and III, Hallcists.

I. A *Dolmen* is the simplest form of the megalithic tomb. It is a more or less rectangular chamber built of three or more huge, upright slabs of undressed stone, covered with a capping or table stone.

II. A *Passage Grave* consists of a central tomb with a covered passage or gallery leading to it.

III. A *Hallcist* is a long, narrow grave with huge, upright stones covered with several capping stones. It may be thought of as a passage grave without the tomb, although it was, in reality, itself a tomb.

Dolmens. (Breton, *dol* table, *men* stone). These are locally called quoits, cromlechs, Druid altars, etc.) When it became the custom to use monoliths in the construction of burial chambers the simplest form of structure (Figs. 75 and 76) was first built. It consisted of three or four upright stones —seldom more—upon which was placed a single capping stone which was generally of great size. The height of dolmens varies from (rarely) three feet to a height sufficient to permit a man mounted on horseback to sit under the roof. The capping stones range from relatively small ones, five feet or less in length, to others, such as one in County Down, Ireland (Liag an Eanaigh), which is eleven feet long and is supported at a height of seven feet by three slender pillar stones, and one in Cornwall, which is eighteen feet six inches long by nine feet six inches wide in the widest part. The greatest thickness of any capping stone which the writer has seen is one

Fig. 75.—Chun Castle, a dolmen in Cornwall, England.
Photograph by the Author.

Fig. 76.—Dolmen near Dublin, Ireland. (Druid Glen, Carrickmines.) The floor of this dolmen is below the level of the ground and the dolmen is consequently not as impressive as it would be were its full height shown. It was probably originally entirely covered with earth.
Photograph by the Author.

near Howth Castle, Dublin, which is about ten feet in maximum thickness. This stone, however, had been moved but a few yards.

Originally, dolmens, passage graves, and hallcists were covered entirely or in part, with mounds of earth (Fig. 77)

FIG. 77.—The barrow or tumulus of Knowth, near Drogheda, Ireland. This tumulus has not been opened and probably covers a passage grave.

FIG. 78.—The entrance to a passage grave and a part of the tumulus, which covered it. Much of the sand of the tumulus has been blown away and carted off. Brittany.

Photographs by the Author.

which, in England, are called barrows but for which the term *tumulus* is generally used on the Continent. In some dolmens, as in Scandinavia, the great capstone was probably never covered but in most regions the entire monument was buried by the builders under a conspicuous tumulus. It is possible, though not probable, that some were never covered. It is, however, extremely difficult to explain the absence of earth about some dolmens (Fig. 75). Although the tumuli of many dolmens and other megalithic tombs have so completely disappeared as to make it doubtful if they ever existed, some are still intact in the Scandinavian countries, France, Great Britain, and Ireland.

An interesting example which shows not only what became of the earth of tumuli but also how the tombs suffer from human hands is that of a Cornish dolmen, "West Lanyon Quoit." [1] This dolmen was not uncovered until near the close of the eighteenth century when it was discovered by a farmer who was removing the earth of the mound to fertilise his fields. Since then, all but two of its great stones have been broken up and carried away for building material.

The simplicity of dolmens—a roofstone resting on upright stones—made any great variation in appearance impossible. The difference is largely in size, and in the kind of stone used.

Dolmens, as well as other megalithic monuments, were erected both in conspicuous and in inconspicuous places: some are in valleys, some on the sides of hills, and some on hilltops. The determining consideration in their location seems to have been the accessibility of suitable stone, although there are some exceptions. In Ireland these structures do not occur where, in Neolithic times, the land was thickly covered with forests, but on nearly treeless areas, along well marked trails, and along treeless coasts. In other words, the distribution of dolmens in Ireland and elsewhere depended directly upon the ancient forestation of the countries which the megalith peoples inhabited and upon the accessibility of suitable stones. The scarcity of megaliths in Western Denmark is due to the small supply of glacial boulders.

Legends. Many legends have grown up about megalithic tombs. The popular belief that they were altars built and used by the Druids was widespread in Ireland and England. An examination of the table or capping stones shows that this could not have been the purpose of the builders. Where

[1] This chamber was probably part of a passage grave.

the upper and lower surfaces of a capping stone differ in convexity or roughness, the upper surface is the more convex of the two, or the rougher, and the flatter surface is on the under side. That some of the dolmens were used in Keltic times as altars, there is no doubt.

An Irish legend of the origin of megalithic monuments is a good example of the more elaborate stories that these pre-

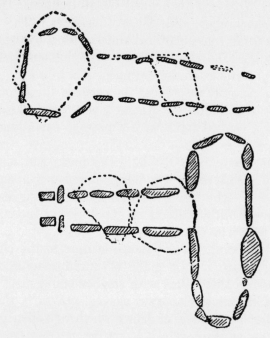

Fig. 79.—Passage graves. After Childe.

historic structures have inspired. According to this story, Gráinne, the daughter of a third century Irish King, Cormac Mac Airt, by name, was betrothed, but without her consent, to her father's favourite general. When the general, a man older than her father, came to claim the princess, she would have none of him. Instead, she induced Diarmuid, a good-looking lieutenant in her father's army, to elope with her.

Tradition says that as the fugitives could not spend more than one night in a place, on account of the pursuit of her father, they fled from place to place, and each evening erected one of these great monuments to shelter them. Because of this these megalithic tombs are sometimes called the beds of Diarmuid and Gráinne. In Cornwall the term "Quoit" suggests that these stones were used by ancient giants in their games.

Passage Graves. (Also called Giant Dolmens, Dolmens à gallerie, Ganggraben and Allées Couvertes.) This type of megalithic tomb consists of a chamber with a covered passage leading to it. The simplest form is a dolmen with two or more upright stones at the entrance, which are covered with a capstone, possibly to prevent the earth of the tumulus from falling into the chamber entrance. The typical passage grave consists of a central tomb with a passage extending to it at right angles (Fig. 79).

A passage grave at Olstykke, Denmark, will serve as an example of such a tomb. The burial chamber is about twenty feet long and eight feet wide with walls formed of eighteen upright stones with boulders on top to bring their height to about six feet. The chamber is covered with three great table stones of red granite. The passage leading to the chamber is about waist high and is made of upright stones with the spaces between them filled with smaller boulders.

One of the most elaborate passage graves is that of La Hougue Bie [2] on the Isle of Jersey which was opened in 1925. The tumulus which covers it has a diameter of one hundred and eighty feet and a present height of forty feet, although originally probably ten feet higher. The plan of the tomb is cross-shaped (Fig. 80) and the greatest length is sixty-seven feet. The passage which is thirty-two feet long, is formed by massive stone uprights with smaller stones forming a dry walling between them, and is roofed with capstones with flat undersurfaces. The average width of the passage is four feet and its

[2] "La Hougue Bie—Its Legend and History." *Bulletin of the Society of Jersey,* 1925, pages 29.41.

height four and one-half feet. It gradually increases in height to five or six feet where it reaches the main chamber which is seven feet high. The main chamber, which is thirty feet long and ten to twelve feet wide, is divided into five compartments by stone slabs, and is covered by five enormous capstones, each about sixteen feet long, and about thirty tons in weight. These stones were conveyed from the seashore about two and one-

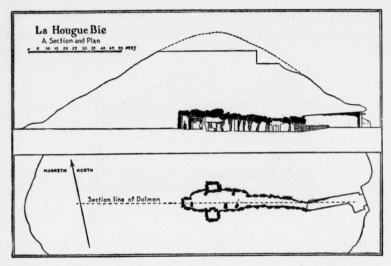

FIG. 80.—Vertical section and plan of the passage grave of La Hougue Bie, on the Isle of Jersey. The original shape of the tumulus is shown by the dashed line. The division of the tomb into five compartments is an unusual feature. Modified from the *Bulletin of the Society of Jersey*, 1925.

half miles distant. The interstices between the uprights in the chamber, as in the passage, are filled up most carefully with small stone dry walling. No carvings or other incisions occur in the chamber except some twenty cup marks, mention of which will be made later (page 180). The main chamber underlies the centre of the tumulus. Portions of at least eight human skeletons, of which two or three were women, are not sufficiently well preserved to make it possible to state definitely their racial characteristics. A U-shaped hand mill two feet in diameter and several vessels of peculiar form were also found. As the inner surfaces of the bowls show traces of fire as if some smoky substance had been burned in them, it is assumed that they were ritual vessels. This tomb, like many other megalithic monuments, had been violated—possibly by the Danes about 829.

One other famous passage grave, New Grange (Fig. 81) near Drogheda, Ireland, should be described. The tumulus, composed of earth and stone, covers an area of about two acres. The passage, which is forty-four feet long, leads to a

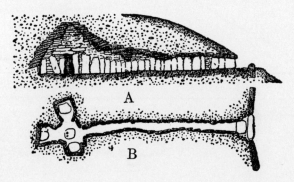

Fig. 81.—The passage grave of New Grange, Ireland, showing: (A) the corbelled roof; (B) the cruciform plan of the tomb. After Déchelette.

cruciform chamber composed of a central chamber with three side chambers or niches opening off from it at right angles. The cruciform chamber measures eighteen by twenty-one feet and is covered by a corbelled vault of rough stones which has a maximum height of nineteen feet six inches. The walls of the passage and the tomb are made of great stone slabs decorated with incised designs. A standing stone (or bætyl) originally stood in the middle of the burial chamber and another on top of the mound. The tumulus is surrounded at its base by stone slabs placed end to end, and at a further distance by a ring of huge boulders (Fig. 82). New Grange is remarkable not only for its size and its elaborate carvings, which resemble those of

Gavr'inis, Brittany, but also for its central chamber with its high corbelled roof (Fig. 82).

An Irish archæologist states that the reason for the erection of New Grange is known. "It was the grave-sanctuary of a great Bronze Age hero whose name probably was something like Oenghus, who was deified after his death, and continued to be worshipped in Ireland at least till the fifth or sixth century of the Christian era. We know something —not so much as we should wish, but still something—of

Fig. 82.—A part of the great circle of stones that surrounds the tumulus of New Grange, Ireland.
Photograph by the Author.

the builders of the mound. They have endeavoured to trace in barbaric hieroglyphs a record of their attitude towards the unseen powers which they dreaded; and though the story is not yet fully unravelled, a good beginning has been made." [3]

Some passage graves are double with separate corridors and in some a single passage leads to a series of chambers which are connected by short passages.

Hallcists. (Hallkists, Cists, Steinkisten, Allées Couvertes.) The third type of megalithic monument consists of a passage without a central chamber (Fig. 83). It is as if the passage

[3] Macalister: "Ireland in Pre-Celtic Times," pp. 364 and 387.

grave had degenerated into a covered passage or long cist. In Scandinavia the contents of the hallcists show that they were erected at a later date than the passage graves. The omission of the central chamber doubtless arose from the fact that the corridor of the passage tombs came to be used for interments and the central chamber in time lost its significance and eventually a long corridor only was built.

Fig. 83.—A hallcist from the vicinity of Paris from which all but one covering stone has been removed. This hallcist also shows a porthole partition. After T. D. Kendrick.

Portholes in Megalithic Tombs. A peculiarity of some megalithic tombs in widely separated regions—Great Britain, Western Europe, Crimea, Asia, and even Oceanica—is the occurrence of a more or less circular hole cut in a slab, or at the inner edges of adjacent slabs of rock. The purpose of such holes in the partitions and in the sides of megalithic tombs has been variously interpreted: as an entrance for the living, as a passage for the soul, and as an opening through which food for the dead could be passed. The variation in size, from holes large enough to admit the body to others as small as the head, may be due to different uses or to local customs. Some of the holed stones have grooves cut on one of the faces to hold a wood or stone covering for the holes.

The porthole is by no means a universal feature of megalithic tombs and has never been found in dolmens. It is more common in Northeastern France, where the rock is a soft, easily worked, chalky limestone, than elsewhere. The porthole is not common in regions where the rock used in the construction of the tombs is hard, as in the granite megalithic graves of Brittany, Cornwall, and Denmark. An exception is to be seen in Sweden, where some twenty hallcists have porthole partitions but as these were erected when the remarkable stone technique of the Swedes was at its height, it is not surprising that holes should have been made in hard stone if it was the custom, elsewhere, to make holed partitions of other materials. This leads one to wonder if portholes were generally made in wooden partitions whose substance has since rotted away, and only occasionally in rocks: or if burial customs differed in different regions, and even in the same region. Great importance has been attributed by some authors [4] to the custom of making portholes.

The Ornamentation of Megalithic Tombs. Most megalithic tombs are without ornamentation of any kind and were constructed of untrimmed stones. Many of these tombs, however, have shallow, cup-shaped depressions on the upright stones and on the under sides of the capstones. What the significance of these depressions is can merely be conjectured. Were they made to hold the blood of some sacrifice which was offered up before the stone was put in place or are they sacred symbols?

In contrast with the absence of all ornamentation on most megalithic tombs, the stones of a few are well covered with engraved designs. The most famous of these are in the passage graves of Gavr'inis in Brittany, and New Grange in Ireland. At Gavr'inis twenty-two of the twenty-nine side stones are almost completely covered with engravings (Fig.

[4] T. D. Kendrick: "The Axe Age," pp. 39-63.

84), some of which have much the appearance of an enlarged fingerprint. Representations of the ax, shieldlike designs, as well as other figures, occur on megalithic monuments. These

Fig. 84.—(*Left*) Carvings on one of the supports of the Table of the Merchants, a late megalithic monument, at Locmariaquer, Morbihan, Brittany. The meaning of the designs has been variously interpreted. After Le Rouzic.

(*Right*) The interior of the passage grave of Gavr'inis, Brittany. The upright stones are elaborately carved. This tomb is of very late Neolithic or early Bronze Age. After Le Rouzic.

engravings have been variously interpreted. As prehistoric men seldom made a meaningless design, these figures probably had a profound religious significance to the people of the time.

The Cult of the Ax has played an important rôle in the

Mediterranean from very early times, and the occurrence of yokelike figures, similar to the schematised horns of the bull which were frequently used in Cretan art may indicate the cult of the sacred horns or of the bull. It is interesting to note that the Cult of the Bull and the Ax are frequently associated. One of the most artistic works of megalithic times is on one of the stones of the New Grange passage grave, Ireland. The stone is embellished with beautifully executed spirals (Fig. 85).

FIG. 85.—Elaborate carvings on the New Grange, Ireland, passage grave. This is perhaps the most artistic effort of the period.
Photograph by the Author.

Contents of Megalithic Graves. Dolmens, passage graves, and hallcists were, with few exceptions, for collective burials, either family or tribal. The "grave furniture" differs in individual graves of the same region as well as in different regions. In Scandinavia, where the study of megaliths has been carried on with great care, it has been found that the earliest monuments, the dolmens, yielded only a few objects, such as characteristic earthenware bottles, flint celts with thin butts (see Fig. 57 (2) p. 136), and ornaments of amber. The later passage graves contained an abundance of objects. For example, in two passage graves in close proximity to each other at Kulby, north of Slagelse, Denmark, were found ninety-six celts and chisels, one hundred and fifty flint flakes, eighty amber beads, and other objects.[5] Another passage grave was full of human bones, and the skeletons of ten adults and twelve children were taken from it. In another, eighty skeletons were removed from the chamber and passage. The hallcists, contained flint daggers, and finely worked arrowheads, but little pottery and few celts and axes.

In Western France (Brittany) megalithic tombs have yielded polished stone celts of rare minerals and stones, such as green jadeite, and fibrolite, beads of the rare mineral callaïs and other materials, knives, arrowheads, scrapers, nuclei of flint, mills for grinding grain, and pottery. A few gold objects have also been found. At Port-Blanc, Brittany, there were forty or fifty skeletons in two layers, separated by flag stones, and in tombs in other places several layers of skeletons separated by slabs have been found. The skeletons in many of the tombs had been disturbed when later burials demanded space, with the result that the bones of earlier skeletons were piled up to make room for the later burials. The passage grave of La Hougue Bie (page 176), on the Isle of Jersey, yielded fragments of at least eight human skeletons, bones of the ox, sheep, and pig, fragments of a dozen ritual vessels. pieces of a red, well baked beaker, two beads, and a few bits of flint. As the tomb had been entered several centuries ago, it is probable that some of the contents had been removed.

Little has been found in the megalithic tombs of Great Britain. The commonest objects are leaf-shaped arrowheads. The little pottery discovered is so poor in quality and crude in workmanship as to suggest that it represents the first attempt of the Britains to make pottery. The most conspicuous characteristic of the British megalithic graves is the great long barrows or tumuli which cover them. The builders delighted in an imposing mound. It is stated [6] that the passage grave type of barrow or tumulus is the oldest in Great Britain and that the other varieties of great barrows are degraded

[5] Guide to the National Museum, Copenhagen, 1921, ¶ 36.
[6] T. D. Kendrick: "The Axe Age," pp. 19-20.

forms. A late type has a megalithic chamber but no stone passage. Finally, there were no stone chambers or passages, but the dead were laid on the ground, perhaps in wooden shelters, or in pit graves of the simplest type.

Fig. 86.—Menhirs or standing stones are of rough stone. Their purpose is unknown. This one is at Carnac, Brittany. After Déchelette.

Standing Stones. The megalith builders not only erected megalithic tombs but they also set up long stones either singly or in long lines, or in circles. These are called menhirs, alignments and cromlechs. (*Menhir*, Breton, *men*, stone and *hir*, long.) The term is applied to the solitary standing stones which are to be seen in many places where dolmens occur, and in a few places where they are absent. They are generally huge stones with their bases firmly implanted in the soil (**Fig. 86**). The fact that so many of them are standing after the lapse of many centuries attests to the care with which they were set up. Their form is chiefly that which they had when first quarried and few show any evidence of having been shaped artificially. Where the granite is exposed at the surface in Brittany it is much weathered, and even decomposed to sand along joints or cracks, leaving solid rock masses of considerable size. The builders of the megalithic tombs, menhirs, cromlechs, and alignments, first removed the weathered rock of the joints and cracks and then by the use of wooden levers and wooden rollers, removed the unweathered block. In most cases the stone was not moved far before it was set up, seldom as much as a mile.

Menhirs are common in Ireland, in parts of England such as Cornwall, in France where 1585 have been counted, especially in Brittany, and in other parts of northwestern Europe. Similar stones, but of much later date, are to be seen in other parts of the world, but as they are not the work of these megalith peoples, they do not concern us.

The largest menhir (Men-er-Hroeck) in France is in Brittany, now prostrate and broken into four or five pieces. It has a length of about 67 feet and an estimated weight of about 330 tons. This menhir is much larger than any of the others, the next highest being about 36 feet. In Cornwall some of the menhirs are little higher than a fence post and are used as "rubbing stones" by the cattle. A menhir about 16 feet high at Quiberon, France, which is in a field with smaller menhirs, has a form which suggests the human figure and may have been artificially shaped somewhat to accentuate the resemblance. Some menhirs are set in the top of tumuli.

The purpose of the menhirs is unknown. Excavations at their bases have revealed nothing which gives a certain clue. Some human bones, ornaments, and stone implements have been found, but as these objects differ greatly in age, and as the oldest ones cannot be dated accurately, they give us little information. Whether they were cenotaphs, monuments to celebrate a great victory or event, boundary markers, or were erected for some religious purpose is a question which cannot at present be answered. The stones are believed to have been erected near the close of the Neolithic, possibly when copper was beginning to be used. They seem certainly to have been the work of the people who erected the megalithic tombs (Fig.

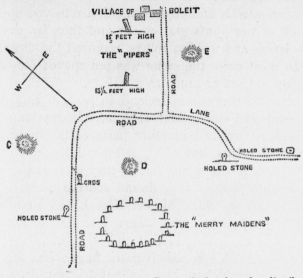

FIG. 87.—A map of a small area in Cornwall showing the distribution and relative positions of various megalithic monuments. The "Merry Maidens" constitute a cromlech, the "Pipers" are menhirs. E, D and C are tumuli or barrows. According to local tradition, the Merry Maidens were turned into stone for dancing on the Sabbath, while the Pipers who were playing for them, suffered the same fate. After W. C. Borlase.

87). The erection of menhirs is associated with old religious practices, traces of which appear in the Bible: Jacob [7] set up a stone pillar where he talked with God and he later set up a pillar on Rachel's grave.[8] Joshua [9] set up twelve stones to commemorate the crossing of the river Jordan. Samuel [10] set

[7] Gen. 35: 14.
[8] Ibid. 35: 20.
[9] Josh. 4: 3.
[10] Sam, I, 7:12.

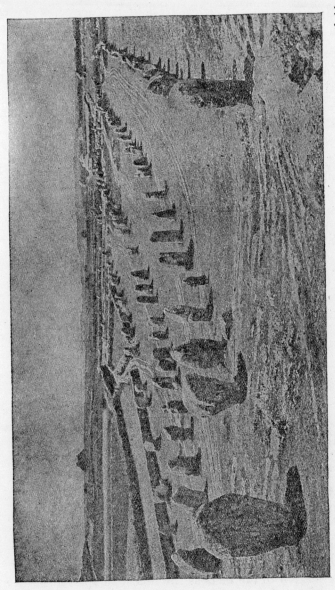

Fig. 88.—Alignment at Carnac, Brittany. There are three alignments at Carnac, consisting of 11, 13, and 14 rows of standing stones respectively.

187

up a stone in memory of the subjugation of the Philistines. The veneration of stones is a form of fetishism common to all primitive people. After the spread of Christianity into Gaul the symbol of the new religion was placed on some of the old sacred stones so that the early apostles would not dare destroy them.

Alignments are even more mysterious than the solitary menhirs. On a poor pasture, situated on fairly high and level land, near the village of Carnac, France, is an alignment (Fig. 88) of nearly twelve hundred standing stones placed in eleven rows or lines which extend for about three thousand feet in an east-northeast direction. At either end there was formerly a circle of standing stones. About a thousand feet further on is another alignment, nearly thirty-five hundred feet long, which contains nine hundred and eighty-two standing stones placed in eleven lines. The orientation is slightly different from that of the first alignment. This also probably ended in a stone circle on the west end. Following an interval of about twelve hundred feet is a third alignment about a half a mile long and some five hundred feet wide, in thirteen lines, on each end of which was a circle of standing stones. The height of the stones of these three alignments ranges from nearly twenty-one feet to less than two feet. It should be noted that these alignments probably have no relation to each other. Alignments are found elsewhere in Europe but none are of the magnitude of those described. In County Fermanagh, Ireland, for example, there is an alignment of four parallel rows of stones about three feet high extending 480 feet.[11]

Again we must use our imagination in an endeavour to discover the motive which induced these prehistoric peoples to spend so much energy and time in digging out, moving and raising these huge stones. There is a legend which has about the same relation to the facts as the theory of special creation has to evolution, which gives a perfect explanation. Accord-

[11] R. A. S. Macalister: "Ireland in Pre-Celtic Times," p. 304.

ing to the story St. Cornély, one of the early Popes of Rome, was driven from Rome by pagan soldiers. For many days he fled toward the west. When he came to Carnac he saw the sea in front of him and the soldiers in battle array close behind. If he went forward he would drown, but being a holy man and a man of resourcefulness and great power, he solved the problem by transforming the whole army into stones. There they stand to this day in battle array. An additional proof offered for the truthfulness of the legend, is that often at night the ghosts of the soldiers can be seen walking between the rows of standing stones. Such is the legend. It seems more probable that these rows of great stones ending in stone circles were erected for some religious or commemorative purpose. With all the mechanical aids of the present it would take a large population many months to take these great stones from the rock, move them, dig holes deep enough to keep them upright, and set them so firmly that most of them would stand upright for more than four thousand years. It seems safe to conclude that they were not built as memorials, unless by some ruler who wished to perpetuate his own greatness, but for some religious reason. Brittany to-day is a poor country—barren for the most part—and yet the peasantry maintain large monasteries and nunneries and have built and support many noble churches. One wonders how they do it, for a considerable portion of the product of their labour must be given to the church. Man will do much, and suffer much, if by so doing he thinks he can secure immortal bliss. Is it not probable that the Breton of to-day is doing for his religion what those people several thousand years ago did for theirs?

Cromlechs. (Welsh, *crom* bent, *llech* a flat stone.) The term is sometimes used incorrectly in Cornwall and Ireland for megalithic tombs.

Scattered here and there in the regions of megaliths, notably in Great Britain, Ireland, Sweden, and Denmark, are numerous circles of standing stones or cromlechs (Fig. 87,

p. 186), even the smallest of which are impressive whether on
lonely moors or in populous places. The number of stones
in the circles varies in different regions; in Ireland circles
of twelve stones are not uncommon, but in Cornwall the number ranges from twenty to more than fifty-five, and the diameter of the circles from about seventy-five feet to one hundred
and fifty feet.

Both in Ireland and Cornwall there is a tradition that
these are dance stones. The ancient religious dance was probably an encircling procession, and many of the stone circles
probably represent a perpetual dance and were for somewhat the same purpose as the prayer wheel. As time went on
other ideas were incorporated and some of the older ones
were dropped so that, in later times, as when Stonehenge was
built, many of the older beliefs had given place to newer ones.
Possibly the stone circle no longer had its former meaning
and was merely the traditional form of a religious edifice. A
possible proof of the purpose of the later stone circles, and
even of Stonehenge and Avebury, is afforded by the well-
known story of St. Patrick and Cromm Cruaich. St. Patrick,
we are told, came during his wanderings in Ireland to Magh
Sleacht, said to be in County Cavan. Here he found "the king
idol of Ireland, called Cromm Cruaich: and he was of gold,[12]
surrounded by twelve subordinate deities of stone. Obviously this is a description of monuments of the class known
as Stone Circles. And in Stone Circles, I see, primarily, the
representations of the abodes of groups of bronze-age deities.
These monuments, of which a large number still remain in
Ireland, are almost always planned on the model of the circle
of Cromm Cruaich as thus described: a circle of stones with
one outstanding stone outside; rarely inside. The outstanding stone is often of commanding size.... This appears at
first sight to be a story of Celtic religious worship...."But
it is clear that the Celtic incomers took much from the religion of their Pre-Celtic predecessors. It was natural that

[12] Not of solid gold, but gilded.

they should do so; for the aborigines presumably would know how the gods of the land should be worshipped." [13]

Stonehenge. The greatest work of prehistoric man in Europe is on the barren Salisbury Plain from which the spires

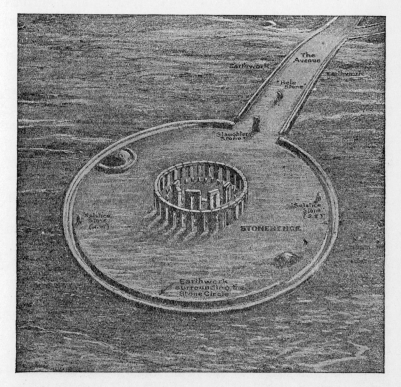

Fig. 89.—This restoration shows Stonehenge at its glory. The Hele stone or "Friar's Heel," the slaughter stone, the outer circle of great stones, the inner circle of "foreign" stones, and the altar are shown. The "avenue" and the road on the right over which the stones were brought from the valley are seen. After *The Illustrated London News.*

of Salisbury Cathedral can be seen. Here is the famous but, to the casual visitor, somewhat disappointing Stonehenge, about which several hundred articles have been written.

Stonehenge consists of an outer circle of dressed mono-

[13] R. A. S. Macalister: "Ireland in Pre-Celtic Times," p. 293.

liths, originally thirty in number, capped by lintels held in place by peg-like projections (tenons) on the top of the upright stones and corresponding depressions in the capping stones. These monoliths are of great size, some more than twenty feet long and weighing thirty to forty tons. Within this outer circle, which is one hundred feet in diameter, is a circle of smaller undressed stones, originally forty in number. Within this is a horseshoe of five trilithons (two stones supporting a third laid on them lintel-wise) (Fig. 89), that is, ten standing stones in pairs with a capping stone on each pair. Within the horseshoe of trilithons is another horseshoe composed of smaller, undressed "blue stones," originally nineteen in number, and within this is a large prostrate stone whose significance is not known but which is called the Altar Stone. The "altar stone" may have had some relation to the Friar's Heel, a menhir at the entrance of Stonehenge, and the so-called "Slaughter Stone" which is on a line with the altar stone and the Friar's Heel and just outside the outer circle of stones. Recent excavations have brought to light two circles of rectangular holes outside the outer circle of stones, indicating that at one time either there were two other stone circles or that a cruder monument of somewhat different design was replaced by the present one or, possibly, that the holes were dug for the erection of poles to form a palisade. A low embankment with a shallow ditch surrounds the outer circle except at one point where it is broken by an entrance avenue.

The larger stones are of sandstone, called sarcen stones, and were quarried in the nearby valley. When the landscape is viewed from an aeroplane a road can be faintly discerned which leads from the valley by an easy grade to Stonehenge and it is thought that this was the path over which the "sarcen" stones were dragged. The "blue stones" are of igneous origin and were brought from Wales. Many of the stones have disappeared, some having been used for bridges and houses.

Megalith art in England and Europe reached its climax when Stonehenge was built. The date of its erection and for what purpose it was made is nearly as much of a mystery as ever. Every date has been assigned to it from "Cheops to Canute." It has been called a fortress, a Buddhist temple, a monument built in honour of a great man, a Druid temple, a prehistoric Westminster Abbey, and a royal exchange and race course combined.

A legend states that it was built as a memorial to the flower of the British Nation which "fell by the cut-throat practice of the Saxons" about 460 A. D., and that the stones were brought from Ireland and set up through the magic of Merlin. As the stones were erected long before the beginning of the Christian Era it is evident that we can find no help in this tradition.

The belief that Stonehenge was a sacred place, probably for the worship of the sun—one of the oldest forms of religion—is based upon the fact that a line extending from the Friar's Heel, at the entrance, through the Slaughter Stone to the Altar Stone, points approximately to the rising sun on Midsummer's Day; *approximately,* yet not exactly now, but when erected, the rays of the rising sun on Midsummer Day fell on the Friar's Heel and Slaughter Stone, pierced an opening in the temple and touched the Altar Stone. Astronomical calculations show that this would have occurred about 1680 B. C., more than 3,600 years ago, and this is the date within two hundred years that has been assigned to the monument. The theory is plausible. The many excavations that have been made at Stonehenge have brought to light no definite clues as to the age of the monument. It is true that with the exception of one small piece of copper which left a stain on the base of one of the monoliths no metal has been found. Chips from the "sarcens," stone mauls for dressing the stones, and deerhorn picks for excavating holes in the chalk which forms the rock of the region have been unearthed, and chips from the sarcens have been dug up in nearby tumuli. Because of the absence of copper and bronze it has been assumed that Stonehenge was built in Neolithic times, but it is possible that for religious reasons, as in Solomon's Temple, no metal was used. Tradition lingers long in the priesthood. In Egypt, for example, flint knives were used in ceremonials long after they were replaced for general use by metal knives. If the tumuli, of which there are many nearby, were built by the same people who erected Stonehenge, the monument is of early Bronze Age since some of the tumuli contain bronze objects.

The recent work of Lieut. Col. William Hawley has shown that a causeway forty feet wide (about half the width of the present Avenue) with ditches on the two sides formerly afforded an entrance and that the causeway is studded with holes which probably held poles to form a palisade. This discovery indicates that Stonehenge was originally a fortified place which later became sacred. Since many sacred places throughout Europe had such an origin this suggestion seems probable. The fact that the ditch surrounding Stonehenge was partially filled with silt without any stone chips indicates that the ditch antedates the dressing and erection of the stones of the structure.

The transportation, dressing and erection of these huge stones would indicate a population of several thousand. The "blue stones" from Wales indicate that there was an orderly government of some kind to which a considerable territory was subject. In a forested country, such as England was then, the people would live in wooden houses which when decayed would leave no record.

Avebury (Fig. 90). Another great megalithic work, in some respects more interesting than Stonehenge, is at Avebury. It consists of a circular earth embankment about twelve hundred feet in average diameter which encloses an area of about twenty-eight and one-half acres. Inside the embankment is a ditch which when first excavated must have been more than fifty feet below the top of the embankment. Bordering the ditch on the inside was a circle of great stones and within this two smaller stone circles, standing side by side, each formed by a double row of smaller stones. From an opening in the embankment at the east a winding avenue of menhirs extended for about a mile and a quarter, and another avenue of stones stretched to the southwest for a mile and a half and ended in a double loop.

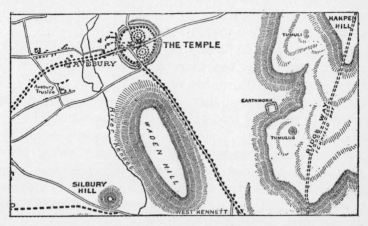

Fig. 90.—Plan of Avebury. The Avebury monument contains 28½ acres. Inside the ditch was a circle of great stones and, within this, two smaller circles formed by a double row of smaller stones. Two long avenues of standing stones led from the embankment. Of the 650 original stones, only 20 are now standing. This has been called the finest megalithic ruin in Europe. After Lord Avebury.

Excavations have brought to light pottery, flint chips, scrapers and a knife. Antlers of the red deer, which were the tools used to dig out the chalk of the ditch, and shoulder blades of the deer—the shovels of the excavators—were found in abundance. Silbury Hill, the largest artificial mound in Europe, about one hundred and thirty feet high, stands midway between the avenues but whether it was a part of the Avebury Monument is not known.

All of the stones are the so-called sarcen stones like those of Stonehenge. When first erected the Avebury Monument must have been considered one of the marvels of the world.

Engineering Skill. The megalith builders used the stones which were most accessible: in Denmark, glacial boulders were employed; in Brittany and Cornwall, the granite of the immediate vicinity; in parts of England, slabs of limestone and sandstone; and in the Paris basin the soft, local limestone. Some of the stones were carried considerable distances: a forty-four-ton block at La Pérotte (Charente) is said to have been transported nearly nineteen miles. The blocks of stone of the dolmen of Moulins (Indre) came from a quarry about twenty-one miles distant. The stones of the passage grave of La Hougue Bie on the island of Jersey were obtained from the seashore, at least two and a half miles distant and were brought up a steep rise of one hundred and fifty feet. The three hundred-ton monolith of Men-er-Hroeck (Locmariaquer, Morbihan) was transported more than a half mile. To transport and set up such a stone as this last—more than sixty-five feet long—would be considered an important undertaking to-day.[14]

Although the task was a difficult one, the work of erecting most of the megalithic monuments has probably been greatly exaggerated. As far as known, the only mechanical aids were wooden levers and rollers and, possibly, ropes. With wooden levers and without rollers two skilled men can move a stone slab weighing one ton, and even the largest capping stones, which weigh possibly seventy tons, could probably be handled by fifteen or twenty men. The chief difficulty would be to raise the capping stones and place them on the standing stones. This could be accomplished by first firmly setting the standing stones, then building a mound so as to cover them, then by moving the capping stone by means of wooden rollers and levers up the inclined slope to the desired position. Later the earth could be removed from the interior of the chamber.

[14] The French evidently considered the erection of the Egyptian obelisk in the Place de la Concorde, Paris, a notable achievement if one may judge by the bronze tablet at its base which shows graphically the methods employed.

As has been stated, the capstones of dolmens originally rested on upright stones, but there are a few exceptions to this statement. Either because of the scarcity of labour, or because of a miscalculation of the labour necessary to move some of the enormous stones, some of the capping stones seem never to have been horizontal but were raised on one end only. This peculiarity is seen in such dolmens as those at Howth, Ireland, and Lower Lanyon Quoit, Cornwall.

The stones of which megalithic tombs are made show little evidence of dressing and, with the exception of splitting, which was occasionally done, they are as first quarried. Some of the stones of the relatively late Stonehenge were not only dressed but had tenons carefully made to fit sockets carved in the stones they supported.

The Origin of the Megalith Idea. There is no question but that the megalithic monuments of prehistoric Europe were built because of some profound religious belief which induced men to expend energy and time in building homes for their dead. The restriction of these monuments to lands adjacent to the coast of Western Europe, and to the islands and coastal regions of the Mediterranean, and Black Seas, suggests that the idea was brought from some centre of civilisation by mariners. The earliest megaliths of Scandinavia (dolmens), for example, are nearer the coast than the later tombs.[15] An attractive theory offered by W. J. Perry and G. Elliot Smith, presents evidence to show that the megalith idea was carried to Europe by Egyptian noblemen, who, with their followers, took long sea voyages in search of gold, copper, tin, amber, and other desired commodities. Upon the death of such a leader a megalithic tomb somewhat like those of the homeland was erected in his memory. Perry and Smith suggest that the mastaba [16] of Egypt is the prototype of dolmens,

[15] It is remarkable that the building of megalithic tombs did not spread over Central Europe, when it is remembered that the custom persisted for many years.

[16] The mastaba is a tomb with a pit below for the body and a chapel above ground for religious ceremonies.

passage graves and hallcists. Perry's argument is as follows: "There seem to be two distinct types [of megalithic tombs]. One consists of a large, flat stone supported by three or more other large stones standing on their edges so as to enclose a space, the large stone often projecting in front so as to form a kind of forecourt or antechapel. In the other type [of megalithic tomb] the chamber is approached by a long gallery formed of rows of large stones set on edge. These two forms of dolmen seem to copy the parts of the mastaba tomb that are above ground and below ground respectively. The essential feature of the visible part of the mastaba grave is the antechapel and the chamber in which the portrait statue is placed. Communication between these two chambers is effected by means of a small hole in the wall of the chamber containing the portrait statue. This feature is often reproduced in dolmens in France, the Caucasus, India, and so forth. The underground part of the mastaba, on the other hand, consists of a chamber of large blocks of stone, or else a chamber carved in the rock, approached by a passage, itself lined with large blocks of stone. This form of tomb is exactly similar to one variety of megalithic tomb [hallcist]. Further, it is found that the practice of making rock-cut tombs is associated with the erection of dolmens. These rock-cut tombs, some of which are to be found in France, are of the same ground plan as the underground part of some of the mastaba tombs." [17]

A study of the megalithic monuments of Western Europe does not show that a striking resemblance to the mastaba exists and, moreover, the earliest tombs, the dolmens, were least like the Egyptian tomb, whereas the latest, the hallcists, resemble them more closely, but even the hallcists bear little likeness to the Egyptian tomb. Burial pits are never found in European megaliths, and the overhanging capstone of the dolmen does not suggest a forecourt or antechapel. Unless it can be shown that the hallcist is the oldest type of megalith

[17] W. J. Perry: "The Growth of Civilization," pp. 64-65. 1923.

and the dolmen a degenerate form, the theory, attractive as it is, cannot stand.

It has also been suggested that the megalith idea arose independently in different regions. It is stated that "Once society had reached a stage where unlimited and intelligently directed labour was available, and there was a convenient supply of detached blocks, then boulder-building was a much faster and more satisfactory method of making an enduring structure than any small stone technique. Other choices of material cannot have been nearly so attractive: earth, wood, and wattle, have no lasting qualities, dressed squares of stones would require infinity of preparation, and mortar was unknown; the practical alternative would be dry-walling, but as a matter of fact the construction of a dry wall of undressed stone sound enough to bear the weight of a heavy roof is probably one of the most difficult tasks that a builder can be set, one requiring not mere physical strength under a single overseer but sustained and laborious skill, all this being in accord with our actual experience that dry work with small stones is a late accessory of megalith construction."

It is further suggested "that there are three centres in northwestern Europe where megalithic tombs were independently invented, namely, the dolmen districts of Portugal, and of Denmark, and of northeastern France where the cist-form with the porthole entrance seem to be copies of neighbouring chalk-cut grottoes. Of these, the culture that exerted the greatest influence on European prehistory was probably that of Portugal which was destined to inspire the great megalith culture of the Peninsula whence, in the flush of strength represented by the larger passage-graves, the megalith fashion travelled to Brittany, and a little later to Ireland and to Cornwall, while a cist-culture was also established across the Pyrenees in the south of France, whence Spanish influence moved eastwards into the Mediterranean and was in part responsible for the megalithic works of the islands." [18]

[18] T. D. Kendrick: "The Axe Age," pp. 101, 102, 105, 106.

There are as serious objections to the independent origin of megaliths as there are to their Egyptian origin. It seems impossible that three nearly identical cultures could have originated independently in nearby regions. We can be confident that the megalith idea, which was vitally associated with some powerful religious cult originated in some one place, and from there spread to the coastal regions of Europe, where local conditions, difference in the capacity of the people, the influence of older or other religious beliefs, and other factors, led to local modifications. Over and over again this has been the history of great religious movements.

CHAPTER VII

THE BRONZE AGE

THE ACQUISITION OF COPPER AND BRONZE
THE BEGINNINGS OF COMMERCE AND ORGANISED WARFARE

Equivalents:
- Full Bronze Age: Minoan in Crete, Mycenean in Greece, Terramara in Italy
- Copper Age: Chalcolithic, Eneolithic, Cyprolithic

Dates in Northern and Central Europe: 2500 B.C. to 500 B.C.
(See table pp. 70-71.)

THE Neolithic merged into the Bronze Age without a break. Indeed, the Bronze Age may best be understood if it is considered as a continuation of the New Stone Age in which stone artifacts are gradually replaced by bronze.

No one can say definitely what first led Neolithic man to use copper, but the reason seems obvious. Such a substance as native copper would attract the attention of the weapon maker because, unlike flint and stone, it can easily be worked into any desired shape by hammering. The North American Indians were in the New Stone Age when Europeans discovered the new world. Nevertheless, for hundreds of years they had made objects of native copper. A remarkable example of such use was brought to light recently when the skeletons of men with copper helmets and with the septa of their noses replaced with thin plates of copper were unearthed when a mound in Ohio was excavated.

The ancient Peruvians had a considerable knowledge of metallurgy. They knew how to cast metal, to solder, and even to plate one metal with another. They mined silver in considerable quantities as hundreds of partly filled shallow shafts show. They mined lead ores and used the lead for making bolas. They smelted copper and had acquired the knowledge that copper alloyed with tin is harder than pure copper. Some investigators however hold that the admixture of copper and tin was accidental. The peoples of the western plateaux of South America were on the threshold of a Bronze Age but had not yet emerged from the Age of Stone.

Copper implements are rare in Europe, both because they were seldom common and also because most of those that once existed were subsequently melted down when bronze came into use. They were not uncommon in Ireland and in Hungary. In the National Museum at Dublin, for example, there are one hundred and twenty-seven copper celts and sixty-five halberds.

The discovery of methods of melting copper and of smelting copper ores was, without doubt, an accident. A lump of copper ore, such as the green carbonate (malachite) or the red oxide (cuprite), which is commonly associated with native copper, may have been used as part of a hearth, or may have been inadvertently dropped into a hot fire. When the fire had died out globules of bright metal would be seen if the globules had been abraded. The Stone Age man would recognise the metal as that which he had found in its native state and which he had used. Such an accident probably happened many times before a man with sufficient native curiosity to take advantage of it had it called to his attention. This man—the one in ten thousand—determined to discover how to obtain larger amounts of copper by heating ore. When, to his great delight, he found that this could be done, it occurred to him that he might make a new copper ax by allowing the molten metal to flow into an ax-shaped depression in the sand. A simple furnace was soon devised because of the demand for larger quantities of the metal.[1]

[1] W. J. Perry suggests that, since the Egyptians painted their faces with powdered malachite, the green ore of copper, in the course of time they found that this green paint, when fused, produced copper, and of this metal they made beads and foils, then pins, and finally knives and chisels. W. J. Perry: "The Origin of Civilization," p. 35.

The discovery of copper smelting had a profound effect in accelerating the upward progress of the human race. Being no longer dependent on the rare native copper for his metal, man could make a greater number of metallic tools. As deposits of copper are restricted, many tribes were obliged to go long distances for the useful metal. As they had to offer something in exchange they were obliged to carry some desirable objects with them, or, they had to conquer the people who lived in the copper region. Copper tools being somewhat better for certain purposes than stone tools, time was saved and man had leisure for other things. "Having no moving pictures or golf to fool away the time thus saved, man very sensibly applied it to inventing means of improving his position in life."

It is evident, therefore, that the discovery of copper smelting was an important event in the development and spread of civilisation. When and where the knowledge of copper smelting was acquired or whether it was acquired independently in a number of places, is not known. It seems fairly well proved that copper came from the Sinai peninsula and was in use in Egypt a thousand years and more before it was known in Central and Western Europe. It was probably smelted in Cyprus and Crete at least as early as 3000 B.C. Copper was introduced into the Nile Valley just before the consolidation of the region under the first dynasty, and bronze a little later. Some statues of bulls, nearly a metre long, made of copper plates riveted to a wooden core and with heads of cast copper were discovered at Ur in Mesopotamia (ancient Babylon) in 1923-24. They are dated at about 3300 B.C., and show that the technique of copper smelting and casting was well advanced, even at this early time. All things considered, Egypt seems to be the centre from which the knowledge of copper spread to Europe. Because of its favourable geographical position Crete became the oldest culture-land of Europe.

Discovery of Bronze. As soon as copper smelting was known, search was made for rich deposits of copper ore. This, as has been stated, was because rich deposits of copper ore are not widely distributed, nor do they cover large areas. In his search for copper, lumps of stream tin, the oxide of tin, (cassiterite), would attract the attention of the prospector because of their high specific gravity. When the stream tin was smelted it would run as a brilliant silver stream. But tin is so soft that implements made of it were found to be of little or no use. How the discovery of bronze, an alloy of copper and tin, was made is not known. Perhaps someone who lacked sufficient copper to fill a mould added a small amount of tin. To his delight he found, when he used his ax, that it was harder and in every way superior to the axes made of copper. The alloy had the added advantage of melting at a lower temperature than copper. Thus another great advance was made. Now came the search for tin ore. Deposits of this mineral are much rarer than those of copper. It should be noted, however, that when the demand for tin first arose, streams in regions where the ore is now too poor to be worked, even with modern machinery,[2] probably had considerable amounts of stream tin, the residue of the weathering of many feet of granite. Only by the existence of such deposits can the great quantities of bronze, in some places, be explained. Most of such deposits however, like those of placer gold, were soon exhausted.

The rarity of large supplies of tin ore compelled the man of the Bronze Age to make long and carefully planned expeditions in search of the metal, and, as a result, commerce on a large scale may be said to date from this time. The principal sources of tin in ancient times were Persia, the Iberian Peninsula, Great Britain, and Bohemia. Early in the Bronze Age, Spain appears to have been the principal centre for tin but later, when the great deposits of tin in Cornwall were discovered,

[2] A good example is to be seen in the Black Hills of South Dakota where, in the vicinity of Harney's Peak, the creeks have much stream tin although the ore is too poor to mine. Had these placer deposits been in Europe they would have been regarded as great wealth by the Bronze Age people.

tin mining in Spain became unimportant and, for perhaps more than three thousand years, thereafter Cornwall supplied most of the tin used.

GOLD IN THE BRONZE AGE

One would expect to find among the artifacts of Paleolithic man at least some made of gold. It would seem that the glitter of gold, its beautiful colour and its malleability would early have attracted him. Moreover, it was abundant as nuggets in the gravels of streams in which he fished. Nevertheless, no gold nuggets or ornaments of gold have been discovered in Paleolithic deposits. After the discovery that copper made useful tools man, in his search for this metal, was doubtless attracted by the bright, readily malleable, nuggets of gold, which resemble untarnished copper, and he chose this metal for objects of personal adornment. At no other time in the history of the world (p. 212) was easily obtainable gold so abundant as in the early Bronze Age. Placer gold, the accumulation of hundreds of thousands of years, occurred in many regions. It was easily obtained but quickly exhausted. It is not surprising, therefore, that Bronze Age graves of Mycenæ, of Crete, and of Troy, yield such a wealth of gold ornaments and gold vessels. One hundred pounds of gold, for example, was found in the "Kings' graves" at Mycenæ. At Ur, of the Chaldees, a great wealth of gold and copper objects, together with some silver, were discovered in graves which are said to be conservatively estimated to belong to about 3500 B.C. One of these graves contained fragments of wrought iron. In this same grave were found a solid gold adz, a gold spearhead, two small gold chisels, a silver jug, a silver belt, carnelian beads, and beads of gold filigree.

Alluvial gold occurred, at that time, in Southern Egypt, Macedonia and Thrace, Transylvania, Hungary, and in Ireland, which was the El Dorado of the time. It was also found in smaller quantities in Spain, France, Germany, and elsewhere. The Irish gold probably came largely from a district south of Dublin (Wicklow County) where, in the eighteenth century, a twenty-two-ounce nugget was found and where, in recent times, more than 7500 ounces have been mined. When first worked the gold was probably very abundant, just as it was in the early days of the "gold rush" in California and the Yukon. The evidence of a large supply is to be seen in the number and massiveness of the gold ornaments found in Ireland and those of Irish manufacture discovered in Great Britain and Europe. These great Irish deposits of stream gold, with the exception of a few that were overlooked and have recently been mined, were exhausted by the close of the Bronze Age. When one takes into account the fact that, ever since gold first attracted man's eye, gold ornaments have been remelted again and again and made into ornaments to meet the taste of the moment, the number still preserved and exhibited in the Irish National Museum in Dublin and in the British Museum affords convincing evidence of the richness of the virgin alluvial deposits. An account of the finds of gold objects of the Bronze Age will be given later (p. 214).

SILVER AND LEAD

Silver objects are very rare in Europe except in the countries bordering the Mediterranean. In the second city of Troy, silver was used for weapons as well as ornaments and an abundance of the metal is indicated. Silver is found in the native state in Spanish mines and, it has been stated, that, at this remote period, silver was more than twice as abundant as tin in one part of Spain. Diodorus says that when the Phœnicians arrived in Spain they found silver being mined in great quantities by the inhabitants and bought it at a low price as the natives did not know its value. In Northern and Central Europe and Great Britain silver was seldom used.

Lead is easily obtained from the ore but is so soft that it is of no use for implements or weapons and was generally disregarded. It was, however, smelted early, as discoveries in the first city of Troy show, but was principally used for votive offerings.

CHRONOLOGY [3]

In our study of the Paleolithic we found that it was possible to determine the relative ages of cultures by their superposition in caves and river terraces, the more ancient cultures underlying the younger. Such evidence is almost entirely lacking in the Bronze Age deposits of Europe. Because of the unsatisfactory character of such criteria, the chronology of the Age is based largely upon the *type* of the object, and upon the stage in its evolution. An excellent example of this method is discussed in a subsequent paragraph. This method has proved fairly satisfactory because, when a new and better type of implement, or a more attractive or useful ornament, was invented in one place, it was soon carried to all parts of Europe. This is especially true in the periods after the invention of bronze because traders, and prospectors in search of copper and tin, spread the knowledge of new inventions wherever they went.

The dates assigned to the periods of this Age by different authors do not entirely agree. This is not surprising as we are dealing, in Central and Western Europe, with civilisations which had no written language and the dates assigned are those determined by students of the Egyptian and the Cretan civilisations.

The absolute dating of bronze objects in Europe depends, ultimately, on the correctness of the Egyptian chronology. In general, the dating is determined in this way; objects of Egyptian manufacture or design, which are known to have been made or used in Egypt during a certain dynasty, are found in Crete or Mycenæ to which they had been brought by traders or colonists or sent as gifts. Such objects were obviously made about the same time as the Cretan and Mycenæan objects with which they occur. If only one object were found,

[3] See chronological table, pages 70-71.

one would generally not place a great deal of dependence on it in dating a find because of the fear that it might not be "in place" but, if a number of utensils, or ornaments and tools of identical design occur both in Egypt and in Crete or Mycenæ there would be little doubt of their contemporaneity. For example, at Tel-el-Amarna, Egypt, Petrie found in the Palace of Iknaton and its environs, Bronze Age potsherds which, for the most part, belonged to the Late Mycenæan or the third Minoan periods. Since this palace was destroyed in 1350 B.C., when the nineteenth dynasty began, the date of these fragments of pottery is known. There have also been discovered at Mycenæ objects of Egyptian origin, such as fayence vases, and gold, glass, and other ornaments. On the Acropolis at Mycenæ there was discovered a scarab inscribed with the name of Queen Teje, the wife of Amenhophis III.

Montelius[4] states the case as follows: "Because many Italic objects have been found in Central and Northern Europe, together with native ones; because in Italy numerous objects of the Ægean circle are found in connection with Italic ones; and because the pre-classical period in Greece can be dated by well-established Cretan chronology, I have been able to determine the age of the different periods of the Bronze Age in Italy and North of the Alps, that is, we can now say to what centuries before Christ the periods of the Bronze Age belong."

In the southern Mediterranean region we find the bronze artifacts poor in tin about 2500 B.C., and the Iron Age about 1200 B.C. In Italy, the Bronze Age begins in the nineteenth century B.C. and ends about 1100 B.C. In Sweden the Bronze Age begins about 1800 B.C. and ends in the eighth century B.C.

Déchelette divides the Bronze Age of Western Europe into four periods as follows:

Period I. This comprises the Copper Age (Eneolithic) and the Earliest Bronze Age. Here belong the earliest flat celts,

[4] Oscar Montelius: "Bronzezeit" in *Reallexikon der Vorgeschichte,* edited by Max Ebert, vol. 2, 1925.

triangular daggers and halberds of copper or bronze with a small percentage of tin. Later there are triangular daggers with a tang or long tongue (the Cypriote dagger), daggers with rivets, and with handles cast in one piece with the blade; pins with heads in the shape of rings; lozenge-shaped awls; olive-shaped gold beads; gold lunulæ; bronze bracers; bell beakers and small vases with handles. Stone artifacts, especially arrow-heads, are still abundant. Date: 2500-1900 B.C.

Period II. Bronze with a high percentage of tin is found. There are celts with slightly raised sides or borders; triangular daggers, with a rounded base and rivets, many decorated with a large median rib. At the end of the period, the blade of the dagger lengthens and the first swords appear. Pins with spherical heads with perforations, open bracelets with pointed ends and pottery with incised decoration are also found. Date: 1900-1600 B.C.

Period III. The typical celts have raised borders, stop ridges (the palstave), with two rings for fastening, and with wing-shaped flanges in the middle. There are also slender daggers; the early long swords with tangs; knives cast in one piece with the handles; pins with long ribbed necks and with wheel-like heads; open bracelets with blunt ends, and flat bracelets and anklets with large spirals at the ends; channelled, incised, and mammillary pottery. Date: 1600-1300 B.C.

Period IV. Celts with wing-shaped flanges at the top and socketed celts appear. There are swords with a tang to pass through the handle, with rivets, or with a long slit, in the tang. Some sword handles have antennæ. In addition, there are daggers with flat tangs and rivets; socketed daggers; arrow-heads with tangs and with sockets; socketed knives; knives cast in one piece with the handle; helmets; twisted and hollow bracelets; pins with spherical and vase-shaped heads; violin bow, bow and serpentine fibulæ; girdle clasps; semicircular razors and double ones with handles; hollow engraved balls; and pottery which is strongly reminiscent of the pile dwelling ware. Date: 1300-900 B.C.

The civilisations of Europe are recent as compared with those of Egypt, Asia Minor, Crete, and Greece. Higher civilisations had been in existence and some had had their rise, development, and fall while Europe was still in the hunting stage of barbarism.

The Great Cretan Civilisation. The people of Europe owe many, perhaps most, of the fundamentals of civilisation to the Orient, but, having obtained them, they adapted and improved them until, before the first millennium before Christ, they had created a distinct civilisation of their own. Europe owes more to the early civilisation of Crete perhaps than to any other country. Lying as it does between the Ægean Archipelago and Egypt, and not far from the coast of Asia Minor, Crete could take advantage of any progress that was made in the South or East without having its native genius overwhelmed and without losing its individuality. Moreover, although largely mountainous there are fertile plains and extensive pasture land capable of supporting a considerable population. As the population grew the Cretans were obliged to turn to maritime trade and, in this way, their culture was carried to distant shores of the Mediterranean and Black Seas. Concerning Neolithic Crete nothing need be said except that the Neolithic inhabitants had little effect on the civilisation of the world. Their sole contribution to the older civilisations of the East and South appear to have been obsidian, which they may have obtained from Melos and which was used for knives.

At the close of the Neolithic a rapid and important change took place and a civilisation, now known as the Minoan, had its rise. The essentials of this new culture appear to be Egyptian but even the impress of the Sumerian civilisation of Mesopotamia is not wanting. This new culture came with the introduction of metal. "Its appearance is marked by the strivings of an artistic impulse which, swiftly changing and

improving, carried the Southern Ægeans in a few centuries
from the rude hand-made pottery of the Neolithic period to
artistic triumphs which have hardly been equalled since." [5]
Crete was the main inspiration although not the only one of
the Ægean civilisation.

The history of this great center of civilisation may be separated into three phases. (1) A period of quiet, during which
mariners sailed to distant lands in their open vessels carrying
with them manufactured articles and bringing back copper
and gold. (2) With wealth came a concentration of power in
the hands of the few, and stately palaces arose. Toward the
close of this period (Middle Minoan) the mainland of Greece
came under the domination of the lords of Crete. But (3)
imperialism was fatal to the mother country for, in late
Minoan times, the colonists from Mycenæ sacked the palaces
of Crete and took over the rule of the island.

Although the Minoan civilisation owed much to Mesopotamia and Egypt it was no mere copy, but an original and
creative force. As such Crete stands out as essentially modern
in aspect. It was thoroughly European and in no sense
Oriental.[6]

Some of the distinctive features of Minoan art should be
mentioned. The art was naturalistic and the vase paintings,
frescoes, and intaglios portray animals, fishes, flowers, trees,
games, and processions with a true sense of line and proportion. The evolution of their tools and weapons shows a creative mind. The flat celt did not pass through a series of forms
as in Europe (p. 225) but quickly gave rise to the ax head
(Fig. 100) with a hole for the insertion of a handle. Slender
rapiers, a yard long, were evolved from daggers and had richly
decorated pommels. The manufacture of swords of this sort
shows metallurgical skill of a high order. The gold jewelry
of the Middle Minoan was remarkable for its abundance and
the excellence of its workmanship. The abundance of gold

[5] H. R. Hall: "The Ancient History of the Far East," 1920, p. 33.
[6] V. Gordon Childe: "The Dawn of European Civilization."

can be explained by the fact that mariners going to countries where alluvial gold deposits had never before been worked, found great quantities of native gold which they brought home. Never, perhaps, in the history of the world, was gold so abundant in any country and more widely used than in Crete and its colonies.

Recent proof of the abundance of gold is seen in the discovery in a beehive tomb in Greece of the skeleton of a "king"

FIG. 91.—The remarkable art of Crete (Minoan) which disappeared before the close of the Bronze Age is shown in these vases: one with a lily design and the other with an octopus.

which was covered almost from head to foot with gold and silver objects. On the breast was a magnificent gold cup seventeen centimetres in diameter, chased with realistic figures of octopuses, dolphins, and argonauts.

The potter used the wheel in the Middle Minoan and made vases and vessels of almost every conceivable form. These he painted with naturalistic designs (Fig. 91). With the invasion of Crete by the Greeks this splendid civilisation began to decline and never again exerted an influence on the world. The Bronze Age began in Crete about 3400 B.C. and reached its artistic climax between 2100 and 1580 B.C., whereas, in Eastern Europe, it began about one thousand years later, and, because of the early introduction of iron, had a shorter time to develop.

The Terramara Settlements. Parts of the Po Valley in Northern Italy were settled by a short-headed (brachycephalic) people who apparently came from the north in late Neolithic and early Bronze Age times. They built huts in rows on level ground and, although the ground was not swampy, they built them on piles. This custom was probably the result of tradition rather than necessity. They built as their lake-dwelling ancestors did but without the reason.

The form of a Terramara settlement is that of a trapezoid cut by two roads at right angles. The settlement was surrounded by a rampart and a moat. The huts were probably built with wattle-and-daub walls and thatched roofs. The inhabitants habitually threw their kitchen waste and other refuse under their huts and, when the pile had grown too high, they either burned down the hut or rebuilt it on the same site. In this way, the superimposed settlements found on some of these sites, and the height of the mounds, can be explained. The terramara (*terra,* earth; *marne,* marl or manure) consists of layers of different coloured earths formed, as has been said, by refuse of various kinds, and it is these layers that have yielded most of the antiquities. The term "terramara" was given to the low mounds of the Po Valley by the peasants who carted away the rich earth to fertilise their fields.

The Terramara settlements were self-supporting; they manufactured metal objects; made pottery, approaching the bucchero of later times; had domestic animals, such as the sheep, cow, pig, goat, and horse, although still hunters; cultivated beans, beets, barley, millet, flax, and the vine; and made cloth. Mention should be made of their pottery with lunate handles because of the religious significance of this symbol (p. 298). The Terremare of Italy belong to the first half of the Bronze Age.

CACHES OR HOARDS

Finds of Bronze Age Objects. Under the terms "hoards" are included collections of implements or weapons which were hidden in moors and bogs, under large stones, or in other places, whether for all time or with the intention of getting them later. Man permanently parted with votive offerings to the gods and he temporarily hid his goods in times of danger. Many of such finds with hundreds of objects of the same type give the impression that they must have belonged to traders. Others which are wholly, or almost entirely, made of broken and worn-out tools must have been the stock of a founder, as moulds for the manufacture of celts, spearheads and other implements are common in such hoards. The care with which bronze fragments, worn-out tools and old metallic objects were preserved is shown by the scarcity of bronze in the débris of villages that had been inhabited for centuries during the Bronze Age. Discoveries, in Ireland, of gold objects of the Bronze Age have been the result of accident and whenever an excavation is made or a peat cutter is spading peat from the bog, there is always a chance that he may uncover a hoard which has been buried for many centuries. Such a cache was the Clare find, made by workmen on a railroad near Limerick in County Clare, Ireland. In removing the stones of a small cairn or rude cist from the side of a railroad cut, they uncovered scores of gold objects, some of which are shown in Plate III, such as bracelets, torques, rings and gold ingots. One of the workmen filled his hat with the precious metal and rushed to Newmarket where he sold his booty which weighed 110½ ounces for £30. Many of the objects went to the melting pot, but some 150 of them, weighing 175 ounces, were preserved and are to be seen in the National Museum in Dublin, and in the British Museum.

Another important find was made at Eberswalde in Bran-

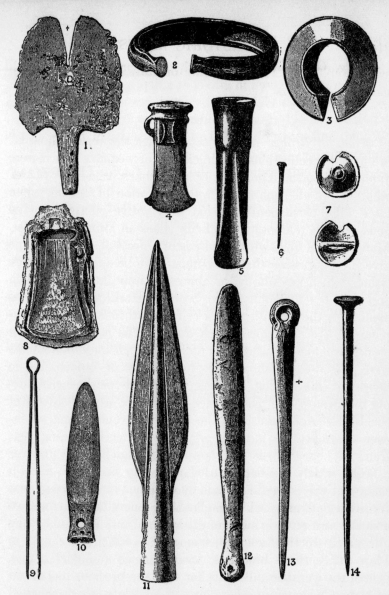

Fig. 92.—Part of the household goods of a family that lived or had taken refuge in a cave when the Bronze Age culture had reached its climax in Britain. Heathery Burn Cave, England. The objects are of bronze, gold, lignite, bone, and deerhorn. (1) razor, (2) gold bracelet, (3) gold ornament, (4) socketed celt, (5) gouge, (6) bronze pin, (7) button, (8) celt mould, (9) tweezers; (10) bronze knife; (11) bronze spearhead; (12) and (13) bone implements, (14) long pin. The objects are not drawn to scale. After Sir Arthur Evans.

denburg, Germany, in 1913, when an urn filled with gold objects was discovered in gravel at a depth of about three feet. In the urn were eight bowl-shaped vessels the size of the hand, a twisted torque, spiral rings of double wire, a small bar of gold, and other objects. The total weight of the gold was eighty-one and three-quarters ounces.

One can only conjecture the reason for the burial of such quantities of gold. It is evident that they did not form part of an interment. "Possibly, they were either the spoils from a vanquished people, a royal tribute, or a votive offering." [7]

An important discovery of the entire equipment of a Bronze Age household was made in a cave in England (Heathery Burn Cave, Durham), where a family lived for a time. The variety of objects (Fig. 92) is rather surprising. Among other things discovered are spearheads, bronze disks, five and one-half inches across, collars of cast bronze, socketed celts, a razor, chisels and a gouge, bone implements, and gold and jet ornaments.

The largest hoard in Denmark was dug up in a peat bog near Copenhagen and consisted of 163 articles, chiefly spearheads and celts.

WEAPONS

The variety of weapons of war used by Neolithic man was comparatively small. This was due partly (1) to the fact that its brittleness and lack of malleability put a definite limit to the size and style of objects made from flint and stone, and (2) partly to the fact that, even in Neolithic times villages were small, there was little movement of population and, consequently, little incentive for the development of the art of war.

With the discovery of copper and the invention of bronze, a great change was wrought in the centres of population. No longer were the people content to remain in one place and

[7] E. C. R. Armstrong: Catalogue of Irish gold ornaments in the collections of the Royal Irish Academy, 1920, p. 19.

to use flint in making tools. They wanted the ores that would make the superior metal implement. To get this metal expeditions were sent out from the Eastern Mediterranean to Spain, Austria, Great Britain and Ireland, to Central Africa and Asia. Where the prospectors and leaders of such expeditions found gold, tin, or copper they doubtless forced the natives to work for them, either as slaves or serfs. They were often, perhaps usually, among hostile peoples and effective weapons of war were necessary. Moreover, having many men and women under their control, they had the leisure to design and improve the weapons which were so essential to their success.

Another result of these expeditions and the exploitation of the backward peoples was the growth of villages and cities of considerable size, such as the first cities of Troy. Thus pride of city and national consciousness arose and, with it, the usual arrogance and feeling of superiority of one city for another, and one people for another. The crowding of populations made necessary the conquering of other peoples in order to obtain plunder or land.

Fig. 93.—Daggers. (1) Cypriote dagger. The tang which passes through the handle is characteristic. (2), (3) and (4) daggers of different shapes and ornamentation. Much reduced in size.

By permission of the Trustees of the British Museum.

Before such expeditions of conquest were undertaken we can imagine that the inventive skill of the military leaders and the metal workers was concentrated on the development of more effective implements of war. It is evident, therefore, that the discovery and use of metal caused a profound change in the mental attitude of tribes toward one another, and that one of the great incentives to invention was the desire for better weapons of attack and defence.

Daggers. Flint daggers were used in the Neolithic and, when copper and bronze came into use, daggers were made

from the metal. The early daggers (Fig. 93) and knives look
very much alike but each soon acquired the form which rendered it best suited for the use to which it was to be put.
As this weapon can be easily carried and concealed it has
continued in use from that time to this.

Halberds. At the close of the Neolithic and in the early
Bronze Age (Copper Age), javelins, and arrows tipped with
stone, were the only weapons
for fighting at a distance. As
the dagger was the only metal
weapon known in the early
Bronze Age it was sometimes
fastened near the end of a
shaft and at right angles to it
(Fig. 94). In this way the
halberd came into use. It
must have been one of the
best weapons of the time for
it rapidly spread over Western
Europe and was used in Italy,
Spain, Ireland, Scotland, and
Germany. A halberd found in
one of the shaft graves at
Mycenæ proves an early use
in Greece.

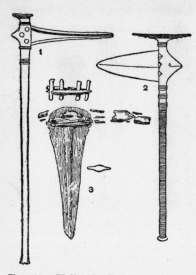

Fig. 94.—Halberds. The halberd was
first made by fastening a copper
or bronze dagger to a shaft, and
at right angles to it. In (3) the
grain of the wood shows that this
blade was part of a halberd as it
is at right angles to it. After
Déchelette.

As the shape of the halberd
blade is similar, or identical,
with that of the dagger it is
often difficult to determine
whether a blade is a dagger or a halberd. Where the marks
of the grain of the wood of the missing handle are impressed
on the rusted surface of the butt of a specimen it is possible
to tell, from the direction of the grain, whether or not the
blade was mounted halberd-wise or was used as a dagger.
The relative length of the rivets which attach the handle to
the blade also shows how the blade was mounted. If the

middle of these rivets is shorter than the others the blade was used in a halberd, as the middle rivet being near the side of the shaft would be shorter than those in the centre of the handle. In daggers the middle rivet, being in the thickest part of the handle, would be the longest. Halberd blades range in length from nine to fifteen inches and in greatest width from three to four inches.

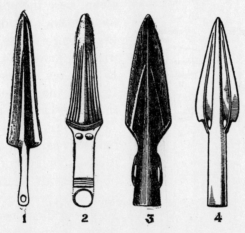

FIG. 95.—Spears. The spearhead, like the halberd, was evolved from the dagger. In Great Britain the head was first attached by a rivet or rivets, later a loop for the insertion of a leather thong (3) was added to hold the head to the shaft. In later forms (4) two ornamental openings in the blade represent the loops.

Spears and Lances. Spear- and lanceheads (Fig. 95) were developed from the dagger by inserting the tang or tongue of a dagger in the end of a long handle, and then by fixing a ring or ferrule around the base of the head, to prevent the tang from splitting the wood. From such a crude form, a head cast in one piece with the socket was evolved. Metal loops to attach the head to the shaft, and ribs to give strength to the head, were next added. Finally the loops appear as openings in the blade of the spear and become merely ornamental features, as the spearhead in its final form was attached to the shaft by a rivet. Some spearheads were of great length, more than thirty inches, whereas others were merely tips on the ends of long shafts. The evolution of the modern bayonet is similar: first a dagger was inserted in the barrel of the gun, later a dagger with a ring was designed, and, finally, the bayonet in its modern form appeared.

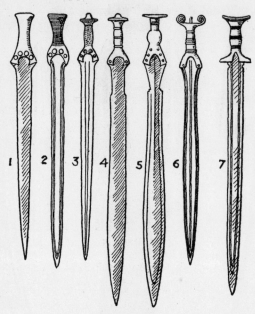

Fig. 96.—Swords. The sword was developed from the dagger. The earlier ones were of the rapier type (1), (2), and (3) and were designed for thrusting and stabbing, but, later, a long, heavy, slashing sword with a wider blade (4), (5), (6), and (7) came into use. After Schumacher.

Swords. From the dagger, there soon evolved, in the South, the short bronze sword (Fig. 96), or rapier, with tapering blade. From the rapier came the long sword, which, toward the end of the Bronze Age, gained more and more ground in the North. In the South, especially in Italy, the short, thrusting sword was preferred. The big Nordic fist fitted the long slashing sword much better.

The change from thrusting to slashing and from a short

to a long blade necessitated a stronger attachment to the handle, and the rounded butt, fastened by rivets to the hilt, was replaced by extending the metal of the blade to the end of the hilt.

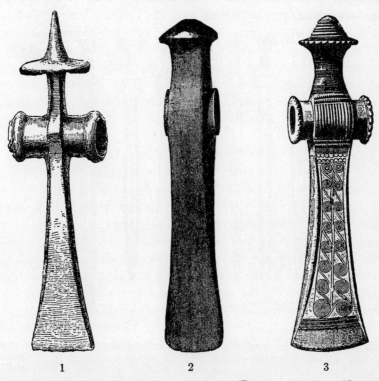

FIG. 97.—Battle-axes such as these from (1) Hungary, (2) from Norway, (3) from Sweden were used in parts of Europe. (1) after the British Museum, (2) after Gustafson, (3) after Montelius. Reduced in size.

The need of something to protect the edge of the sword and to prevent injury to the wearer, brought about the invention of the scabbard. Few scabbards are made entirely of metal and it is probable that most of them were made of leather, tipped at the point with metal. The metal tips, or chapes, were, as a rule, small, but toward the close of the Age they were so large as to suggest that they served as a foot purchase in drawing the sword from the sheath.

Battle-Axes. Bronze battle-axes, some beautifully made and ornamented (Fig. 97), were favoured weapons from Asia Minor and the Caucasus to Denmark but were never manufactured west of the Rhine and the Alps. Those found in Western Europe were introduced by invaders or traders.

Arrow- and Javelin-heads. The use of flint arrow-heads lasted into the Bronze Age and in the early part the height of technical perfection was reached. They continued in use for a long time, probably to conserve the valuable metal, until the art of flaking stone was lost.

DEFENSIVE ARMOUR

Shields and Armour. Circular shields (Fig. 98), generally ornamented with raised (*repousée*) concentric bands of knobs or dots and ribs were carried by the warrior in the later Bronze Age. Some shields made of wood, and even of leather, have been found in bogs, but bronze shields are commoner, possibly because they are less destructible. There is no record of bronze helmets in the early part of the Age and none may have been worn, as the swords of the time were for thrusting and not for cutting and slashing. If there was any protective covering for the head it was probably merely a cap made of leather or cloth. Toward the close of the Bronze Age when the heavy, slashing sword became an important part of the equipment of the soldier of Northern Europe, it became necessary to protect the head and body. This need brought about the invention of bronze helmets and cuirasses which were widely used in subsequent periods.

TOOLS

Agricultural and household tools of wood, horn, and stone were very slowly replaced by bronze as the metal became cheaper. Indeed, stone and wooden tools, of the same general design as those used by the Neolithic peoples, were employed

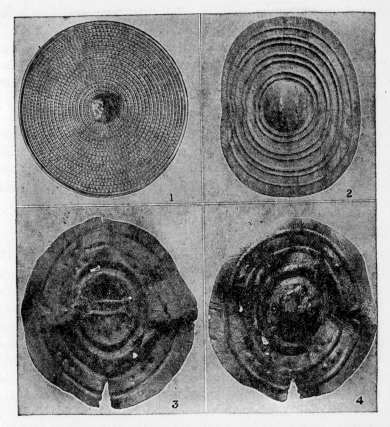

FIG. 98.—Bronze Age Shields. (1) A bronze shield with characteristic ornamentation. England. (2) A wooden shield 2 ft. 2½ inches by 1 ft. 9 inches.
Ireland. (3) and (4) Back and front views of a leather shield 1 ft. 8½
inches by 1 ft. 7½ inches from Ireland. (2), (3), and (4) are from
photographs by courtesy of the National Irish Museum.

throughout the Age. This is proved both by the absence of
bronze tools in some Bronze Age deposits and by several finds.
The wooden plough is represented in rude Swedish carvings
and in rock carvings in Liguria and one actual specimen found
in a Danish peat bog is probably of this Age. The bronze ax
was used both as a weapon and as a tool and soon replaced the
stone ax at least in the South, except for ceremonial purposes.

The stone knife was used for ceremonial purposes long after bronze knives were in general use.

Such tools as knives, sickles (Fig. 101), saws, chisels, and awls were, in time, made of bronze; after old stone models at first, but later of designs which experience had shown to be better.

New types of tools were created, such as hammers, files, anvils, punches for the metal workers, knives, bronze razors, toilet implements, and ornaments.

Much of our knowledge of the common tools and implements of everyday use is obtained from the Bronze Age lake dwellings (p. 154) of Switzerland and Southern Germany, where they were lost in the mud of the lake and thus preserved. Bronze chisels, gouges, socketed celts, saws, fish-hooks, bridle bits, vessels and dishes, rivets and nails, buttons and many long hairpins have been among the important objects discovered in such deposits.

Stone, Horn, and Bone Implements. Flint and bone implements were common early in the age but gradually gave way to bronze. Stone was used by the lake dwellers of this Age for the manufacture of a number of things, such as hearth stones, sharpening stones, stones for grinding grain, arrow-heads, hammers, and moulds for bronze implements. Although in less demand than in the Neolithic, staghorn and bone were favourite materials for combs, horsebits, fish spears and harpoons. Wood was used for many purposes such as dug-out canoes, oars, bows, dishes, and ladles.

Bronze Celts. The importance of the bronze celt in making man more independent of Nature should be emphasised; with it he was able more rapidly to cut down forests and make clearings for his crops. With the stone ax and aided by fire, his Neolithic ancestors could also extend their domain but the stone celt was easily broken and the progress was slow. When man began to use copper, his first celts were made of the same shape as his stone ones (Fig. 99) and were fastened to the handles in the same manner. Near the close of the "Copper Age" a celt with flat sides (not convex as in stone celts) was made. A flat celt is both more efficient and requires less metal than the stone type. It, however, presented one disadvantage: when inserted in the hole of a wooden handle there was no longer a bulge to prevent its slipping too far. Moreover, because it was thin, it quickly split the handle when blows were struck. To obviate this defect a different kind of handle was invented. Instead of making a hole for the insertion of the celt, a tree branch from which projected the stump

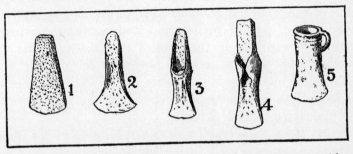

FIG. 99.—Evolution of the bronze celt. (1) a flat celt; (2) a celt with marginal flanges to prevent lateral movement; (3) a celt with a transverse stop ridge to prevent the head from embedding itself in the handle (palstave). (4) In this celt the flanges have become wings, and in (5) the partition has disappeared and a socketed celt is formed. After the Leipzig guide to the prehistoric collection of the Museum.

of another branch was chosen. This stump was split and into the cleft the celt was inserted and firmly bound to the wood with thongs (Fig. 100). With time the shape of the celt was modified (1) by making flanges on the sides to prevent so much lateral motion. Later, (2) by making a stop ridge, the head was prevented from sinking too far into the handle and thus splitting it. This form is called a *palstave*. Still further improvement was effected (3) by increasing the flanges until a sort of socket on each side of the blade was developed. Another feature was the addition of one or two loops at the side for the attachment of a thong (Fig. 100) to hold the ax more securely. Finally, (4) the wings meet, the dividing piece disappears and a socketed celt results. The side loops were retained in the socketed ax. The evolution of the bronze celt is well-shown in Figures 99 and 100.

The earliest celts were not ornamented but soon the workman began to embellish them with simple and characteristic designs. This was done by hammering, chiselling and by patterns made in the mould before casting.

The ax did not go through the stages just described in all regions. In the Eastern Mediterranean the flat celt did not lead

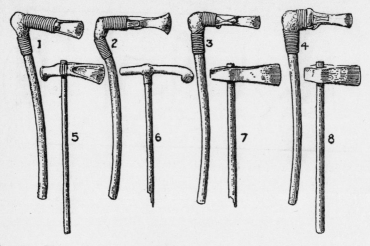

Fig. 100.—The method of fastening bronze celts and axheads to their handles is shown. After C. Schumacher.

to the palstave and the winged type, as in Western Europe, but directly to an ax with a hole for the insertion of a handle. In Scandinavia the socketed celt was not preceded by the winged type but was created out of the palstave, by casting the bronze ring which held the palstave to the handle in one piece with the head.

Knives. Bronze knives (Fig. 92 (10), p. 215) replaced flint ones for practical purposes before the end of the Bronze Age. They are rather rare in the first half but more common in the second half of the Age. The blades of most of them were attached to a handle of bone, horn, or wood but some had the handle and blade cast in one piece.

Sickles. The large number of bronze sickles (Fig. 101) found in Swiss lake dwellings is an indication of the importance of agriculture, at least in some places. Early in the Age grain was cut with sickles made of flint as in Neolithic times.

Pins and Needles. Pins of various shapes and sizes (Fig. 92, p. 215), some more than a foot long, were used. They are more common in women's graves and are generally on the

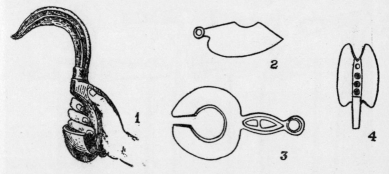

FIG. 101.—Sickles were smaller than those of to-day but were of similar shape. The figure (1) shows a bronze blade with a wooden handle. After E. Chantre.

Bronze razors of several shapes (2, 3, and 4) are illustrated. After Déchelette.

breast. They were used both for fastening garments together and as an ornament for the hair. The heads of the pins are of considerable variety: disk-shaped, ribbed, wheel-shaped, spherical, and crosier-shaped.

Bronze and bone needles were employed. The eye is either at the end or nearly midway.

Toilet Articles. The people of the Bronze Age used combs made of such materials as bone, horn, wood, and bronze. They had tweezers evidently to remove superfluous hair, but as far as is known, no mirrors were in use north of the Alps. The beautifully engraved and enamelled bronze mirrors appeared in the Hallstatt period.

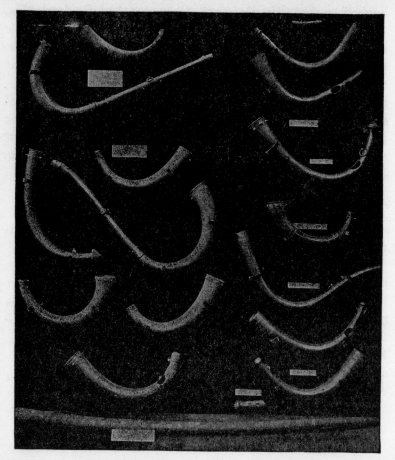

FIG. 102.—Trumpets were probably used a great deal in Ireland and Scandinavia during the Bronze Age. Three types are shown, one of which has the mouth opening at the side instead of at the end.

Photograph by courtesy of the National Irish Museum.

Razors. Bronze razors of a variety of shapes (Fig. 101), some with one, and some with two edges, were in common use. When ornamented, sun symbols were favoured (Fig. 116). A leather sheath enclosing a razor, found in Ireland, shows the means employed to protect the edge of the blade.

Trumpets and Rattles. Trumpets, made of cast bronze,

have been found in Denmark, Germany, and England (Fig. 102). The trumpets discovered in Denmark are remarkable examples of the metal worker's art. They have been found in pairs, each pair producing the same tone. This indicates that they were not made for noise alone but for musical tones. So graceful are these Danish trumpets that two allegorical statues in front of the Rathaus in Copenhagen are represented as blowing them. In Ireland there are three types of trumpets: (1) horn-shaped, open at both ends, (2) of similar shape but with an aperture on the side, and (3) horn-shaped but with a long straight tube.

Hollow, gourd-shaped balls, called bells, because they rattle when shaken, enclosing bits of metal or stone, have been found but do not give forth musical sounds.

Bronze Vessels. Probably because of mechanical difficulties bronze vessels did not appear in Northern Europe until about the middle of this Age. At this time small cauldrons and cups generally decorated with dots in *repoussée* were used. Before the close of the Bronze Age large cauldrons and situlæ (Fig. 103) were imported to Germany, Czechoslovakia and Scandinavia. Such a vessel was found in a bog in Denmark. It is a vessel of Etruscan workmanship on wheels which was originally intended for wine, but was employed here as a receptacle for burnt bones.

Pottery. The traders, tinkers, and prospectors who went about Europe, introduced new implements and weapons and the technique of metal working, but they had little effect in improving the pottery. This was probably due to the fact that women were the potters of the time and that these wanderers did not take their women with them. We consequently find that the Bronze Age pottery of Great Britain and Ireland is little better than that of the Neolithic, notwithstanding the long duration of the Bronze Age. It is only in this way that one can explain the failure of the peoples of Northern Europe to adopt the potter's wheel which was used at the end of the

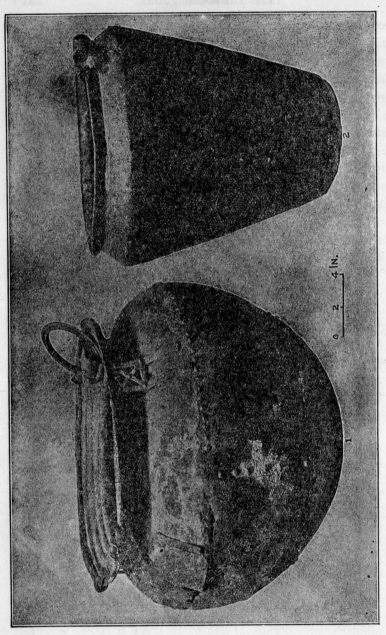

Fig. 103.—Bronze vessels imported to England (1) and Ireland (2) from Italy. Note the riveting and ornamentation of number (1).

Courtesy of the Trustees of the British Museum.

Early Minoan period in Crete many centuries before the Bronze Age of Europe began.

One of the most striking differences between the Neolithic pottery and that of the first period of the Bronze Age of Great Britain and Ireland is in the handles. The Neolithic pottery had (Fig. 47, p. 99) knobs, ribs and perforated ears for suspension, but, at the beginning of the Bronze Age, these gave way to handles. The general characteristics of the Bronze Age pottery of Great Britain and Ireland are: (1) The clay is coarse and commonly gritty; (2) the potter's wheel, although used in the Eastern Mediterranean, was unknown. As vessels were modelled by hand they are only approximately symmetrical; (3) the ornamentation of the vessels was made free-hand and is generally crude.

The instruments used in making designs were: (a) a twisted cord, (b) a sharp or blunt point, (c) the finger nail, and (d) a stamp. The patterns were engraved or modelled in the clay. (4) As the vessels were not baked in a kiln but in an open fire the colour is generally uneven. (5) With few exceptions there was no glaze, colour or other applied ornament.

Fig. 104.—Model of a cinerary urn showing its position over the burnt bones, and a small vessel. Ireland. After National Museum of Ireland.

Pottery vessels were used for cinerary urns (Fig. 104) in which were placed the burnt bones of the dead, for household purposes and, in Great Britain and Ireland, for example, to hold food offerings for the dead, and for incense, or possibly for some other religious ceremony. The pottery of continental Europe (Fig. 105) was much better than that of Great Britain and a large number of shapes were manufactured.

Fig. 105.—Examples of Bronze Age pottery from Germany and Hungary. (1) and (2) from Germany; (3), (4), and (5) Mammillary jars (Lausitz type), Germany; (6) A jar with white inlay (Hungary); (7) A jar of middle or late Bronze Age, Germany; (8) Late Lausitz type, Germany.

Photographs by courtesy of the Berlin Museum of Ethnology.

A wealth of pottery has been found in lake dwelling sites. Some jars for the storage of food are more than three feet in diameter. There are also small vessels of many forms, some of which are made of a fine biscuit with a polished surface of jet black, like the Etruscan bucchero ware. This shiny black surface was acquired by smoking and polishing the ware. Some of the jars are surprisingly symmetrical and are almost as perfect in this respect as those made on the potter's wheel. Some of the later pottery of the lake dwellers was decorated with bits of tin fastened to it with rosin. Pottery perforated for cheese-making, nursery bottles and many spindle whorls and loom weights for weaving are known.

ORNAMENTS

The ornaments of the men consisted, for the most part, of pins and clasps for holding together their mantles, and leather belts, and, occasionally, an arm band. The ornaments of the women were richer, in the North, than in the South, although they likewise consisted of gleaming bronze, and gold, of amber, shells, and glass beads. Pins of great variety were worn in pairs to hold together the mantle by means of cords threaded through them. Ornamental bronze plaques and pendants, earrings, necklets, armlets, anklets, and finger rings, show the pride in the new metal among the northern people and especially among the lake dwellers. The hunters and herdsmen, who were poorer than the people of the rich lands, were forced to be satisfied with amber. The Germanic people of the North wore torques, several bracelets on each arm, earrings, finger rings, and rings for their hair. Especially conspicuous were the beautifully ornamented girdle plaques (see Frontispiece) of the women. In the girdle was stuck a short knife. The women of the lake dwellings were often overladen with rings and pendants of many kinds but the different ornaments were less artistic and varied than in the North. The broad leather belts of these women were covered over and over with small bronze studs or with ornamented bronze plates.

For garment pins, the Nordic women wore a sort of bodkin which was early replaced by the bronze fibula.

Fibula or Safety Pin Brooch. Early in the Bronze Age man invented a sort of safety pin or fibula to hold his clothing together at the neck. In construction and appearance these earliest pins (Fig. 106) do not differ greatly from the modern

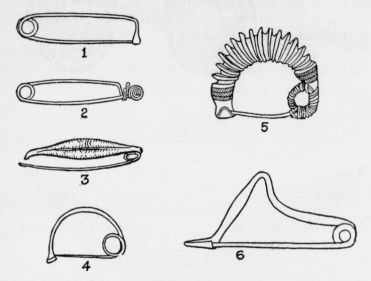

Fig. 106.—The fibula or safety pin was an important fastener for clothing as well as an ornament. Because of the progressive change in shape and ornamentation they are especially valuable in fixing the date of the objects with which they occur. They are here arranged in chronological order. After Déchelette.

safety pins, which were patented more than three thousand years later as a modern invention. The fibula used in southern countries was in one piece and consisted of three parts: the ornamental back or bow, the spring, and the pin or tongue. As the shape and ornamentation changed from time to time, and as the same type was used contemporaneously over wide areas, the fibula is important in fixing the date of objects with which it occurs. Four principal types were used successively in Western Europe. Their characteristics can best be recog-

nised from the illustrations: (1) the "violin bow" fibula
(Fig. 106 (1)), (2) the fibula with a simple bow (Fig. 106
(4)), (3) the fibula with a ribbed bow (Fig. 106 (5), and (4)

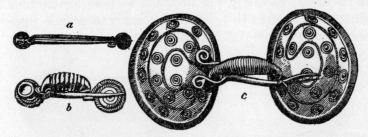

FIG. 107.—Scandinavian fibulæ were made in two pieces which were developed from a pin with an eye. Later a metal bar replaced the cord (*a*);
then (*b*), in order to have more room for the cloth, an arched back was
made. Still later (*c*), it became brooch-like.

FIG. 108.—Necklaces of amber, jet, bone, and other substances were popular.
This one of jet is interesting because the decoration is reminiscent of the
Irish gold lunulæ.

the serpentine fibula (Fig. 106 (6)). Fibulæ of the second type
appear to have been especially useful for the thick coarse
cloth of the time.

The fibulæ of Scandinavian countries differed from those elsewhere in lacking the spring, the fibula being made in two pieces with the back passing through a hole in the end of the front piece. The evolution of the Scandinavian fibulæ and the construction is shown in Figure 107. The spectacle brooch

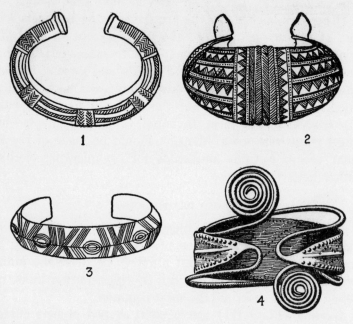

Fig. 109.—Bracelets (1), (2) and (3) ornamented with geometric patterns were worn. Anklets (4) were less common. (1-3) After Déchelette, (4) after the British Museum Guide.

was the final stage and was widely used in the Bronze Age and in the Hallstatt period.

Fibulæ may have been invented in Central Europe and from there brought to Greece where they became popular. From Greece they spread to Sicily. They were early adopted in Scandinavia, not until late in Gaul, and no fibulæ are known to have been used in Great Britain during the Bronze Age.

Head and Neck Ornaments. Ornaments were worn, as now, on the more conspicuous parts of the body. Around the neck were worn *torques* (see Plate III), twisted or plain pieces of gold or bronze. These ornaments were especially popular in Eastern and Northern Europe, but rare in Gaul until later periods. They also adorned themselves with necklaces (Fig. 108) of amber, jet, bone, and occasionally beads, some of which were very artistic. A few gold earrings have been found.

Other Ornaments. On the arms they wore bracelets (Fig. 109) of bronze, jet, lignite, and, more rarely, of gold. The bronze bracelets were ornamented with characteristic chevrons, lines, concentric circles and spirals, and some of the open bracelets ended in spirals. Anklets were used both for decoration and for protection but they did not have the vogue that bracelets—the most favoured of all ornaments—had. Finger rings were worn. Mention should be made of the frequent use of buttons and studs for ornamenting clothing, leather belts and girdles.

GOLD ORNAMENTS

A large number of gold objects of the Bronze Age has been found but with the exception of Crete and the Ægean, Ireland has furnished the largest number. Of these the lunulæ, gorgets, torques, open or penannular rings, button links, ring money and sun disks are the most common.

Lunulæ (Plate III) are crescent-shaped objects cut out of thin plates of gold with the ends expanded and turned at right angles. They are rudely engraved, on one face only, with bands composed of lines, cross-hatchings, chevrons, triangles and lozenges. One peculiarity is that the engraving is most elaborate near the ends. The use to which lunulæ were put is not clear. None show marks of wear and none have been perforated so that they could be fastened to clothing or leather. In most of them the gold is so thin that they could not have been suspended. To the writer, their most probable use was as ornaments for the dead, possibly to be used only during the funeral ceremony. It was the custom, in the approximately contemporaneous Mycenæan civilisation to place highly ornamented objects made of thin plates or sheets of gold upon the bodies or on the wooden coffins of the dead. The possibility that the strange decoration of the lunulæ is derived from necklaces of jet (see Fig. 108, p. 235), in which the decoration is restricted to triangular pieces at the ends, must not be disregarded.

Lunulæ were probably used in Ireland before bronze was known, that is, in the "Copper Age." At least sixty have been found in Ireland, nine in Scotland and England, six in Western France, one in Belgium, two in Denmark and one in Western Germany, indicating a considerable trade.

Another striking object is the *gorget* which resembles the lunula and was probably derived from it. It differed from the lunula in being curved and not flat, in its larger size, in the character of the ornamentation, which is *repoussée* and not engraved, and which consists chiefly of raised ridges, dots and rope patterns, and in the large, highly ornamented disks which decorated the ends. They have an average diameter of eleven inches and weigh from four to sixteen ounces. No gorgets have been found outside of Ireland and none have been discovered with other objects which give a clue to their date.

It is possible that they belong to the Hallstatt period but the similarity of the ornamentation to that of two bracelets which are probably of the Bronze Age, indicates the Age of Bronze.

Open rings (see Plate III) with cup-shaped terminals, also called penannular rings, have been found in considerable number and in a variety of shapes. Their use is problematical as they range in size from eleven inches in length with cup-shaped terminals five inches in diameter to small ones three and one-fourth inches long with very small disks. It has been suggested that some were bracelets, some were links for fastening garments together, and that some of them were used as money. That they were held in high regard is shown by the fact that some, at least, were kept in wooden cases. Some small

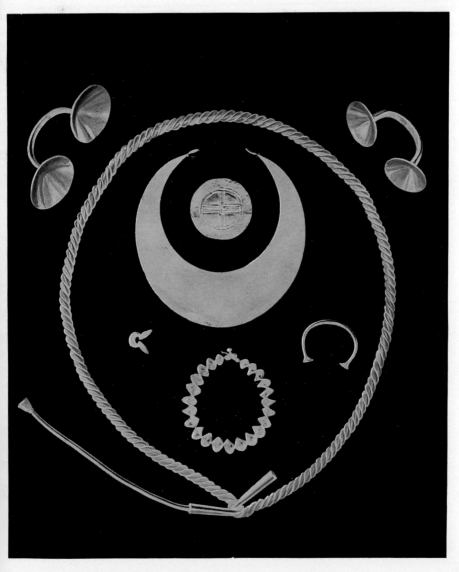

Gold ornaments from Ireland, the Eldorado of the Bronze Age.
Photograph by courtesy of the National Irish Museum.

open rings may have been the money of the time and are called "ring money."

The typical torque is made of a bar or a flat strip or strips of metal, twisted like a screw, but the name is also applied to neck collars that are not twisted. Most torques were apparently made for neck collars but some were probably bracelets and some large ones in the National Museum in Dublin are believed by some to have been worn about the waist.[8] The largest torque is fourteen and one-half inches in diameter and weighs more than twenty-seven ounces. Where it was worn is not known but as a small representation of the Keltic god Nodens or Nuada has a torque about his waist it may be that this was made to adorn a huge wooden statue of some god. A torque similar in shape and weight, but bent in a spiral like a bracelet was found in Cornwall and these large torques may be bracelets which have been straightened or have not yet been made into a spiral bracelet. A heavy spiral bracelet with recurved ends on the arm of a terra cotta figure of an Etruscan woman, from Chiusi (now in the British Museum), although of later date, shows the probable shape and use. The use of neck torques as ornaments and as a badge of distinction extended over many centuries (pp. 283 and 320).

Disks ornamented with the well recognised sun symbol—the cross in a circle, resembling the four-spoked wheel of a chariot—have been found, usually in pairs, in Ireland. Their resemblance to the disks on a sun chariot found in Denmark (p. 254) indicates that they are of the same age (before 1000 B.C.) and that the people of the time were sun-worshippers (p. 253).

The variety of gold ornaments is not great. In addition to those described above, mention should be made of gold beads, plain and spiral bracelets, pins, plain and ornamental gold bands, earrings and large hollow gold balls two and seven-tenths to three and nine-tenths inches in diameter.

[8] R. A. S. Macalister: "Ireland in Pre-Celtic Times."

ART

The art of the Bronze Age in Western Europe is little in advance of that of the Neolithic. The remarkable naturalistic art of the Magdalenian hunter (p. 32) left no impress on the later peoples and was as completely forgotten as if it had never existed. Instead of life-like paintings and engravings of animals we find designs in the form of triangles, zigzags, dog-teeth, lozenges and other geometric figures (Fig. 110).

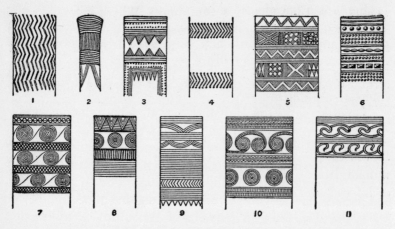

FIG. 110.—Bronze Age Designs. The designs used at this time in Northern and Central Europe are for the most part simple geometric figures made of parallel lines, chevrons, diamonds, herringbone patterns, circles, and spirals. Almost the only originality is in the combination of the designs. These drawings show the more important motives: (1) Ireland; (2) England; (3) Ireland; (4) France; (5) France; (6) England; (7) Denmark; (8) Ireland; (9) France; (10) Scandinavia; (11) Scandinavia.

Later, circles and segments of circles and spirals appear. Some of the combinations of designs are original but most of them are monotonous. The Bronze Age artist showed little creative genius. The spiral, which became so widely used in the Hallstatt period, may have originated in the North and may have been introduced to Ireland and Scotland from Scandinavia. Once introduced, however, the spiral was evolved into original designs, and new designs such as concentric circles joined together with connecting lines appear. The spiral decoration did not, however, reach England or Gaul although some rings and bracelets terminating in spirals were used in eastern Gaul. A characteristic seen on pottery and other broad surfaces, such as wide bracelets, is the arrangement of different designs in parallel rows.

The lack of art in Western Europe was in striking contrast to the beautiful art of Minoan Crete. Why this southern art did not spread north and exert an influence is not clear.

Perhaps a parallel is to be seen in New Mexico and Arizona where the Indians still make geometric designs on their baskets and pottery although they have been more or less in contact with Spanish culture for some 350 years. Tradition lingers long and exerts a strong influence on people whose interests are narrow.

Possibly, as in the Hallstatt period, some religious prejudice may have prevented, just as that which kept the Moors and other Moslems from making representations of living things. It is conceivable, too, that, with the introduction of metal, man's thought and ingenuity was absorbed in developing skill in metal-working and in designing new and better tools. Possibly, too, the demands of agriculture, cattle raising and house building diverted his attention.

PICTOGRAPHS IN SWEDEN

Scores of roughly cut figures occur on rocks (Figs 111 and 112) in many parts of Sweden. These were, with little doubt, made by Bronze Age folk and portray the important events of that time. Incidentally, they give a picture of the life of the period. We learn from them (Fig. 113) that the wooden plow was used, and was drawn by two oxen; that the sleigh had been invented; that man rode horses, that in his combats (Figs. 111 and 113) he used the bronze ax, sword, dagger, and spear; and protected himself with an ornamented bronze shield; that he had trumpets and trumpeters; that there were religious dances in honour of great events, that the people

FIG. 111.—Photograph of a Swedish pictograph of a prehistoric battle.
Photograph by courtesy of the Swedish National Museum.

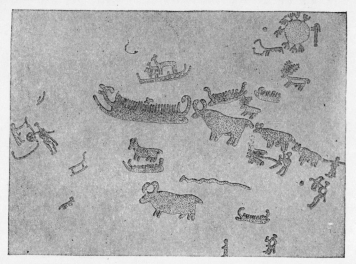

FIG. 112.—Photograph of a Swedish pictograph showing boats, sleighs,
warriors, farmer, domesticated animals, etc.
Photograph by courtesy of the Swedish National Museum.

kept cattle, pigs, goats, and dogs, and were interested in birds,
deer, reindeer, and snakes.

But the pictures that recur again and again and of which
many are preserved are those of large and small boats with
oarsmen. Some of the boats have as many as eighty men and
some depict the leader as taller than the others and with a
special headdress to show his relative importance. The great

FIG. 113.—Pictographs from Sweden which show the daily life and customs of the people; (a) They rode horses and carried metal spears; (b) they fought with battle axes; (c) they had wheeled vehicles; (d) they had long curved trumpets which were used on state occasions; (e) and (l) they used the bow and arrow in hunting; (f) the spear was used by men on foot; (g) metal (bronze) shields like those found in Great Britain and Ireland were carried by warriors; (h) they had herds of domesticated cattle; (j) they had large, elaborately decorated boats and went on forays as did their Viking descendants, and (k) they had ceremonial dances; (i) they used the plow and had oxen to draw it.

number and size of the boats indicate that the great historical events of the time had to do with seafaring. Boats of this kind were not used for fishing but were evidently for warfare and it is safe to say that the Bronze Age people, like their Viking descendants, were doughty sea-rovers who plundered the coasts far and near.[9] [See Figures 112 and 113, *j-*]

The explanation for the presence of bronze, and of high Bronze Age art in a country which yielded no tin or copper is thus indicated. The sea robbers went to Denmark, and probably to England and the western coasts of Europe, and appropriated what they wanted or could get. They melted the bronze implements or pieces of bronze which they obtained in their raiding expeditions and made objects to suit their taste. Cupels of pottery with globules of copper still adhering to their sides have been found in Western Sweden and may have been used for this purpose.

The pictures from the standpoint of art are poor. The sides of some of the boats are ornamented with the characteristic Scandinavian scrolls and spirals with dots and circles, vertical and crossed lines. The proof of the age of these drawings is in the type of the weapons which are portrayed. The bronze axes, trumpets, and swords are of the Bronze Age and may represent the products of raiding expeditions or new inventions.

Many of the human figures, especially those of Western Sweden (Bohuslän) shock the modern sense of decency but the figures probably had a religious significance and were in no sense lewd.

The engravings vary in size: some of the boats are as much as eight feet long, and human figures are from about eight inches to five and a half feet tall. They are made on the smooth glaciated surfaces of rocks, some of which are flat, and some inclined.

ITALIAN PICTOGRAPHS

Rock engravings in Liguria, Italy, occur on surfaces which have been smoothed and polished by glaciers. They are even

---

[9] The South Sea Islanders formerly took voyages of 1000 miles and more in boats that were not more seaworthy.

cruder and more conventionalised than those of Sweden. They have one noteworthy characteristic: many of them are the outlines of objects *seen from above,* and not in profile, as elsewhere. They were made with great labour in inaccessible places far from the habitable lands. Were they engraved in these inaccessible places for religious purposes and to preserve them from destruction or to keep them from the eyes of the curious? Among other objects portrayed are hammers, axes, daggers, halberds, arrowheads, sickles, two-wheeled carts, human figures, many heads of cattle, and oxen drawing plows. In one figure, there are seven oxen drawing a plow. The designs show that they were made by people devoted to agriculture and cattle raising. The figures of the halberds, a weapon used in the early Bronze Age, would indicate that the drawings were made early in that age, but of this there is some dispute.

CLOTHING

The costumes worn in the Bronze Age in Denmark are known because of the amazing preservation of the clothing of both men and women. The uniqueness of these discoveries is rendered more striking when we find that almost nothing is preserved of the clothing and little of the cloth of the early Iron Age. In excavating a tumulus in Denmark, a coffin, hewn from the split trunk of an oak tree, was found. In the coffin had been buried a warrior (Fig. 114) with his sword and all his clothing. His garments, made of simply woven sheeps' wool mixed with deer-hair, consist of a high cap, a large mantle of circular cut, a sort of tunic which reached to the knees and, on the feet, traces of leather, probably the remains of shoes. The tunic was held in at the waist by a woollen belt. Although the woollen garments were remarkably preserved, the body had completely disappeared and even the skeleton was decomposed. The bronze sword was in a wooden scabbard covered with leather. Other implements were a horn comb and a bronze razor.

The extraordinary preservation of the woollen cloth and the hair of the head is due to the moisture charged with tannic acid from the oak coffin, and to the northern climate.

A garment has recently been found deeply buried in a peat bog in Sweden which has an unusually interesting his-

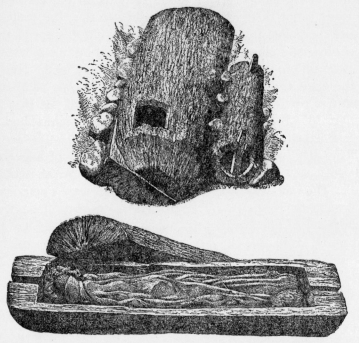

Fig. 114.—When Bronze Age graves in Denmark were excavated, oak coffins were unearthed and, in one, the hair and clothing of a man were found in an excellent state of preservation. From this clothing and that of a woman from another grave it is possible to make correct restorations of the clothing of the Scandinavians. After Madsen.

tory. It was carefully folded and weighted down with stones. The cloth is of good quality and is made of a mixture of wool, and the hair of some such animal as the deer. Holes in the cloth may have been made when the owner was stabbed to death. This suggests that a wealthy man was attacked and killed and his mantle stripped off. The murderer then hid the mantle in a ditch after weighting it down with three stones. Either because he was overtaken by Justice or because he was unable to find his booty, it remained in the ditch until to-day, when it was found with five feet of peat covering it. The time at which the crime was committed is revealed by a study of the pollen grains found clinging to the garment. An exact count of the pollen grains showed that the proportion of the pollen from the oak, linden and elm to that of the pine, birch and alder, is larger than it would be in a Swedish "pollen rain" to-day, indicating a milder climate in the North at the time the mantle was hidden. It is known that the climate of Sweden was milder at the beginning of the Bronze Age (p. 165) than it was in the Early Iron Age which had a severer climate than now.

The dress of the Northern women consisted of a short-sleeved jacket and a long skirt fastened at the waist with a girdle. The hair was held in place by a hair net. Their love of ornaments is shown by large belt plates, bracelets, and other jewelry. The girdle, with tassels, was artistically woven and partly dyed. See the frontispiece for a restoration of the clothing and ornaments of the men and women of Northern Europe.

The people of the more civilised parts of the world did not wear the simple, heavy garments of Northern, Western, and Central Europe, but the costumes of ladies of high rank were probably as elaborate as that shown on a Bronze Age idol from Serbia (Fig. 115 (1)) and the flounce-skirted figurines from Crete (Fig. 115 (2), (3), (4)). In some regions, however, the custom of going naked persisted a long time, as is shown by the fact that the custom of tattooing and painting the body continued until historic times in Europe, Asia, and Africa.

In the South, the lake dwellers raised flax and some of their clothing was doubtless made of linen. The position of bronze objects on the skeletons in the South shows that the clothing was of about the same style as in the North. The heavy pin found lying on the shoulders of the skeletons gives evidence that a heavy mantle was worn. Belt ornaments show that a girdle was used to draw in a tunic which probably reached to the knees, and the remains of linen cloth indicate an underskirt.

It is probable that the hunters and poor wore skins, at least in part.

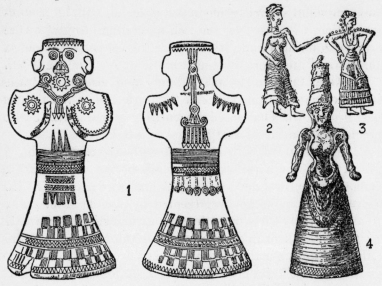

FIG. 115.—The costumes worn in Central and Southern Europe differed greatly from those of the North as is seen in this (1) idol from Serbia which shows both the female costume and the manner in which the metal ornaments were worn, and in (2), (3) and (4) idols from Mycenæ and Knossos. Compare with the figures in the frontispiece. These figures are not drawn to scale and all are reduced in size.

The clothing was better than that worn by the Neolithic peoples and the men, especially in the North, took great pains with their hair and beards as is shown by numerous bronze combs and razors in men's graves.

HABITATIONS AND FORTIFICATIONS

Little is known about the houses of this age in Western Europe because, unlike the palaces in Crete and the temples in Egypt, they were made of wood. Fortunately the custom of living in pile dwellings on the borders of lakes persisted into the Bronze Age in Switzerland and Germany, and the remains of the houses, preserved in the mud of the lakes, permit the student to reconstruct them. As in the Neolithic they were rectilinear in plan and were gathered into quite imposing villages. Houses of similar style, but without the pile foundation, were used on the rich agricultural lands of Germany. Round huts and pit huts were the usual habitations of hunters and the poor.

In Great Britain, as in Germany and elsewhere, traces of houses dating from this Age are rare, but four types at least are known. One was built entirely above ground, with circular walls made of vertical stakes interlaced with wattle-work and plastered with clay, and with a thatched roof. A second type was a pit dwelling, sunk in the ground like a shallow well with a flat roof or a leaning roof meeting at the top. A third type is now represented by circular stone walls, fifteen to twenty feet in diameter, with upright stone door posts about four or five feet high. This third type may originally have been a corbelled, beehive hut or the roof may have consisted of turf supported by poles. A fourth type found near Berlin is on the megaron plan.

Parts of Europe were densely populated. During the Urnfield period in Germany, for example, the land was thickly settled and the large and numerous villages were continuously inhabited for many years. The high bronze technique of Denmark surely required a large and stable population for its development. Some villages of the Bronze Age in Western Europe were on sites which had been occupied by Neolithic villages and which were continuously settled until well into Roman times. Even cave shelters in the French Dordogne were inhabited from Paleolithic to Roman times, though not continuously.

Defensive works are rare in the remains of this Age. Human cupidity and ambition being much the same then, as now, but with society less organised, it was doubtless necessary to pay more attention to defensive works for individual houses and for villages. The Terramara settlements (p. 213) in the broad Po Valley were protected by earthen ramparts and a moat—in one village nearly 100 feet wide. The lake dwellings of Switzerland could be easily defended. In Spain some Bronze Age villages were on hills protected by substantial walls of unhewn stone, under which stepped galleries led to springs.

THE BRONZE AGE PEOPLES

Little is definitely known about the races of the Bronze Age. This is due to some extent to the practice of cremation which was adopted in many regions and the resultant destruction of the skeletons. That there were repeated invasions or infiltrations in parts of Europe of new peoples who brought new cultures is proved by the appearance of new pottery, weapons, and implements. In some regions the Neolithic stock remained unchanged. The Bronze Age lake dwellers, for example, were undoubtedly the descendants of Neolithic lake dwellers. This is shown by a study of their skulls.

In general, it can be said that the Bronze Age in Western Europe, particularly in France, may be characterised by the arrival of new and extensive inundations of brachycephalic peoples. The bronze industry seems to have been imported (into France) by men of the Alpine type, though this does not necessarily mean that they were the inventors of it. These new floods of brachycephalic people penetrated at this time into the British Isles.[9]

The population of Great Britain, which, during Neolithic times, was dolichocephalic (long-headed), in the Bronze Age was an admixture of dolichocephalics and brachycephalics with the latter predominating, showing that a new people had come in. As a rule the long heads belonged to a race of small stature, as is, indeed, true to-day, and the short heads

[9] M. Boule: "Fossil Men," p. 342.

to a taller and physically stronger people. The typical Bronze Age man of Britain has been compared to the modern Dane.

The Danube Valley appears to have been the most important cultural centre in Continental Europe. It was from here that, in Neolithic times, domesticated animals and plants, and industries were brought to the peoples of the west. It was from here, later, that metal tools were introduced into the west. (It should be recalled that metal tools had long been in use in Asia Minor.)

The first Bronze Age culture, called the Aunjetitz, after a cemetery near Prague, was developed from these elements. This culture is of especial importance because it is the basis of both the Nordic and Danubian Bronze Age civilisations. The Aunjetitz peoples had long heads and used the flanged ax, the dagger with a rounded base, and amber beads. Not only did they furnish the basis for the Bronze Age culture of the western peoples but they developed a distinctive and characteristic civilisation of their own. Their greatest achievement as metal workers is seen in their graceful and beautifully ornamented battle-axes. The discussion of Bronze Age races is a thorny one and, as many essential points are still in dispute, and may never be settled, it would be out of place to consider them in this volume.

Burials. Care for the dead was an important consideration in the Bronze Age. The burial customs differed from time to time, from place to place, and even at the same time and in the same place.

The most striking sepultures are the tumuli or barrows. They differ little in external appearance from those of the Neolithic except in shape and in their smaller size. In Great Britain the dead were buried in round barrows and the peoples were short-headed (*brachycephalic*) whereas the Neolithic barrows are longer than wide and the dead are long-headed (*dolichocephalic*). Some barrows contain burnt, others unburnt interments, and still others have both burnt and unburnt burials. The Bronze Age barrows of Great Britain are, as a rule, two to six feet high and have a diameter of fifty to one hundred feet. Many barrows show no trace of an interment but most of them have several burials. The explanation for the absence of skeletons in some barrows is that the bodies formerly covered by them have completely disintegrated. As it is known that under favourable conditions a body may completely disappear in a comparatively short time especially in sandy soil, the explanation is doubtless correct. When a body was buried unburnt it was generally in a "contracted" position. When cremation was adopted the ashes and burnt bones were deposited either in urns (see Fig. 104, p. 231) or in hollows in the floor of the grave.

The problem of megaliths has already been discussed. This form of sepulture seems certainly to have been used. Beehive or corbelled chambers, which appeared in Central and Western Europe, were used long before in the Eastern Mediterranean. Some natural caves and grottoes and tombs hewn out of soft rocks contain skeletons of this age. In Scandinavia several burials in coffins made of hollowed tree trunks have been discovered.

A burial custom prevalent in Southern Russia should be mentioned: the skeletons are thickly covered with red ochre, a practice similar to that employed by the Magdalenians, though probably having no relation to it.

When cremation was practiced the body was generally not burnt on the grave but the burnt bones were later gathered up and buried. Traces of the bones of animals, such as the pig, goat, horse, hog, and ox, and of human remains in some cremated burials may indicate the custom of sacrificing animals, slaves, and wives in honour of the dead. Food vessels in graves indicate that food was buried for use in the spirit world.

Few of the English barrows and Bronze Age tumuli elsewhere contain many objects. One great tumulus (Arbor Low) contained only a bone pin, a piece of iron pyrites, a flint implement and two vases; a barrow excavated in 1925 contained a few flint chips and pointed bone implements. Several reasons for the burial of articles with the dead may be suggested. (1) Objects of personal adornment, and objects especially used or admired by the dead were doubtless sometimes buried with the body as a token of affection. (2) Objects may have been placed in the grave to be used in the other world. (3) A superstitious dread of using what belonged to the dead may have been the motive. Certain it is that great tumuli would not have been erected and so much labour would not have been expended unless the living had felt great affection for the dead, as, for example, a large tumulus in Great Britain which covered the earthly remains of a twelve-year-old boy.

Religion. About three and a half thousand years before our time a great religious movement must have taken place in Europe—a revolution in beliefs which can be seen in the changed cult of the dead. In the Stone Age and the early Bronze Age the dead were generally buried without cremation. Great structures, like the pyramids, were erected to protect their rest. According to the belief of their contemporaries the dead still lived and the soul was likewise bound to the body. But now this belief changed. Body and soul were evidently believed not to be so closely connected after death. This is seen in the desire to destroy the body by fire and thus set the spirit free. Therefore the bodies of the dead were cremated and only the burnt bones were buried in a vase or an urn. However, the belief in a connection of the freed spirit with the remains of the body was not yet extinct. In the bottom or lower part of some of the Bronze Age burial urns there is a small, carefully made, hole, called the "soul hole," which was probably made to permit the return of the soul to the remains of the body. Moreover the burnt bones were not placed in the urn helter-skelter, but at the bottom are the leg bones, on these the remains of the trunk, and at the top, the fragments of the head, so that the dead, as it were, sat in his urn.[10] Not only was the body burned but the tomb furniture also was destroyed in the same way in the belief that implements in their material form could not serve the departed in the other world, but that the spirits of the ax and other objects would be useful.

The sun as the bestower of all blessings was worshipped in Ireland on the west and throughout the greater part of Europe. The most important discovery which bears on this sun cult of the Bronze Age is one found in Denmark. It consists of an engraved bronze disk six inches in diameter, covered with gold foil, mounted on a wheeled carriage drawn by a horse. There is no doubt that this was a ceremonial object and was connected with sun worship. The design on the disk is almost identical with that on several disks in Ireland and shows that the sun cult was widespread. The sun disk carriage just described had been broken intentionally before it was buried and may be regarded as a votive offering. The date of this sun chariot is about 1300 B.C. The Irish disks have lugs on the margin exactly as in the Danish specimen, the lower one for fastening it to the axle and the upper one for holding the reins. Two of the disks found in Ireland [10a] have a cruciform design, a well-known solar symbol, which occurs commonly on the pottery of the time. Other discoveries of two horses, portions of a chariot, and of a solar disk strengthen the belief that the sun cult was widespread. According to ancient myths the sun made his daily journey across the sky in a chariot drawn by horses and when he had to return from the place of his setting to the place of his rising, the god left his chariot and was conveyed in a boat on the Ocean river. Some engravings show sun disks on horses' heads. Although the horse was associated with the daily solar journey, it was the swan that drew the divine bark on the return journey. It is not

[10] J. Richter: "Führer durch die Praehistorische Abteilung," Leipzig Museum.

[10a] R. A. S. Macalister expresses the opinion that the so-called sun disks found in Ireland may have had no religious significance and may have been ornaments which were sewed to the clothing.

surprising that in Scandinavia where the long winter nights and short summer ones are so noticeable, that the symbol of the sun bark is so common. The prows and sterns of many of the Scandinavian boats shown in pictographs and on engravings on razor blades (see Fig. 116) end in the neck of

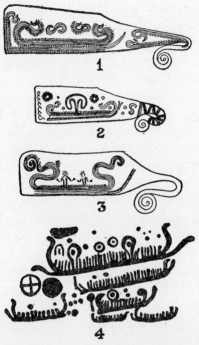

FIG. 116.—(1, 2, 3) Conventionalised boats on Scandinavian bronze razors. (4) A pictograph from Sweden for comparison.

a swan. The swan was the principal companion of the sun during the second half of the Bronze Age, and of the first Age of Iron, in Southern and Central and Northern Europe. The sun cult must have been in honour throughout Europe for at least 1500 years, and was consequently one of the most enduring religions the world has known. It was widespread and was adopted throughout a large part of the ancient world.

The reason that the sun bark symbol is almost exclusively

associated with knives seems to be because the god of the sun
and of fire was also the god of medicine and surgery, as is true
also in Greek Mythology.

The cult of the sun was mixed with beliefs that had penetrated from the East and South, such as the cult of the double
ax and the bull, which in the North is usually represented
by the horns alone. It also included practices of magic and
sorcery which, if the priestly caste were strong, may have
occupied a large part of the religious life of the people. Their
physicians were probably medicine men, as the contents of a
grave in Denmark seems to show. This grave contained a
small leather box in which were objects similar to those used
by the medicine man of the American Indian: the tip of a
snake's tail, a shell from the Mediterranean, the claw of a
bird, some small stones, a flint spearhead, a pair of small
tweezers, two razors, and an amber bead. There was, too,
doubtless, a worship of natural forces as is the practice of
primitive peoples.

The swastika is a religious symbol of great antiquity and
was, as far as is known, first used in the Copper Age in
Europe where it was frequently employed until the tenth century. It was used in ancient Persia, in India, in Japan and
China, and is employed by the Indians of the New World.
It probably represents a sacred fire or the sun in its daily
movements and is one of the few designs for which we are
indebted to the people of the Bronze Age.

The reason for believing that Stonehenge on the Salisbury
Plain was a great temple of the sun which was used early
in the Bronze Age has already been discussed.

Idols were seldom worshipped, if at all, and one no longer
finds crude pottery figurines such as those of the Neolithic.

Trade Routes and Commerce. Commerce [11] may be said
to have begun in the Bronze Age. Before this there was little
need for trade. Paleolithic man doubtless secured something

---

[11] H. F. Cleland: "Commerce and Trade Routes in Prehistoric Europe."
Economic Geography, III, 1927.

by exchange, when, in his wanderings after game he met people who had flint or bone implements which he wanted. But there is no evidence that he had commercial relations other than these with his neighbours. The permanent villages and settlements of the Neolithic would make some trade imperative because few villages would be entirely self-sufficient. There is evidence that a trade in obsidian, or volcanic glass, was carried on to some extent between the islands of Santori and Lipari and the mainland, and that there was possibly an interchange of pottery. But, at most, it was unimportant. When, however, the demand for copper and tin for making bronze arose, the peoples of Europe became keenly interested in all places where the ores of these metals occur. Copper was found in Cyprus, Spain, Czechoslovakia, Roumania, the Eastern Alps, France, England and elsewhere but in each of these regions it was confined to very limited areas and had to be transported to populous centers. Tin was much rarer and at the height of the Bronze Age probably came largely from Cornwall, England.

Transportation was carried on by men with packs on their backs, by pack horses, in wagons, and by boats. Definite routes (Fig. 117), determined by the topography of the country, as well as transport by sea were soon established. The location of these old trade routes has been determined by the caches or hoards of traders which furnish important sign posts. Such caches are found in lonely places in the neighbourhood of old trade routes, along river courses, at the foot of mountains and across plateaux. In Rhenish Hesse, for example, a route follows the highway which cuts off the great curve of the Rhine from Mainz to Bingen. In these traders' caches, as we have seen (p. 214), are found a great variety of articles for exchange, such as weapons, implements and ornaments and, not infrequently, raw materials like bronze ingots, damaged articles and cakes of cast metal and, occasionally, the moulds and tools of the metal worker. Possibly some of the traders were also metal workers and exchanged

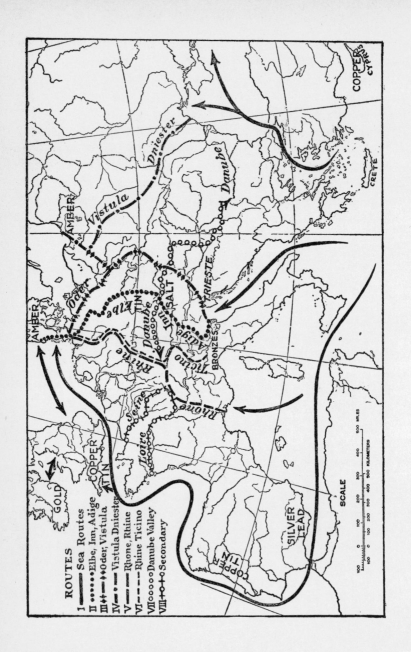

ROUTES

I ———— Sea Routes
II •••••• Elbe, Inn, Adige
III ♦ ← → ♦ Oder, Vistula
IV — • — Vistula Dniester
V ———— Rhone, Rhine
VI – – – – Rhine Ticino
VII ooooo Danube Valley
VIII +o+o+ Secondary

SCALE

AMBER

COPPER

TIN

GOLD

AMBER

Vistula

Dniester

Dniester

Danube

Oder

Elbe

Danube

TIN

SALT

Inn

TRIESTE

Adige

Ticino

BRONZES

Rhine

Seine

Loire

Rhone

SILVER

LEAD

COPPER

TIN

CRETE

COPPER

CYPRUS

FIG. 117.—PREHISTORIC TRADE ROUTES IN EUROPE

ROUTE I.—The sea was used as early as the New Stone Age and mariners from the Mediterranean reached Great Britain, Ireland, and as far north as Denmark, before metals were known. In the early Bronze Age, mariners were attracted to Denmark by the amber, to Ireland by the gold, to Cornwall by the rich deposits of tin and copper. When the Irish gold deposits were exhausted, trade with Ireland practically ceased and civilisation stagnated or decayed. Cornwall was the principal source of tin for 3,000 years and the metal was transported, chiefly as bronze, across the English Channel to Gaul, and thence to the Mediterranean and elsewhere. There was also a trade between Great Britain and Denmark. Marine trade with Denmark became unimportant after the opening of the land routes, especially the great Elbe route (Route II). When metallic iron came into use, land routes became less important and sea trade increased.

ROUTE II.—The Elbe route (the Elbe, Moldau, Inn, Adige) and Route III were the most important thoroughfares in prehistoric times. The Elbe route was first used about 1800 B.C. and continued in use until after the beginning of the Christian era. Along it amber was transported to the south and exchanged for the bronze of Bohemia and the manufactured bronze weapons and vessels of Italy. The civilisation of the Bronze Age in Europe (which was far from barbarous) was largely due to the ideas and wares carried over this route by traders. When salt was mined at Hallstatt and Salzburg in the early Iron (and doubtless in the Bronze) Age, it was probably carried long distances to Bohemia on the North, which is destitute of salt, and east and west along the great Danube route (Route VII).

ROUTE III.—The Vistula, Oder, March route became important when the amber of East Prussia was rediscovered early in the Iron Age, and along it a brisk trade was carried on, beginning about 700 B.C.

ROUTE IV.—The Vistula-Dniester route to the Black Sea was opened when Greek colonies were established on the Black Sea.

ROUTE V.—The Rhone-Rhine route became an important artery of commerce, especially after the establishment of the Greek Colony at Marseilles and along it the arts and crafts of the south were carried to the north. However, it had been used for many centuries before this.

ROUTE VI.—A route of some importance which led into Italy passed along the upper Rhine, over the St. Bernard Pass and down the Ticino to the bronze workers of the Po Valley.

ROUTE VII.—The Danube Valley has been populous since early Neolithic times; along it there have been repeated movements of peoples, and trade routes have traversed it. The salt of Hallstatt and Salzburg and the iron workings of the early Iron Age gave it a greater importance than it had previously had.

OTHER ROUTES.—The Seine, Loire, and other rivers in France, the Werra, Fulda, and Saale in Germany, and other stream valleys were used for local trade.

new things for broken ones which they later melted and recast. Traders' caches in Germany contain bronze swords of Swiss and Italic origin, and gold ornaments, some of which may have come from Ireland. Along the Danube route to Germany came ribbed and ringed bars, and axes with heart-shaped openings.

A study of the distribution of flat celts of the Early Bronze Age in the British Islands shows that they are fairly numerous and widespread on the open grasslands but elsewhere, where the land was thickly wooded and probably uninhabited, they are strung out in long lines which, if produced, would converge at Dublin. They are evidently paths taken by traders on their way to the Irish gold fields.[12]

What was given in exchange for the precious bronze, a metal which was costly both because of the distance it had to be transported and because of the labour involved in smelting and casting it? There were, of course, broken bronze objects for remelting, but salt, skins, horses, possibly cattle and female slaves, were doubtless important articles of trade. In the North there was amber, the beloved "Gold of the North." That copper came to Scandinavia from Central Europe is shown by the composition of the bronzes, some of which contain one and five-tenths per cent or more of nickel, the same percentage of nickel as the copper ores of the South. Some of the bronze contains little or no nickel and this probably came from Great Britain where copper is deficient in this metal. As the bronze objects are of Scandinavian manufacture it is evident that crude bronze was imported.

Salt was mined near Salzburg, Austria, and in the French Juras, and was also probably evaporated in the coastal swamps. As salt is an indispensable condiment for people whose diet is largely vegetarian it must have been obtained in exchange for other commodities.

Amber and gold were desired for ornaments and amulets

[12] O. G. S. Crawford.

by the wives and sweethearts of the lords of Crete and elsewhere, and were obtained in exchange for bronze.

Ireland's gold, while it lasted, brought bronze to that
island, but when the richer placers were exhausted, trade
from other countries languished and civilisation and art
stagnated.

The high civilisation of Scandinavia in the Bronze Age
depended upon the Baltic amber which was exchanged for
bronze and without the amber of the west coast of Jutland,
it is possible that there would have been no northern Bronze
Age culture. Because of its stock of amber Denmark was
able to buy an abundance of bronze, with the result, that
bronze-working and art reached its climax in the Baltic
region.

The cultures of the islands of the Mediterranean—Crete,
Cyprus, Malta, Sicily, Sardinia and the Balearics—show that
not only did migrations take place but that the new settlers
chose sites for their settlements with a view to trade and
commerce. For example, that great centre of continental
Cretan culture, Mycenæ, was on a site that commanded an
important trade route between the South and Northwest.
Maritime routes radiated westward from the Eastern Mediterranean. This is shown by the distribution of pottery and
other objects of Eastern origin. In Sicily for example, are
many imported Mycenæan vases and metallic objects. The
Ægean civilisation did not penetrate far inland; its influence
was largely coastal. A comparatively short distance from the
shores of the Continent the cultures are largely those of
Central Europe, proving that continental trade routes were
already well established.

The Mariners of the Bronze Age had open boats only (Fig.
116) but they nevertheless took long sea journeys. Not only
was the entire coast of the Mediterranean known to them, but
they went to Great Britain for copper and tin; to Ireland for
gold; they visited the coasts of the English Channel, and the
North Sea; and traded for amber with the inhabitants of Den-

mark. To make such long voyages in open boats propelled by oars and small sails was an undertaking which required great courage and endurance.

Two principal land routes (see Fig. 117) to the amber deposits of the North were established at this time. One began on the Adriatic near Venice, thence up the river Adige, over the Brenner Pass, and down the Inn to Passau where it joins the Danube. From here it crossed the Bohemian Forest to the Moldau River and followed the Elbe to its mouth.

A second principal route began at the Gulf of Trieste and went northeast to Laibach, thence to Gratz and down the Leitha to the Danube at Pressburg. The tributary March was then ascended and, after crossing Moravia, the route passed through Silesia and followed the Oder to the coast. Another route diverged from this one at Posen and followed the Vistula to Danzig. A third less important route led to the North Sea from the Mediterranean, by way of the Rhone and the Rhine.

Besides these main "Amber routes" there were routes across the Alpine passes to France and Germany which followed the Rhone, Loire, Seine and Rhine, and routes to and along the broad Danube Valley by way of the Inn, Save, and other tributaries.

There is some evidence of a currency. This consists of gold, and bronze rings or ingot torques. In the National Museum, in Ireland, there is a large number of small, thick, open rings, which are called "ring money," and in Vienna great numbers of bronze rings. In Switzerland, small bronze rings strung on a braceletlike bronze bar has been interpreted as a purse. A similar large gold ring with smaller gold rings strung on it, in the British Museum, may be a bracelet.

Commerce would soon lead to a uniform system of weights and measures. The Terramara people used the foot, which was later adopted by the Romans. At first, metals were bartered as ingots of irregular shape and weight, of which some in the form of double axes have been found, and as manufactured objects. This was found to be unsatisfactory and masses of metal were later given definite weights and a uniform shape. Evidence of scales for weighing is offered by the discovery in Swiss lake dwellings of weights composed of lead and tin which were probably used on a balance.

SUMMARY

Objects from the sites of Bronze Age dwellings are so numerous and so many objects of bronze and bone have been found elsewhere that it is possible to construct a fairly accurate picture of the life of the people. Although customs varied in different parts of Europe the essential features of the life of the time were probably the same over large areas.

The daily life of the lake dwellers of this Age was fuller and more varied than that of the Neolithic. The men still hunted a great deal as the remains of wild animals, such as the bison, elk, stag, roe deer, wild boar, fox, beaver, skunk, hare, squirrel and other animals, show. The abundance of bronze fishhooks prove that the men, or the women, spent much time in fishing. That they depended largely upon domestic animals for food and clothing is attested by the numerous bones of the cow, sheep, and swine. The dog, as now, was a favourite companion. That horses were broken and drew wagons or chariots is definitely proved by the discovery of several wooden wheels, by Swedish pictographs, and also by the sun chariot (p. 254) found in Denmark. Horses may have been domesticated in the Neolithic, and probably were, but there is no positive proof of this. The Bronze Age people cultivated their fields with much the same agricultural implements as did the Neolithic people, and added rye and oats. Meal was ground, as in Neolithic times, in hand mills that consisted of a large flat lower stone of hard rock and a movable grinding stone which was either cylindrical or flattened on one surface. The upper stone was either rolled as a cylinder or was pushed backwards and forwards, the latter method being the usual one. For the greater part of prehistoric times, in fact, until the late La Tene, grain was ground in this way. The millstones were made of any suitable hard rock such as granite, trap, porphyry, quartzite, sandstone, and, when a better material was not available, even limestone. When the rubbing surfaces became too smooth to be effective they were roughened by cutting shallow grooves in them. Similar millstones are employed by some backward peoples to-day. Because of the stone dust from the mill, which they did not know how to remove, the meal was so gritty as to rapidly grind down the teeth. As a result the teeth of the skeletons, even of young people, are greatly worn.

Crucibles, molds, ingots and pieces of slag show that the inhabitants were able to reduce ores and to make their own weapons and implements. Spindle whorls, loom weights and pieces of cloth, some of which is very fine, show that the women were skilful weavers. Though the potter's wheel was not known north of the Mediterranean basin, nevertheless thin and well-proportioned pottery was made. In some out-of-the-way places, however, such as Great Britain, the art of making pottery was much less advanced and the pottery was extremely crude.

Fires were lighted by sparks made by striking flint against pyrites but, doubtless, usually from carefully tended fires.

For hunting and defense at close quarters the men had daggers and swords, and for attacking at a distance, javelins and yew bows.

That the young women made themselves as attractive as possible to the young men is shown by the abundance of beads, rings, armlets, bracelets and other jewelry. Most of the jewelry was bronze but we can be sure it was polished until it shone as gold. The young men, on their part, shaved, and plucked out superfluous hair with bronze tweezers.

Life, with its diversified industries must have been a full, and, probably, a happy one. The women were occupied with their weaving, pottery making, cooking, and the rearing of their children; the men with hunting, fishing, the care of their domestic animals, and with the raising of crops with which they were doubtless assisted by the women, if indeed the women did not do the greater part of the work. Too few skeletons have been found to enable one to say whether the people lived to a good old age or whether they died young but they probably seldom lived to be more than forty years old.

The doctors doubtless tried to drive out the evil spirits that was believed to cause the sickness, in ways common among primitive peoples.

The skill in metal working was somewhat remarkable when one remembers that each village probably made most of its own metal tools and ornaments. The moulds they used were made of clay and stone. Bronze moulds were employed to make wax models which were then surrounded by a clay paste, when the paste hardened the wax was melted out and a second mould was formed in which molten bronze was poured. The skill required to make rapiers (one in the National Irish Museum is three feet long and three-fifths of an inch wide) and long thin lance heads (one in the British Museum is thirty-one and one-half inches long), for example, was of a high order. In making the open gold rings with cup-shaped terminals (see Plate III) the Irish goldsmith had to have a general knowledge of the whole field of metal working. He first melted the gold in a charcoal fire, next he poured the molten gold into a mould. The ring thus made was then shaped in a mould by "swaging," the hammer being applied not directly to the gold, but to a stone similar to, but smaller than, the mould. The cup-shaped ends were formed on anvils of special shape, and were joined to the ring by surface melting. The ornamentation was made by means of a chisel and hammer. In manufacturing such an ornament the workman had to have a furnace, flux, bellows, several hammers, anvils, swage anvil, swages, chisel, and a sectional tool for making concentric rings.[13]

It is evident that the peoples of the Bronze Age in Eu-

[11] Edmond Johnson, quoted by R. A. S. Macalister, "Ireland in Pre-Celtic Times," pp. 179-180.

rope were not savages but had developed a civilisation of
no mean order. That they had not invented or acquired a
written language is somewhat unexpected, especially as they
were in communication with the cultures of the South. But
as a knowledge of writing in the Eastern Mediterranean
was confined to the few, and the traders who brought wares
to the North were not of that class, they had no means of
learning it.

CHAPTER VIII

THE HALLSTATT—FIRST AGE OF IRON

THE ACQUISITION OF IRON

Equivalents: Hallstatt in Western and Central Europe; Villanova in Italy; Dipylon in Greece
Date: 1000 or 900 to 500 B.C.

THE Bronze Age did not come abruptly to an end when methods of making iron were invented, but the transition was gradual. In some localities, especially where iron ore was worked, the change was comparatively rapid; in others it was slow. The pile dwellers of Switzerland and the Upper Rhine, and the peoples of Scandinavia and Hungary, for example, kept on developing art in bronze and reached the "bel age" of bronze long after iron was introduced. The beauty and glitter of bronze still appealed to the people even though they were not blind to the greater cheapness and greater practical advantages of the more modest iron. Moreover, tradition doubtless had grown up about the use of bronze for ceremonial and religious objects, and it was employed for certain implements centuries after the superiority of iron was recognised. In the manufacture of ornaments, bronze long kept its place and even to-day is better suited for certain purposes, statuary for example, than any other metal.

When iron was still quite costly it was used only as an inlay in sword handles, for bracelets and for such other purposes as a rare material is employed. Later it was used for the blades of swords and for such things as bridle bits (snaffles), fibulæ, needles, and rings. It was spread by traders

267

from the South and East or was passed from hand to hand. The merchants and iron workers travelled around as the tinkers have in recent times; they brought iron hoops, half- and wholly-made objects, gathered native iron ore, smelted it and gradually taught their art to the natives. Iron was preferred for utensils and weapons because bronze was more difficult and more costly to make and was unsuitable for many purposes.

The region of Central Europe where iron was first manufactured was Noricum (Austria and Eastern Bavaria) and it was from here in the tenth and ninth centuries before Christ, that the knowledge of the new metal spread in all directions. Here lay Hallstatt whose thousands of rich graves first gave a knowledge of the culture of this epoch. Because of its traffic in salt, Hallstatt early became a rich trading post, but it was not such a centre for the iron industry as was Carniola. The Hallstatt culture spread rapidly along the Danube to the Rhine, and took foothold wherever the necessary raw materials were found, as for example, in the German and Swiss Juras and on their slopes in Burgundy and Lothringia. The traders and smiths were followed by armed bands with long bronze and iron swords who settled in larger or smaller groups wherever the country especially pleased them. They were hunters, herdsmen, and cattle breeders who took possession of the Swabian Alps, the foothills of Lake Constance, and the Upper Rhine districts which even to-day are noted for their cattle breeding. They also travelled into Northwestern Switzerland and towards France and settled there.

The new Hallstatt people came in several waves and were of different tribes but not in all places were they able to overcome completely the old Bronze Age people. In some places they intermarried with them and such districts retained their old characteristics for a long time, even though they adopted some elements of the new culture. This is what happened in the pile dwelling stations on Lake Constance in

Northern Switzerland, along the banks of the Upper and Middle Rhine, and in the mountains and Rhine forests.

The German word for iron, according to Kossina, goes back to an Illyrian-Keltic word "isarnon" and is therefore interesting because it indicates from what source the Germans of the North obtained the metal that was so highly prized by them. It came partly from the wares of traders, as the iron bars from the station of Wahren near Leipzig show, and partly by direct contact with their neighbours. But the Germans quickly learned to mine and to smelt the iron ore in their crude furnaces, and thus to develop an independent culture.

The Discovery of Iron. Metallic iron rarely occurs in nature, and it is improbable that prehistoric man in Europe ever found the native metal except as meteoric iron. There was little chance, therefore, of his learning its value until he had discovered a way to reduce the ore. It seems at first thought remarkable that copper should have been in use more than a thousand years before iron since copper is much more difficult to smelt than iron. The question as to why iron was not discovered first is an interesting one and the answer seems fairly evident. During the thousands of years of the Stone Ages ,as has been stated elsewhere (p. 202), man must occasionally have used among other stones a piece or pieces of copper ore in making his hearths. When these were heated by the fire to such a temperature that globules of copper were formed, an alert man would notice this bright coloured, malleable metal and would wonder whence it came He would search for its source, which could readily be traced to the copper ore. This discovery would, in time, lead to the invention of methods of smelting copper. Doubtless iron had often been made in the same way; but as iron, when cold, is so hard as to be nearly unmalleable to the stone hammers of the time and as it is not bright and soon rusts, it would be left unnoticed. The reason then for the lateness of the discovery

of iron is probably to be found in its hardness and in the fact
that it rusts rapidly.

The first iron furnaces were, doubtless, a single excavation on the side of a hill or bank, facing the prevailing direction of the wind, with an opening at the bottom for draft.
In this appliance the ore was heated, and in contact with
the charcoal, a small, pasty mass of iron was obtained.

When and Where Iron Was Discovered. The date at which
iron was first discovered is not known and probably never
will be known. A lump of what may once have been iron but
is now iron rust was found in Egypt wrapped in a piece of
cloth, with a mirror and tools of copper and is known to have
been buried 2700-2500 B. C., that is, during the sixth dynasty.
Some iron beads, the oxidised remains of which have been
found in pre-dynastic tombs, date back to about 4000 B. C.
This iron which antedates any other record by more than a
thousand years, was probably meteoric iron. The use of
meteoric iron was known to the American Indian in pre-
Columbian times as is proved by implements hammered out
of this material which have been found in Ohio mounds. About
1350 B. C., during the nineteenth dynasty, a tribute of iron as a
rare metal was sent from Syria to Egypt, but as no mention
is made of it in a long tribute list of the eighteenth dynasty,
about 1500 B. C., it is probable that iron was not manufactured
as early as that date. The oldest iron knives (at Tell Jemmeh,
the ancient city of Gerar) date back as far as 1350 B. C., and
by 1200 B. C. there were furnaces for iron-smelting, and large
tools, such as picks weighing seven pounds, and hoes were
made. It is possible that iron was known in Egypt as early
as copper was. It was used by the Hittites about 1300 B. C.
Several hundred years before the end of the Bronze Age,
iron was known in Crete but for a long time it was rare and
costly and was used as a precious metal for finger-rings. It
may have been meteoric iron.

The events described in Homer's "Iliad" apparently took
place when iron was first coming into use and was a new

and suspicious metal, as both weapons of bronze and of iron were used, and iron appears to have been rare.

Examples of the Spread of Iron. The comparative merits of bronze and iron are well shown by the rather surprising slowness with which the latter was spread over Europe. On the other hand, the great superiority of iron over stone is well exemplified in the rapidity with which a knowledge of this metal was carried over America. The physical obstacles to travel in Europe, for example, were not greater than those in North America and, moreover, the people of the Bronze Age in Europe had horses and wheeled vehicles and well-established trade routes (p. 256), advantages not possessed by the American Indian. In his voyage to the South Pacific Islands and to the western coast of North America (1777-1778), Captain Cook found that a knowledge of iron had already spread from island to island in the South Pacific. Of all the things the natives saw on their visits to his vessel, it was the objects of iron that they most desired. Captain Cook cites a number of incidents which illustrates this. On one island, for example, several small pigs were purchased for a sixpenny nail; and on a number of occasions natives were willing to exchange almost anything they possessed for small pieces of iron such as nails and iron hoops. At the South Pacific island of "Oneeheow" the natives readily parted with all their commodities for pieces of this precious metal. On the coasts of Northern California, Canada, and Alaska, the natives were also more desirous for iron than for any other of our articles of commerce, appearing to be perfectly acquainted with the use of that metal. His explanation of the presence of iron among the Indians of the Alaskan coast is that it was obtained after passing through many hands from the far distant Hudson Bay posts.

Whether this is the correct explanation or whether iron was brought north from the Spanish missions which had been established in California about 1770, the striking fact is, that to these people in the Stone Age, the most remarkable things carried by the white explorers was iron, a substance which would make implements for cutting and boring. When the difficulties of travel in North America and the South Pacific are considered, the spread of a knowledge of iron is little less than marvellous.

To the users of bronze in Europe, iron could not have seemed such a wonderful substance as it did to stone-using Indians and South Sea Islanders because they already had cutting tools of bronze which, though not as good as those of iron, would serve the same purpose. This may explain the conservatism of the lake dwellers of Switzerland and Germany, and the Scandinavian peoples in adopting iron.

THE HALLSTATT CEMETERY

The Hallstatt epoch receives its name from a cemetery in the Austrian Tyrol. For hundreds of years salt has been mined there, and it was one of the earliest centres of ironworking in Europe. More than 3,000 sepultures have been uncovered. Of nearly 1,000 burials excavated before 1864 about one-half were cremations and half inhumations. Incineration was dominant at the beginning and inhumation at the close, but both rites were practiced throughout the epoch. The contents of the graves show that the cremations belong to the ruling or wealthier class as all but one of the swords and most of the bronze weapons, vessels, shield bosses, and brooches with pendants were found with cremated remains, whereas iron lances and axes were generally found with skeletons (inhumations). Some graves contain more than one body or incineration; and, in a few, both incinerated and inhumed remains were found. The skeletons were usually oriented east and west.

Most of the objects found in the graves at Hallstatt are of bronze; next in abundance is pottery, and then iron, amber and glass and, least common, trinkets of gold. Objects for personal adornment are most abundant both because they were the intimate possessions of the dead and also because of their value; and accordingly, necklaces of amber, beads, chains with pendants, fibulæ, ornamental pins, bracelets, and bronze belts are common.

THE VILLANOVA CIVILISATION

At Villanova, near Bologna, is a cemetery of the Hallstatt epoch in which pottery designs like those of Hallstatt (see Fig. 132, p. 287) and the Greek Dipylon (Fig. 118) occur. The people were in the early Iron Age and are thought to be the Terramara people of the Po Valley who had moved south after they had acquired a knowledge of iron. Their iron weapons are skilfully made, and everything indicates that they were an industrious and prosperous people. They lived in villages, cremated their dead, and buried the ashes in urns, some of which were hut urns.[1] Their small, roughly circular dwellings had their floors sunk three feet or more below the level of the ground.

FIG. 118.—A Dipylon mixing bowl with characteristic geometric designs.

THE DIPYLON CIVILISATION

A geometric style of art called the Dipylon for a cemetery northwest of Athens, outside the "double gate," where many vases of this style (Fig. 118) were unearthed, spread over a large part of Europe. The civilisation of the peoples who made these vases was much inferior to that of the Mycenæan culture, with its naturalistic designs or patterns (see Fig. 91, p. 212), its

[1] Schumacher places the hut urn culture at the close of the Bronze Age, 1200-1000 B.C. "Siedelungs- und Kulturgeschichte der Rheinlande," p. 61.

wall paintings, its metal objects, and architecture. With
apparent suddenness this Mycenæan civilisation vanished
and was replaced by the inferior Dipylon culture. A
plausible explanation for the disappearance of the higher
civilisation is that a people with an inferior culture had
learned the use of a new metal, iron, for their weapons,
and especially for their swords and knives. Sword in hand,
these invaders cut their way through the men armed with
bronze weapons, became their masters, and imposed their
art and civilisation on the conquered. In this way the artistic culture of the Mycenæan people was probably destroyed.
The destruction of this high civilisation was probably not
due to the fact that the invaders were of a higher type or
that the conquered had degenerated, but because one was
armed with superior weapons against which the users of
bronze were helpless. Without doubt, if the events of prehistoric times were better known, it would be found that such
tragedies as that which destroyed the Mycenæan civilisation
happened again and again as tribes learned to use iron.

WEAPONS

Swords. As swords were buried with the wealthier and
ruling classes of this epoch and as the shapes changed with
time they afford a means of determining the relative age of
the graves in which they occur. The uniformity of the shapes
and the ornamentation of the weapons over large areas in
this epoch is in striking contrast to the variety of the sword
designs in the Bronze Age. The early iron swords are merely
reproductions of those of the Late Bronze Age. They were
first manufactured in Austria and Eastern Bavaria. From
there they were carried by traders and invaders. In time the
technique of iron smelting and working was acquired in
Western Europe and iron centres arose where iron ore deposits occurred. Iron was scarce and valuable at the beginning;
and some swords were made with iron blades and bronze

handles; but as iron became cheaper, the blade was made larger and heavier and the pommel of the handle increased in size until, about the eighth century B.C., the slashing or cutting sword wa sevolved (Fig. 119). After a time, seventh

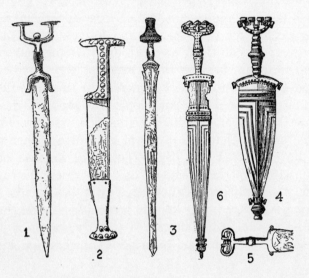

FIG. 119.—Swords and daggers of Hallstatt type. (3) An iron slashing sword with ivory pommel, about 3 feet 8 inches long, Hallstatt. Such huge weapons were replaced in the seventh century B.C. by the short sword (1) with branching horseshoe pommel, and the knife (2). The characteristic branching pommel (antennæ) is shown in the short sword and dagger of (4), (5) and (6). (1), (2), (3), (4) after Sacken; (5) after Lindenschmidt. Reduced in size and not drawn to scale.

century B.C., the slashing sword was replaced by the shorter, thrusting swords with a horseshoe-shaped pommel. The earlier scabbards were made of wood or leather, but later some were made of beaten bronze.

Daggers. As the dagger was a short arm, with an average length of about one and one-half feet, it was more constantly worn and became not only a weapon but an article of personal adornment and it consequently varied more in ornamentation than other arms. The handle generally ended in a branched pommel or antennæ, and the grip in some cases was made of alternating disks of iron, copper and ivory or bone. The habitual use of daggers led also to the development of metallic scabbards, which, at first, were of bronze and later of iron. The blades of the early daggers were generally narrow, but later they were made with a tendency toward a wider and triangular shape. The tips of most of the scabbards were made in the form of a hollow sphere or

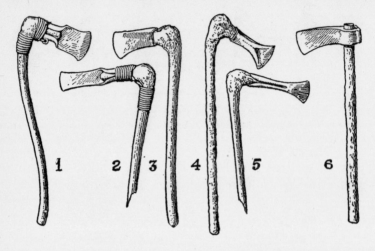

FIG. 120.—The method of attaching celts and ax heads to their handles and the variations in shape are well shown. After Schumacher.

ring, much like some of those of the Near East to-day. With a few exceptions the handles terminated in the characteristic antennæ, of which there are three principal types (see Fig. 119, (1), (4) and (5)). The details of the metal work of the scabbards and handles show that the armourers possessed considerable skill.

Lances and Arrows. Like the earliest iron celts and swords, the first iron lances were merely reproductions of bronze models, but as the armourers became more skilful in iron working, the form and ornamentation changed, and long, slender, thin spearheads were made. So few arrowheads have been found that it seems probable the bow and arrow was little used; but, if so, it is surprising, for the Hallstattians had no other weapon, as far as is known, which could be propelled against distant objects.

TOOLS AND IMPLEMENTS

Axes, Celts, Sickles. As tools of everyday use were seldom placed in tombs, our knowledge of the implements commonly

FIG. 121.—A contemporary vase from Certosa, near Bologna, Italy, shows a mounted warrior with no shield but with a celt, and four foot soldiers with shields, helmets, and javelins. The celt is best shown in the last figure.

employed, such as iron celts (Fig. 120), sickles, and knives is rather meagre. Figures embossed on a situla (Fig. 121) show axes carried by soldiers possibly as weapons, but with

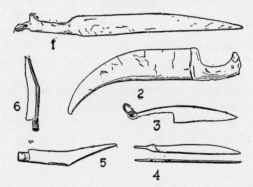

FIG. 122.—Iron knives of various shapes, some with rings for suspension. From Southern Germany, Alsace, and Southern France. After Déchelette. Much reduced in size.

equal plausibility as tools. In this figure the axes are broad and flat. Some socketed iron celts are reproductions of Bronze Age tools (compare Fig. 100, p. 226, and Fig. 120). Flat axes

with trunnions were made of bronze in the British Isles but
were forged from iron where iron was better known.

Knives. The knives (Fig. 122) with iron blades are not
unlike the bronze knives of the Bronze Age; but the Hallstattians brought out a new invention: they made knives, the
prototype of our pocket knife, with blades that folded into the
handle.

Razors. The razors of the Hallstatt epoch are much like
those of the Bronze Age and are generally made of bronze but
some are of iron. Some have holes for suspension. That shaving
was a privilege of the aristocratic warrior is indicated by the
association of the razor with the sword.

Toilet Articles. Small toilet articles consisting of tweezers,

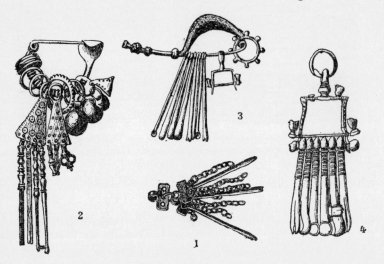

Fig. 123.—Tweezers, earspoons, and other implements of the toilet. In (2)
and (3) the instruments are strung on fibulæ. Juras and Northern Italy.
After Déchelette. Reduced in size.

earspoons, and scratchers fastened to a ring or fibula (Fig.
123) appear in the later Hallstatt epoch.

Bronze Buckets, Situlæ, etc. The people of the Hallstatt
epoch seem to have found bronze vessels especially desirable
media for expressing their artistic taste, and on them they

embossed and engraved designs, and to them they later attached figures cast in bronze. During the early part of the epoch no figure decoration is known, but later, at about the time the iron sword appeared, bronze pails were decorated with horizontal bands or friezes consisting of rows of men and animals and with dots and bosses, inherited from the preceding period. There were two types of vessels with bails, the cista or bucket with vertical sides (Fig. 124), some of

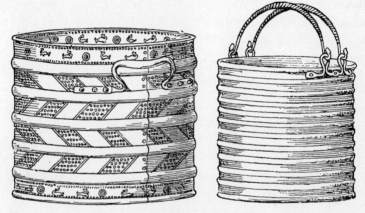

FIG. 124.—Bronze buckets from Hallstatt, Austria. This style of bronze vessel was not uncommon over a large part of Europe.

which were ribbed, and the bucket with bulging sides called the situla (Fig. 125). The figures and designs on situlæ were outlined with the chisel and were brought into relief by hammering from the back (*repoussé*). Details were added with punches by means of which dots and bosses were made.

A few elaborately ornamented caldrons have been found in France, Switzerland, and elsewhere. One of the most striking is nearly two feet high and has attached to it between the shoulder and the rim a figure of a winged deity of the so-called Persian Artemis type holding in each hand a hare —a motive which is frequently found on metal and clay objects of the Greek archaic period. On each side of the central figure is a lion; and above, on the rim, are two other lions, a double-headed serpent, and an eagle. The contact with the culture of the East is thus well shown.

Caldrons supported on tripods have also been found in tumuli. A remarkable one (Fig. 135) from Eastern France, Garenne (Côte d'Or), has a tripod made entirely of iron with the exception of the feet and small cylinders for binding the parts together. The squat caldron is surmounted by four griffin heads made of cast and chiselled bronze which are attached to the rim by rivets. The fact that similar objects were discovered in Olympia and assigned to the seventh century B. C. gives an approximate date.

Bronze vessels were first made of sheet metal bent and hammered into shape and held together by rivets, for solder was not invented until about 490 B. C. When the casting of bronze became prevalent, about 700 B. C., an active trade in bronze vessels was carried on with Italy where an important centre of the bronze industry existed near

Fig. 125.—A bronze situla from Certosa, near Bologna, with figures of marching soldiers, labourers, agriculturists, and overlords. After Hoernes.

Padua. Oriental motives such as sphinxes, centaurs, winged griffins, similar to those found on contemporary Greek pottery, appear. At this time athletic events and chariot races and religious ceremonies (Fig. 125) are represented. Other designs such as animals in heraldic opposition indicate the influence of the Near East.

In addition to situlæ and buckets, basins, dishes, water jars, amphoræ, wine pitchers, goblets, and bowls were used by the people; and so many have been preserved that it is evident that great quantities were carried by traders from the South and East. There were also local metal industries in Germany and in the Alpine districts where simply-ornamented objects like fibulæ, and rings were manufactured, but the finer fibulæ, ear rings, and other objects of skilled manufacture came from a greater distance.

ORNAMENTS

Fibulæ and Pins. Various types of fibulæ which were developed during the Bronze Age (p. 234) continued in use in the first epoch of the Iron Age. New styles appeared (Fig. 126) but they were generally rather simple in design. Few

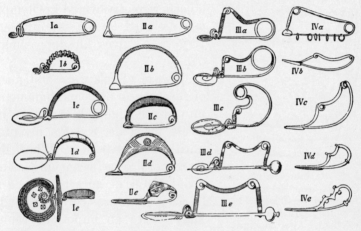

FIG. 126.—The evolution of Italian fibulæ before 500 B.C., that is, before the beginning of La Tene times. The four series are arranged vertically. The primitive (earliest type) (*a*) closely resembles a modern safety pin. The bow of the earlier pins is plain. The later fibulæ are heavier and are more arched to provide more room for the cloth. The late forms I e; II e; III e; and IV e; are greatly ornamented.

of the graves of men at Hallstatt yield fibulæ but some fibulæ of the spectacle type (Fig. 127) as well as those with the semi-circular arch and short sheath occur. The craftsmen displayed greater skill and originality in making fibulæ than in any other products of the epoch. As fibulæ underwent a gradual change in shape, a study of them has made it possible to date, with considerable accuracy, the graves in which they were found. The series shown in Figure 126 gives the development before 500 B.C. of Italian fibulæ.

Long pins with ornamental heads much like those found in Lake Dwelling deposits and "swan neck" pins (Fig. 127) also occur in the graves of men.

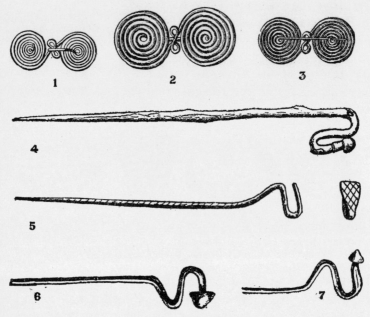

FIG. 127.—Bronze fibulæ of the spectacle type showing the front (2) and the way the pin is attached (3). After Déchelette. (4), (5), (6), and (7) are "Swan neck" bronze pins. The kink in the stem is to prevent the pin from falling out when in use. Pins of this style were used in widely separated regions. After Déchelette.

Necklaces. As necklaces and pendants have been favourite ornaments or charms ever since the dawn of the Stone Age, it would indeed be surprising if they were not worn in the Hallstatt epoch. Amber beads have been found at Hallstatt by the thousands and, judging from the grave furniture, they were worn by rich and poor. In addition to amber, bronze, ivory, coral, glass, and bone, either in combination or separately, were employed. The necklaces were generally plain but some were more ornate and were made of carved amber and stone. Some had engraved hollow bronze bells hanging from rings, while other necklaces with chain pendants forming a kind of breastplate six or seven inches across have been found. It was not until La Tene times, however, that they became really elaborate.

Bracelets, etc. Bracelets, anklets, torques, and finger-rings were much more common in the later than in the earlier part of the epoch under discussion. Individual taste in jewelry differed at this time, as it does to-day, with the result that various forms and designs were created. Some bracelets

FIG. 128.—Bronze Bracelets. (1) A rather unusual type; (2) a hinged bracelet; (3) a wide arm bracelet or brassard; (4) a bronze anklet. (1), (2), (3) after Déchelette; (4) after British Museum. Much reduced in size.

(Fig. 128) are hinged so as to admit the wrist, but most are of one piece; some are ornamented in such a way as to give the effect of beads of different sizes. Large brassards made of hollow bronze (Fig. 128 (3)), and rings, possibly bracelets, two inches across, were favourite ornaments in Germany. Bronze ribbonlike spirals which must have covered the whole of the forearm were also worn. Such spirals are now popular with some African tribes. Anklets were also used and can generally be distinguished from bracelets by their shape. Finger-rings with spiral terminals were inherited from the preceding age.

Torques. Torques were commonly worn as ornaments but the variety is not as great as in the next epoch. A peculiar type, made by twisting a three ridged bar of bronze, which is typical of the latest Bronze Age in Scandinavia, was popular

in Hallstatt times in Germany. Neck ornaments have been
found which consist of six or more neck rings attached to
an ornamented plaque. Some of these plaques have additional holes for the insertion of other rings; one in the Berlin Museum has places for 14 such rings.

Gold objects were rare in Central Europe during the Early
and Middle Hallstatt epoch. Toward the end of the epoch,
as trade with the South became better developed, gold was
more widely employed. When the Hallstattian goldsmiths

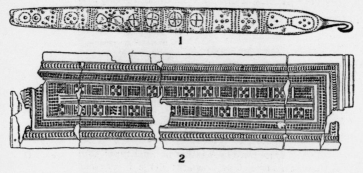

Fig. 129.—Bronze Belts. One of the most characteristic ornaments of female
   attire of the first Age of Iron was the belt ornamented with bronze.
   (1) shows how the belt was fastened. (2) Characteristic ornamentation is
   shown in the bronze covering of a belt in which the designs are in
   repousée. (1) after Lindenschmidt; (2) after the Museum of St. Germain.

made earrings, torques, bracelets, and pendants, they did not
make them heavy and massive but hollow and light in order
to conserve the precious metal as much as possible.

Belts. Wide leather belts (Fig. 129) covered with thin
sheets of bronze were much favoured by the women of the
later Hallstatt epoch, and constitute one of the most widespread ornaments of the time. The belts varied greatly in
width from less than an inch to eight inches but most of
them were wide. As some are more than a yard long, it
seems possible that they were worn a little above the hips.
Some of the belts were covered only at the back with bronze,
but in others the leather was nearly or quite hidden by

metal sheets. Another form of decoration was produced by riveting rows of bronze buttons on leather. Geometric designs stamped with a punch and arranged in longitudinal

FIG. 130.—Restoration of the clothing of a warrior. Note the spectacle fibula, the iron sword, ornamental belt, and probable design of the tunic and trousers. Central Museum, Mainz. Model by F. Wagner.

Photograph by courtesy of the Central Museum, Mainz.

bands, separated by parallel strips, were common forms of decoration. The motives are for the most part crosses and diamond- and boat-shaped figures. Several belts with engraved decorations have been found. Most of the belt buckles or clasps were made of bronze, but some were of iron.

Glass. Glass beads which were introduced in the Bronze Age, were also favourite objects in this epoch. In the middle of the epoch, vases of glass first made their appearance, although such objects had long been in use in the Mediterranean countries. Since the technique of glass blowing had not yet been discovered, all glass vessels were moulded.

Clothing. Remains of clothing (Fig. 130) are rarely found in the graves and when found are so poorly preserved as to

afford little knowledge of their character. A little more is learned from the cloth in which iron and bronze objects were wrapped because the oxidation products of these metals act as a preservative. Besides the thicker textures there are some which are not unlike some of the finest weaves of to-day. Most of our knowledge of clothing for this epoch is derived from representations on situlæ Fig. 125), belts, and pottery. The costumes shown on these ob-

FIG. 131.—An urn from Odenburg, Hungary, which depicts women in hoop skirts, and men in tight fitting trousers. After Hoernes.

jects represent the attire of the people of Northern Italy and the Alpine settlements, but it is possible that the clothing worn in Central and Western Europe differed little from it. Some vases from Odenburg, Hungary (Fig. 131), depict men with close-fitting trousers and women with hoop skirts. Fibulæ were common from the middle of the epoch and were probably used to fasten the floating mantle which was like the "sagum" of Roman times. Earrings, necklaces, bracelets, anklets, and belts in the graves of women give a true picture of their ornaments. The wide belt decorated with stamped copper and bronze was perhaps the most conspicuous and valued of their finery. Razors and hair shears indicate that

Fig. 132.—These typical Hallstatt platters from Württemberg are decorated in red and black with incised geometric patterns.

Permission of the Trustees of the British Museum.

the young men shaved and that the mustache was probably the vogue.

Pottery. Technical skill in pottery was in general more advanced than in the Bronze Age, and when it had reached its climax large vessels decorated in black and red with incised geometric designs (Fig. 132) were made. Some of the Bronze Age people in Central Europe, however (Lausitz) (Fig. 105, p. 232), made beautiful black mammillary jars, some with feet, that are nearly equal to the best Hallstatt ware. Some tribes (the Urnfield) liked thin, well-polished and black coloured vases, made in imitation of bronze vessels. Not only were pottery vessels made in imitation of bronze ones but bronze vases were made to imitate pottery. Other tribes (Salem) preferred coloured vases which were decorated with white, red, yellow, and black inlay. Still others (Lower Rhine) were unskilled in the art of making pottery. One specimen from Württemberg, Germany, measures twenty-one

Fig. 133.—A face urn with incised fibulæ. Some face urns have bronze earrings, and one is ornamented with an iron torque.

Photograph by courtesy of the Berlin Museum of Ethnology.

inches in diameter and has its surface blackened with graphite and grooved vertically and horizontally. In it were thirteen vessels which may represent typical household utensils. In parts of Germany face urns with caplike lids were made (Fig. 133). Some of the jars had bronze rings in the ears, torques on the necks, and representations of pins and other ornaments incised on the body of the urn.

Salt. Salt is craved by all herbivorous animals and by man, and just as the deer will go long distances to a salt lick so man made special efforts to get salt. The reason for the settlement of Hallstatt was the presence of salt. A trade in this indispensable commodity sprang up (see Fig. 117, p. 258) which brought back many articles in exchange. The method of obtaining salt by the Hallstattians is interesting. Brine was poured over or allowed to drip on an apparatus consisting of bars of baked clay. After the water had evaporated a deposit of salt was formed on the bars and when the layer had accumulated to sufficient thickness it was removed. In modern times salt has been mined at Hallstatt where the beds are estimated as 1100 feet thick. Salt has therefore been obtained from this locality for more than 2500 years.

Amber and Trade Routes. Given a substance beautiful in colour, which is easily carried and polished, and yet hard enough to resist wear, light in weight, and valuable because rare; endow it with supposed magical and medicinal properties, and we have a substance which would be greatly desired by man. Such a substance is amber. It is not surprising, therefore, that from Neolithic times to the present day this fossil gum should have been an article of commerce. In the history of the world no other substance, not a metal, has for so long a time had so great an influence on the whole of Europe. For more than 4000 years amber has been brought from the shores of the Baltic and carried by traders to all parts of Europe, including Greece, and even more distant countries. Because the source of amber was the west coast of Denmark and the shores of the Baltic, in East Prussia, traders brought there articles for exchange from Britain, from the South, and from the East. In the Bronze and Iron Ages, it enabled the inhabitants of Scandinavia to secure large quantities of tin and copper for their bronze industry and made it possible for them to develop a characteristic art in bronze which is as unexpected as it is skilful. It was probably largely in exchange for amber that bronze objects such as situlæ, buckets, swords, and ornaments, which were so frequently buried in the graves of their owners, were obtained. The possibility, however, that cattle were also used in exchange must not be omitted.

Amber beads found in graves and in caches where they

had been buried by traders or other individuals while temporarily absent or in time of trouble and then lost give a clue to the routes followed in this amber trade. There are five principal routes (Fig. 117, p. 258): (1) by the sea through the Mediterranean to the coasts of Spain, France, Britain, Denmark, and Sweden; (2) one along the Rhone, Doubs, and Rhine rivers; (3) one from the Po Valley (the great centre of the bronze industry in the Late Bronze and Early Iron Ages) by way of the Tessin Valley, the Alpine passes, and Swiss Lakes to the north; (4) a very important one from the head of the Adriatic along the Moldau and the Elbe to the Baltic. This last route should be especially considered because halfway along it lay the east-west Danube Valley which afforded communication in one direction with the Black Sea and in the other with the upper Rhine Valley. It permitted the distribution of amber by various branches to the Adriatic, the Balkans, and the Ægean countries. Its existence is the reason for the high civilisation of the Bronze Age in the north. So great a trade in amber was carried on by this route that, according to tradition, the Po was the "river of amber" and the Amber Isles (Electrides) were believed to be at its mouth. In the First Age of Iron the products of the iron industry, and soon the technical skill of the industry, were spread throughout the Keltic world by means of this route. (5) A fifth route extended from the Black Sea along the valleys of the Dniester and Vistula to the Baltic. From all of these routes trails of lesser importance radiated to settlements and villages.

Amber has been especially mentioned because of its early importance and because for thousands of years it was a much desired article of commerce. Bronze, as has been seen (p. 204), was carried long distances; and the size of some of the objects such as situlæ three feet high, for example, show that well marked trails were in existence. There was also a considerable trade in gold, silver, jet, ivory, coral, and objects of glass such as beads, goblets, and bowls. Salt from Salzburg, Hallstatt and other centres was probably transported many miles; and salt mines became important centres of trade and industry. When centres for the manufacture of iron were established, roads led from them to the old established trade routes shown on the map, Figure 117.

Merchandise was transported on the backs of men, on horses, in wheeled vehicles for short distances and in boats. One would not be justified in assuming that good roads were in existence, for even to-day in countries such as Mexico a considerable commerce is carried on trails over which wagons cannot pass.

Houses. The failure of the prehistoric peoples of Central and Western Europe to build houses of stone when the contemporaneous Mediterranean peoples were erecting noble stone buildings was evidently due to the abundance of wood in the former regions, just as in modern North America, wooden houses are the rule whereas in Mexico houses are built of stone or adobe. The megalithic monuments of the Neolithic and Early Bronze Ages seem an anomaly but were, with little doubt, erected by a ruling class whose religious cult had a foreign origin and came from a region where stone was used.

As a result of skilful excavations much is now known about the houses of Hallstatt times. It is found that some were huts of the crudest kind but that others compare well with the houses of prosperous farmers of to-day. An example of the best type of house is one at Neuhausel, Czechoslovakia. The group of buildings of this estate (Fig. 134) covers an area of about ninety by ninety-five feet and consists of several attached houses for living and farm purposes. The roofs were covered with thatch, and the framework of the buildings was constructed of carefully jointed timbers. Some of the partition walls were covered with clay as is shown by fragments of this material with impressions of brush, but that others were probably made of split boards is indicated by the absence of clay. The earthen floors were covered with sand. The long halls, stables, and barns leave little doubt that this establishment was the property of a wealthy farmer.

In the city of Hallstatt the houses were small, about sixteen by twenty feet; most of them are with one room, and an entrance vestibule, either open or enclosed. A wooden grave chamber at Villingen, Germany, probably gives an accurate

Fig. 134.—(1) Restoration of a house of this epoch at Neuhausel, Czechoslovakia; and another (2) at Grossgartach, Germany. Model in the Central Museum, Mainz. After Schumacher.

picture of these small houses with the possible exception of the floor, which in the houses of the living was generally of earth. The carefully hewn timbers of this grave chamber are eight by fifteen inches in cross section, the floor is made of timbers laid side by side, and the walls of timbers laid one above the other. The rather high gable roof was made of beams fitted together. In some districts the foundations of the houses were made of dry masonry.

In Rhenish Hesse there has been found an oval pit dwelling twelve and one-half by fourteen feet, with the floor five feet below the surface, whose walls were made of thin strips of wood woven together. Another pit dwelling, with the floor three feet below the ground level, had a plastered entrance eleven feet long and five feet wide which led down to the floor. In general it can be said that, as in Europe to-day, the houses of different districts had characteristic peculiarities of architecture. In some backward regions, as in the vicinity of Rome (Latium), the people lived in one-roomed houses of straw and branches or of skin stretched on a light framework. The ground plan of these huts was roughly circular, and the walls and roof formed a continuous curve. The shape and construction of these houses is shown in the funeral urns, some of which show that the roofs were thatched.

Agricultural villages and the clustered villages of the herdsmen were laid out much as to-day. They were generally surrounded by a palisade or stone barrier which was less for protection than for the purposes of a corral. The absence of strong fortifications and the location of the villages on the valley floors indicate peaceful times in the Rhine Valley during a large part of the Hallstatt epoch. Elsewhere, encircling walls and walls with the additional protection of trenches were employed by some tribes. A highly developed skill and technique in defensive works is seen in a fortification near Langen, Germany, which has a double wall and ditch with woven breastworks, ditch obstacles, and projecting barriers. Entrenched fortifications seem to have been preferred, especially in the later Hallstatt.

Peoples. Our knowledge of the Hallstattian peoples is derived from ancient authors, from place names, from the names of ancient tribes, from archæological finds, and from a study of skulls. According to ancient writers the Ligurians lived in a region extending from the Western Alps to the mouth of the Rhone, although exact boundaries if they ever existed are doubtful, and the Iberians west of the Rhone and in Spain. The Raetians lived in the Central Alps and seem to have occupied a territory extending to the north, beyond the Danube and the Swabian Alps into the upper Neckar Valley. They are believed to be a branch of the great Thracian people; and from them came many place names such as Rhine, Jura, and Alps. The Illyrians, who were related to them, occupied the Eastern Alpine district as far as the Balkans and spread out from there to the northeast and northwest. The Kelts occupied a large region in France and Western Europe from which they later spread. All of these races intermingled with their neighbours. In general it can be said that the Hallstatt civilisation is associated with the Keltic and Alpine races.

FIG. 135.—Bronze basin with griffin heads from a chariot burial in the tumulus of La Garenne. After the Museum of St. Germain. Much reduced in size.

The same type of skull is found in the older Hallstatt graves as in Bronze Age burials, an indication of the continuity of the races. After a time, however, a new type of skull appears, especially in the warriors' graves, which resembles that of the Illyrians.

Burials. A brief description of the graves at Hallstatt has already been given on page 272. As in the Neolithic and Bronze Ages and also in the La Tene epoch, the dead were buried in tumuli, sometimes several burials being placed in the same mound. The tumuli at Hallstatt are not especially conspicuous; the maximum height is about twenty feet, and the diameter is seldom more than 100 feet. Burials without artificial mounds were exceptional. In the latter half of the Hallstatt epoch chariot burial was practiced, the body of the warrior being buried with his chariot and horses, implements of war, and other cherished objects, a practice which survived into the next epoch.

One of the most famous of the Hallstatt tumuli with chariot burial is that of la Garenne near Châtillon-sur-Seine, Côte d'Or. Originally about 13 feet high and 250 feet long, it was levelled by a peasant who found in it the remains of a chariot, a bronze basin (Fig. 135) ornamented with griffin heads of cast bronze, of Greek workmanship of the seventh or sixth centuries B. C., and a much broken tripod of iron and bronze. If more care had been taken during the removal of the earth and stones, more objects would probably have been found. A more detailed description of this basin is given on p. 280.

Another tumulus in the same district, that of La Butte, contained the remains of a rich person buried on a four-wheeled chariot or funeral car. Two gold earrings, two gold bracelets and an iron hatchet constituted the grave furniture. The workmanship of the iron objects, especially the spokes of the wheels, is remarkable. In the middle of the mound there was a circular arrangement of stones, within which were three skeletons, those of a man, a woman, and a child.

In a Keltic tumulus five feet high and eighty feet in diameter, in Matzhausen, Upper Palatinate, dating from the second half of the Hallstatt, were three burials. The skeleton in the man's grave had a large iron knife in the left hand and a small iron lancehead near the left side. The child's remains had a bracelet on the right forearm, two small fibulæ on the breast and a hairpin near the head. The skeleton of the woman had a head-ring above the head, a torque on the neck, and three bracelets, one on each of the upper arms and the third on the right forearm. She had four rings on her right and two on her left hand. On her breast were four fibulæ and two large pins, more than two and a half feet long. In this last

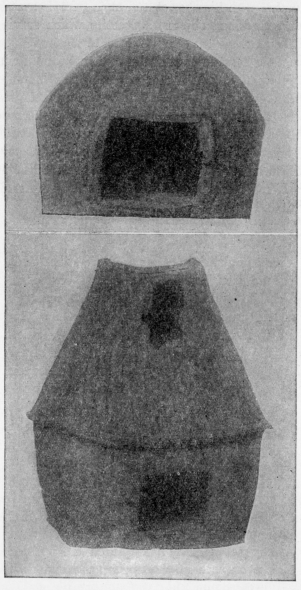

FIG. 136.—Funeral hut urns from Germany.
Photograph by courtesy of the Berlin Ethnological Museum.

grave there was a very fine vase shaped like a decanter, made to imitate bronze and engraved with animal and bird designs.

The practice of burying the dead in tumuli was widespread; and these funeral mounds occur in Central and Western Europe, and in Spain.

A peculiar custom, prevalent during a part of the Hallstatt epoch, was the burial of the ashes of the dead in urns made in imitation of the dwellings of the time (Fig. 136). These urns are made of pottery and range in height from seven to twenty-two inches. Some of the hut urns are simply jars with covers shaped somewhat like the arching roofs of the huts of the period. Almost without exception the ashes of the deceased were introduced through the door on the side and not through the top by the removal of the cover. The hut urn was not exclusively used, but jars of other shapes were employed also. Inhumation as well as cremation was practiced. With the remains of the dead, objects of personal use were also inserted, such as fibulæ, hairpins, bits of amber, or bone for necklaces or to ornament fibulæ. Bronze tweezers, rings, lances, small iron swords, vases, and glass beads have also been found but as a rule little was buried in any one urn.

Hut urn burials were practiced in the Rhine Valley and its tributaries, Scandinavia, Italy, Crete, Cyprus, and North Africa. In Italy, the custom extended from the ninth to the eighth centuries B. C. but was more common in the eighth century. It is not definitely known from what region the people with the hut urn culture came to the Rhine Valley, but they are thought to have come from the southeast. The strong resemblances between the houses as well as the grave rites of the people of the hut urn culture of Italy (Villanova) to that of Austria and Germany is striking.

Religion. The worship of the Sun continued into this epoch and was probably the most important cult of the time although there is little doubt that the polytheistic religions of the South had spread north and were adopted by a part of the people or were in some degree incorporated in the earlier religious beliefs. The evidence for the cult of the Sun, as in the Bronze Age, rests largely on the occurrence of symbols of the sun disk and crescent and the swan and the horse which are occasionally associated with them (see p. 253). The frequent occurrence of the moon figure or ox horns suggests the worship of the bull-headed deity which had long been practiced in Crete and the Ægean countries. This cult would especially appeal to primitive peoples as the bull was the highest embodiment of force, the emblem of the male godhead.

Superstition and the belief in charms and amulets had a stronger hold on the people then than now. This is shown by the widespread use of various materials, especially amber and coral, to ward off the evil spirits. Astral representations, especially the solar disk or forms derived from it were also believed to have some marvellous virtue.

Music. Evidence that music was enjoyed and that it was employed in ceremonials is so strong as to leave little doubt that the people were lovers of music. A vase from Odenburg, Hungary, depicts two men playing on lyres while two women dance (Fig. 131, p. 286). On another vase, a woman (or man) sits before a loom and plays for two dancing women. Situlæ made in Italy and transported to the North show that there was a great deal of music at sacrifices and banquets.

The Debt of Civilisation to the Hallstatt. Modern civilisation owes to the Hallstatt the introduction of iron in commercial quantities. It was no longer a rare and precious substance but a metal for ordinary tools and weapons. The dependence of modern man on iron is so obvious that further discussion is unnecessary. Aside from this great achievement, the Hallstatt gave little to the world but continued the traditions of the Bronze Age.

CHAPTER IX

THE LA TENE EPOCH—THE SECOND AGE OF IRON

Equivalent: Late Keltic in Britain.
Date: 500 B.C. to the Christian Era.[1]

THE La Tene culture is partly a development of that of
the Hallstatt, partly a modification of that obtained from
other peoples, and partly a new creation, consummated by
the genius of a vigorous and untrammeled people. The end
of the Hallstatt and the beginning of the La Tene was coin-
cident with the spread of the conquering Kelts (Gauls) and
the passing under their domination of the Illyrian-Alpine
peoples. One of the most striking facts brought out by a study
of the objects of this epoch is the similarity of Keltic culture
over the entire territory of Keltic rule. The people of Eastern Gaul possessed the same ornaments and tools as those
of Czechoslovakia, Bosnia, and Hungary.

Just as the English and German settlers of the United
States and Canada and the Spaniards of Mexico and California gave the place names of the country of their birth to
the villages and towns they founded in the New World, so
place names of Gaul (France) were given to villages as far
east as Silesia.

[1] Déchelette: La Tene   I, 500-300 B.C.
                  II, 300-100 B.C.
                  III, 100 B.C.-1st Cent. A.D.
                  IV, (Brit.) 1st Cent. A.D.
    Montelius (France): La Tene   I, 450-250 B.C.
                          II, 250-150 B.C.
                          III, 150-1 B.C.
    Schumacher: La Tene   I, 500-400 B.C.
                  II, 400-300 B.C.
                  III, 300-100 B.C.
                  IV, 100 B.C.-Christian Era.

"The Greco-Roman culture knocked with more and more insistence than hitherto on the doors of Central Europe and found a more receptive people in the Keltic races. The Rhone route (Map, Fig. 117, p. 258) gained in importance and the influence of the Danube waned. This culture quickly extended from Southern France to the Rhine, to Southeastern Europe and even into Asia as the great Keltic migration spread." [2]

During the sixth and fifth centuries B. C. the Keltic tribes of Germany and Eastern Gaul were prosperous and active. They had important iron and salt industries, their agriculture was of a high order, and they were skilled workers in bronze and iron. They were not content with articles of their own manufacture but sought articles of Greek and Roman workmanship which they obtained either by exchange or by war.

The heart of the Keltic domain in Early La Tene times was that region lying between Northern France and Czechoslovakia. It probably centered in the basin of the Middle Rhine, for only in this restricted region are found objects of Greek and Roman workmanship of Early La Tene date and it is from it, therefore, that the Keltic culture was probably diffused.

In the fourth and third centuries the frontiers of the Empire were extended by conquests and migrations into Western and Southern Gaul, into Upper Italy, and into the valley of the Danube. Some Kelts even reached the Bosphorus. On the west they crossed the Straits of Dover and established themselves in Britain which was already occupied by tribes speaking a dialect of the same language.

The La Tene culture did not spread to all parts of Central and Western Europe simultaneously as is shown by the fact that in some places the earliest La Tene culture belongs to the second and third stages of the epoch. This is especially true of isolated and easily defended valleys.

[2] Karl Schumacher: "Seidelungs- und Kulturgeschichte der Rheinlande."

The second stage, La Tene II, was the period of the greatest expansion of the Kelts and it was then that their culture reached the Scandinavian countries and Northern Germany. Later, about the middle of the third century B. C., decadence set in. The gold ornaments and beautiful bronze torques so characteristic of the earlier stage are completely lacking in the last stage, and few graves contain any articles except those of native workmanship. At this time, too, the Kelts had lost their aggressiveness and initiative and were driven across the Rhine by the Germanic tribes and elsewhere they were being conquered or pushed back. Such times did not encourage commerce or the industrial arts.

The La Tene closed with the conquest of Gaul by Cæsar. The written history of Northern, Central, and Western Europe begins and prehistory ends with the passing of the Keltic Civilisation and the coming of the Roman.

In Déchelette's [3] résumé of the La Tene culture, he says: "The culture of the La Tene which prepared the way for Roman unity was born about 500 B. C. thanks to southern influence on the territory of ancient Keltica.[4] Two main causes coöperated simultaneously for its wide diffusion, especially in the fourth century: (1) the political, industrial, and commercial prosperity of the Kelts, and (2) the extent of their conquests. It was established in Europe wherever their arms were carried. Then, from the third century on, it spread gradually by a sort of diffusion among the Germanic nations of Northeastern Germany and Scandinavia, where it presented itself in a peculiar and more barbaric character.

"Conquered and absorbed by the Romans, the inhabitants of Gaul, in losing their independence, at least received from their conquerors the benefits of the Greco-Roman cul-

---

[3] J. Déchelette: "Manuel d'Archéologie," vol. II, Part 3.
[4] Moritz Hoernes: "Urgeschichte der Bildenden Kunst in Europa " disagrees with Déchelette and holds that the Keltic civilisation was largely due to the genius of a people who, free from the traditions of the Hallstatt and with little influence from the South, developed a new art and civilisation.

ture. During the Imperial epoch, the traditions of the culture of the Iron Age were kept among the free peoples of Germany on the right bank of the Rhine."

When the barbarians of Central and Western Europe were developing the La Tene culture, Greece was at the apogee of her artistic career. At this time the Parthenon was built, and the superb Greek statuary, the finest product of human skill, was being created. At this time, too, the Etruscan civilisation was disappearing and Rome was starting on its career of world domination. Without the artistic impulse which emanated from Greece and Rome it is doubtful if the Kelts would have advanced far; but with this impulse they rapidly developed a characteristic and beautiful art.

The Station of La Tene. A short description of the station of La Tene should be given both because of its historical interest and because it gives an insight into the life of the times. Its situation was ideal for a fortress as it was on the bank of a navigable stream, at the junction of three lakes, Neuchatel, Bienne, and Murat, and as it was one of the centres to which routes from the Alps converged. Careful excavations have shown that La Tene was a fortified post which was abandoned between 100 and 50 B. C., after an existence of nearly 200 years. The reason for believing that it was a military establishment is that the objects discovered are largely weapons and harness, and that there are few women's ornaments and little evidence of fishing and agriculture. The absence of forges, anvils, and hammers indicate that the swords and other weapons were made elsewhere and stored here. As La Tene was only occupied between 250 and 50 B. C., excavations bring to light the objects of only a part of the epoch, that is, of La Tene II.

Divisions of the La Tene Epoch. The La Tene Epoch is separated into three or four divisions by different authors. The bases upon which such divisions are made are well shown in a classification for Central and Western Europe as given by Schumacher:

La Tene I. The earliest La Tene culture is characterised by Greek red-figured vases, Greco-Roman bronze vessels, short and long iron swords, daggers, hacking knives, masks, fibulæ ornamented with animal heads, lenticular vases, etc. Burial mounds. Date: about 500-400 B. C.

La Tene II. In the Early La Tene Greco-Italic bronze vessels and ornaments continue to be used and short iron swords, hacking knives, signet rings, fibulæ with recurved foot, large earthenware flasks are characteristic. Burial mounds and flat graves. Date: about 400-300 B. C.

La Tene III. The Middle La Tene is characterised by long iron swords, shield bosses with wings, glass rings, and dishes with moulded bottoms. Graves without mounds. Beginning of incineration. Date: 300-100 B. C.

La Tene IV. The closing division of the La Tene is characterised by long iron swords with iron or bronze scabbards, glass rings, fibulæ with a closed foot, and pail-shaped pottery jars, some of which are painted. Incineration burials in mounds and also without mounds. Date: 100 B. C. to the Christian Era.

Peoples. The Keltic peoples, the creators of the art of the La Tene, did not have a national organisation; but they belonged to a number of tribes with a common language, who sometimes acted together in a common cause. More is known about their bodily appearance, clothing, and ornaments than about those of the peoples of previous epochs because, in addition to the evidence from graves, the writings of ancient authors and representations in art give a fairly complete picture. The Kelts or Gauls and West Germans were of nearly the same physical type. They were tall, with fair or reddish hair, blue or grey eyes; a very different type from the short, dark-haired dolichocephalic peoples of the Mediterranean region. The older men wore beards and had long hair. Some of the Germanic tribes wore their hair tied in a knot. The younger men had clipped hair and were shaven. The Kelts usually wore moustaches. Cæsar found

that the inhabitants of Britain near the Straits of Dover
were as civilised as the Kelts of the mainland and had the
same culture but that those of the interior had no agriculture, used milk and flesh for food, and skins for clothing.
They wore their hair long, had moustaches, and stained their
bodies blue to frighten their enemies. It is interesting to
note that the tall fair type which, according to Cæsar, occupied Gallia Celtica (Central France) has disappeared from
that region and that the native population now is of the
dark-haired Alpine type. There are two possible explanations
for this apparent change in the physical type of the people:
(1) that the description of ancient writers applies only to
the Keltic leaders with whom Cæsar and his officers came in
contact in their conferences, and that the mass of the Gauls
were dark-haired men who had been recruited for their expeditions for plunder or land, or (2) that the Nordic characteristics have been lost by intermarriage.

Habitations. The wooden houses of the La Tene, as well
as those of the Bronze Age and Hallstatt epoch, had much
the same construction as those of to-day; and all differ little
in their structural details from those of Neolithic times. The
style of architecture differed from place to place. In regions
of heavy snows or of heavy rains, of strong winds, or where
the land was swampy or stony, certain modifications in the
shape or slope of the roof were found desirable. Although
utility was the determining factor in the shape of the houses,
the artistic sense of the community had its effect. Especially
was this true of details or ornamentation which were the result of tradition or tribal superstitions.

Pit dwellings continued to be used by the poor. They differed little from those of the Hallstatt and, indeed, such huts
were common habitations in Roman times. In these wretched
huts, families lived from generation to generation, notwithstanding changes in overlords. Hut urns, so frequently employed in the Hallstatt epoch (Fig. 136, p. 296), were used in
La Tene times and reproduce the appearance of these huts.

In parts of Germany (Grossgartach, near Heilbronn, Württemberg)there were fine farm buildings (Fig. 137) consisting of several small rectangular or round wattle-and-daub houses for living and farm purposes.

In the construction of some of the better houses iron clamps were used to bind the wooden posts to the stone foundations. This method of building may have had a classical origin as the stones of the superb Greek temples were fastened together in this way. The methods of heating the

Fig. 137.—Buildings of La Tene times in Germany. (1) Grossgartach; (2) Handschuhsheim. After Schumacher.

houses improved with time. The poor lived in pit huts because of the protection from cold which the excavation afforded. These huts were also warmed by small hearth fires. That the living rooms of some of the houses of the well-to-do may have been heated by fireplaces is indicated by primitive fireplaces. Later, chimneys were built and stoves were used to heat the rooms. The stoves were clay pyramids with oaken frames walled in with bricks on a clay foundation and were built either in the middle or at the side of the room. Toward the close of the epoch, a few of the larger buildings had a heating system like the Roman hypocausts, that is, with air spaces in the floors and walls through which the heat from a subterranean fire circulated. This method of heating was without doubt introduced from Italy.

Enough is known of the towns or oppida of Gaul to enable one to form a fairly true conception of the larger towns which existed at the close of the La Tene epoch. One of these, the oppidum of Bibracte near Autun, France, covered 135 hectares or about 333 acres and was surrounded by a wall and a rampart. The houses were rectangular in plan and were constructed either of wood or of dry masonry held together with clay. The corners were made of carefully dressed granite blocks. The majority of the houses were half under ground, a necessary feature because of the severity of the winters. The floors were ordinarily covered with a layer of clay or with a layer of broken tiles. The roofs of most of the houses were doubtless covered with thatch but some of them were roofed with Roman tiles. The number of rooms in a house varied: the forgers, artisans, and other workingmen had one-roomed houses, whereas the homes of the rich, built on the classical plan of the Pompeiian houses, had as many as thirty rooms arranged around an atrium. As no springs were available, water was obtained from several wells. The wells were cut in the solid rock and some of them were walled up. As some of the wells were later used as rubbish pits, they have yielded all sorts of archæological objects. Bibracte was inhabited until Augustus' time, when the inhabitants were moved by the Emperor's orders to Augustodunum (*Autun*).

At least toward the close of the La Tene, wheeled vehicles were much used as the ruts in the streets, about four feet six inches apart, clearly indicate. It has been suggested that the ruts were made artificially to make it easier to drag the wagons through the streets. One road which crossed the Keltic town of Alesia was made by smoothing the rocky soil and by laying a herringbone pavement in some places.

Fortifications. A warlike people such as the Kelts, who attacked and in turn were attacked and who invaded hostile countries, were obliged to know how to defend themselves. As a result of their habits they developed an effective system of defense. On their marches of conquest they fortified all military and strategic points such as fords, mountain passes, and mountains commanding plains, etc. Such fortifications were both concentration points and places of safety for the peaceful inhabitants of the immediate vicinity. The encircling walls of such camps consisted of dry masonry several metres in thickness bound firmly together by beams of timber. In some fortifications there were two or three encircling walls built one behind the other. As these walls were fifteen to thirty feet high and had breastworks of wood or wickerwork, and as they surrounded hilltops, they formed strong defensive works and were safe enclosures for the inhabitants and their herds. The water supply was a serious problem in many of these strongholds, and as a rule it precluded a large population. In addition to such large fortifications there were many small ones for sudden emergencies. These consisted merely of a wall of earth and a ditch. One advance in the construction of the fortresses of this epoch was the binding of the stone blocks by a dove-tail mortise.

WEAPONS

The contents of graves show that in their migrations and conquests both the Keltic soldiers and the noncombatants carried arms, but that, in the more peaceful times which followed, weapons were seldom borne except by soldiers. When, however, the Germanic tribes became aggressive, weapons again appear in the graves.

Swords. The short sword was used in early La Tene times (Fig. 138) and is merely a modification of the short sword with antennæ of the Hallstatt epoch (see Fig. 119, p. 275). Many of these short, thrusting swords had handles decorated with the figure of a human head, an indication, perhaps, of the prevalent custom of beheading an enemy. These were generally used throughout Central Europe in the first half of the epoch. The typical sword of the later La Tene (La Tene III) is long and double-edged, not tapering but with a rounded end, and adapted for cutting and slashing instead of thrusting. Some swords from Northern Germany have blades nearly three inches wide and with the tang for the hilt at one side, so that they are like huge cleavers or knives

(Fig. 138 (5)), The position of the swords at the right side of the skeletons indicates that this weapon was not worn on the left side as now. The fact that the edges of some swords are sharp and well-preserved when unearthed, whereas the rest of the blade is badly corroded, shows that two kinds of iron were

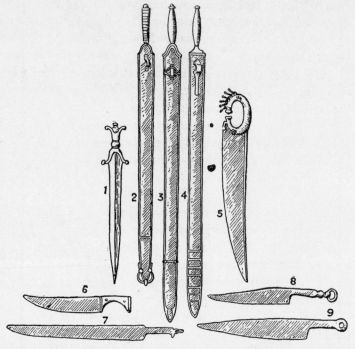

FIG. 138.—Swords. The sword was the most important arm of the Keltic warrior. (1) A short sword of the Early La Tene with handle decorated with the figure of a human head; (2) to (4) long swords; (5) to (9) knives. After Schumacher. Greatly reduced.

used; a soft kind for the edge which could be easily sharpened, and a harder kind for the body of the blade. The grips of swords were ornamented with gold or bronze and other substances, but most of them were quite plain. The swords were suspended from the belt by a buckle and straps.

Knives. Long iron knives Fig. 138 (5-9)) were sometimes carried by warriors. Their length and weight indicate

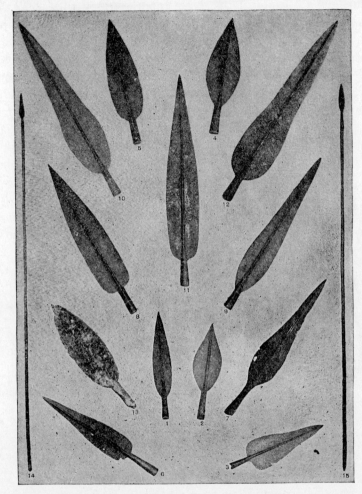

FIG. 139.—Next to the sword, the lance was the important Keltic weapon. Some of the simpler ones are shown here. Numbers 14 and 15 show lance-heads with wooden shafts. After P. Vouga. Reduced.

that they would have made useful weapons and it is probable that, on occasion, they were used instead of swords just as the machete is used in Central America and Venezuela.

Lances. The lance and javelin (Figs. 139 and 140) were, next to the sword, the favourite weapons of the Kelts. It is difficult to distinguish between them as they differ chiefly in use, the javelin being hurled and the lance being held in the hand. Some of the lance- or spearheads are as much as twenty inches long, while those of the javelins are as short as five inches. A complete lance with the head and wooden shaft, discovered at La Tene, measures about eight feet. The early lanceheads had regular edges but later those with wavy and

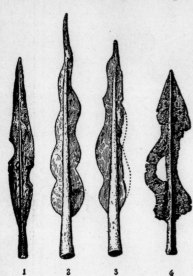

notched edges appear (Fig. 140). Some of the blades were decorated with designs like those on the swords. The lance was the favourite weapon of many of the Germanic tribes and considerable individuality in form and ornamentation is shown.

The bow, hatchet, and sling were not in general use during this epoch.

DEFENSIVE ARMOUR

Shields. With the exception of shields, which are quite common in the graves of warriors, defensive armour is rarely found. At the beginning of the epoch, shields were prob-

1   2   3   4

FIG. 140.—The love of curves is shown in the shape of some of the lanceheads as is seen in these specimens. After Déchelette.

ably made solely of wood (Fig. 141), leather, or wickerwork as few remains of them have been preserved. In the second stage of the La Tene, shields were common equipment for the soldiery, as is proved by the frequent discovery of the metallic bosses or umbos with which the shields were decorated. One umbo usually ornamented the centre of the shield, but in richly decorated shields there were two or more additional ones. A group of figures set up on the Acropolis of Athens by Attalus to commemorate his defeat of the Gauls in 240

B. C., gave a fairly accurate picture of the dress, arms, and appearance of the Keltic warriors. The shields, as shown in such works of art, are oblong or polygonal and slightly curved, and with a longitudinal ridge.

Some of the most artistic work of the epoch is preserved in the bosses. In Britain the characteristic and beautiful curvilinear designs consisting of intricate scroll patterns are skilfully executed on them (Plate IV). Some of the bosses were further embellished with red enamel and coral. The shape of the bosses gradually underwent a change. In La Tene II they were generally in the form of a half cylinder, but later this simple shape disappeared and circular, conical, and hemispherical ones became characteristic.

Helmets of various shapes have been found but are not common. Some were horned, some had somewhat the form of a jockey cap with the "visor" for the protection of the neck, while others were not unlike the helmets worn in the World War.

As armour is known to have been worn in the Bronze Age in Central and Western Europe,

FIG. 141.—The outside of a wooden shield with bronze umbo, from Lake Neuchatel, Switzerland. The shield was the principal defensive armour of the Kelts. After Vouga. Greatly reduced in size.

one can perhaps assume that this invention would continue to be used by some of the warriors of the La Tene Epoch, since offensive weapons had not greatly changed. Nevertheless only a few archæological finds bear out this assumption. The ancient writers, however, state that some of the Gauls wore iron coats of mail and some fought naked. Varro (116-27 B. C.) states that iron coats of mail were a Gallic invention.

When the Kelts marched to battle they carried with them shafts surmounted by symbolic figures of which the wheel and boar were preferred (Fig. 142). The boar was a sacred animal among the Kelts and was believed to give protection from the weapons of the enemy. Its religious significance is further seen in its representation on amulet figurines. The wheel probably was a religious symbol, possibly connected with the ancient sun-worship. These emblems had a religious significance and were also the rallying points of the soldiers.

Fig. 142.—A fragment of a Gallo-Roman frieze ornamented with Gallic arms. Note the wild boar on a standard and the shields. After Esperandieu.

The Kelts went into battle with yells. They pounded on their shields with their lances, and made as much noise as possible in order to strike terror in the heart of the enemy. The noise was further increased by the rough notes of the trumpet, an instrument of which figured representations are known.

Chariots. Chariots found in burials of this epoch seem certainly to have been for war purposes and not merely for funeral rites. They were lightly constructed, possibly because of the smallness of the horses of the time, had two wheels, and were like the Gallic war chariots described by Latin authors. The wheels varied in diameter from about thirty to thirty-six inches and had very narrow iron tires, a little more than an inch wide. The distance between the wheels was between four feet one inch and four feet four inches. The chariots and harnesses were ornamented with bronze, and the woodwork was probably painted in bright colours. The chariots were drawn by two horses by means of a yoke and tongue.

The use of chariots in warfare was possibly somewhat like that employed hundreds of years before at the siege of Troy. The chieftains did not fight from their chariots but used them in order to carry themselves to that part of the battle line which they judged was most advantageous. When driven to a chosen position, the warrior would descend from his chariot, hurl his lance at his antagonist or the enemy foot-soldiers, and when hard pressed would run back to his chariot and be carried out of range. The use of war chariots was discontinued on the continent shortly after the middle of the epoch but continued in Britain until the second century of our era.

Toward the close of the epoch wheeled vehicles of several kinds were made and utilised for transportation and, especially in the North of France, their manufacture became an important industry.

Spurs were used from the beginning of the La Tene, but usually one only was worn by a rider.

TOOLS AND TRADES

Iron tools of many kinds and of excellent workmanship were manufactured, so that before the end of the La Tene they are not inferior to those of the Romans. The tools of the farmer did not differ greatly from those used to-day in parts of Europe. Iron plowshares were apparently a Keltic invention, and, together with sickles, were exported. It should be noted that no bronze plowshares are known from the Bronze Age. Iron scythes, some thirty inches long, sickles (Fig. 143), hooked knives, hatchets, and handmills (Fig. 144) made of basalt were in common use. It is evident that the cultivation of cereals and the process of milling were well

Fig. 143.—Agricultural implements: (1) is a sickle, (2) and (3) are scythes intended to be used with two hands; (4) and (5) are probably pruning hooks; (6) and (7) are knives with blunt points bent at right angles to the blade which were used for cutting leather. After Vouga.

advanced, and Gaul must have been a fertile and well-culti-
vated country, as described by ancient writers.

Fishing gear consisted of fishhooks (Fig. 145) of considerable variety, some of them linked, and fishspears.

The carpenter had a full complement of tools: chisels
like those of the Bronze Age, awls, gouges, saws, files, com-
passes, and planes. The forgers and blacksmiths had a variety
of tools such as hammers, anvils, and tongs.

In addition to the iron tools mentioned above, iron calks
to be fastened on shoes to prevent slipping on the ice, pokers,
pothangers, cauldrons, forks, andirons (first made in the Hall-

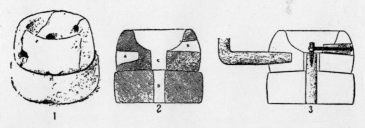

Fig. 144.—Hand mill (1) for grinding grain, France. It is composed of two
stone (basalt) parts, the one fixed and the other movable. Number (2)
is a section to show the construction and Number (3) shows a restoration
of the wooden parts. After Déchelette.

statt epoch) and other hardware were manufactured. Toward the close of the epoch, iron keys were made. Large and
small knives (Fig. 146) were in common use and in one
cemetery a knife was buried with every woman and child.
Axes and socketed celts nearly like those of the Late Bronze
Age were used but axes of nearly the modern type were more
common. An outfit of some twenty instruments which probably belonged to a goldsmith was found at La Tene. The
equipment for iron working on the farm is shown by the remains of a small foundry of early La Tene times at Grossgartach near Heilbron, Germany. The simple forges give evidence of a highly developed and widespread technique. The
cast iron, in the form of narrow, double pyramidal bars with

Fig. 145.—The tools of the fisherman. The fishhooks (1) to (12) are like those of to-day. (13) and (14) are harpoons; (15) is a fish spear or trident; (16) to (23) are boat hooks. After Vouga.

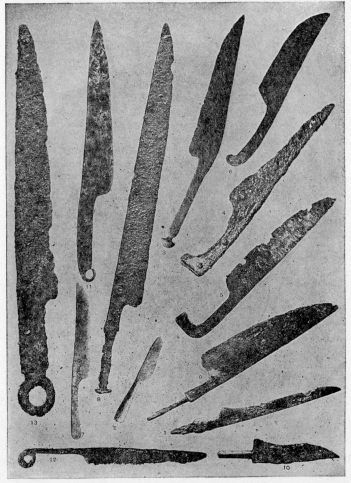

FIG. 146.—Knives of various shapes and sizes. The largest are 16 inches long. One-fourth natural size. Lake Neuchatel, Switzerland. After Vouga. Reduced in size.

sharp points, was an article of commerce. The Kelts in Gaul and the Rhine districts were masters of the art of mining.

Salt was obtained from a large number of places and a network of "salt routes" was established. Instead of an apparatus made of pottery bars such as was used in the first Age of Iron, earthenware jars and wooden containers were employed for the evaporation of the salt water.

Games of chance were probably as popular then as now as is shown by the occurrence of dice and counters made of bronze, bone, pottery, and stone.

Pottery. The ceramics of La Tene times, for the most part, is superior to that which preceded it (Plate V). The pottery is, in general, made of a fine paste and is smooth and with little or no ornamentation (Fig. 147). The technical excellence was in

1   2

Fig. 147.—Photographs of (1) a jar made in imitation of an iron pot. It contained burnt bones, an iron buckle, knife, lancehead, and strike-a-light. From Germany. (2) A jar made in imitation of bronze, Rhineland. Both photographs are reproduced by courtesy of the Berlin Museum of Ethnology.

large part due to the introduction of the potter's wheel, which enabled the potter to make with ease perfectly symmetrical shapes, as well as vases with hollow bases. With the exception of flagons (œnochoe), few of the vessels had handles. All sizes were made, from small goblets to storage jars. The artistic forms of many of the vases were due to the fact that they were made in imitation of bronze vessels (Fig. 147). The vessels of the common people, however, continued to be made by hand and of coarse materials. The poor probably were unable to buy the machine-made ware and continued to use the technique of ancient times.

Although, as has been stated, La Tene ware was generally

without ornamentation (the pottery discovered at the station of La Tene, for example, is plain), some clay objects were embellished. In the early days of the period the brush was occasionally used to make the La Tene scroll. In England, the scroll was sometimes engraved and stamped. Geometrical designs recalling those of the Hallstatt were sometimes employed.

At the beginning of the period the shapes and ornamentation varied from place to place and there was, consequently, a considerable diversity of types. Evidently trade in pottery was not important then. As time went on, regional differences became less and less marked until, toward the close of the period, many identical forms were made from France to Czechoslovakia. If we may judge from this, international trade in the modern sense began at this time.

The abundance of pottery in some graves and grave trenches of the Early La Tene should be mentioned. In the Marne district, France, graves have been opened in which pottery was scattered over the corpse from head to foot or was grouped about the head. In a chariot burial (Chalons sur Marne) at least fifteen vessels were found. The burials in later times, however, are poor in pottery.

Clothing. The characteristic clothing of the wealthier Gauls and Germans was a woollen mantle, heavy for winter and light for summer, fastened in front with a fibula, long, close-fitting trousers held up by a leather belt, and shoes of leather or cloth, as in the Middle Ages, which were fastened to the trousers. The upper part of the body was clothed with a sleeved tunic or shirt. The cloth of the mantles was dyed in bright colours and, according to Pliny, was woven in plaids, like that of the Scotch Highlanders.

The dress of the women varied according to their station in life. The Gallic gentlewomen early adopted Greco-Roman styles; the German women wore a dress which exposed half of the breasts. The dress of the poorer women was much like that of the men and consisted of shirt and trousers. The fact that some female skeletons had bracelets above the elbows (Early La Tene) indicates that the sleeves were short. It is rather remarkable that although the clothing of the Bronze Age—many centuries earlier—has been preserved, no La Tene clothing has survived. It is known, however, that some of the richest clothing was embroidered with gold. The Gallic women used a great deal of rich jewellery.

ORNAMENTS

Torques. When the Keltic tribes first came in contact with the Romans the torque or metal neck ring of gold, bronze, or iron, was so generally worn that it came to be regarded as their characteristic ornament (Fig. 148). This singular decoration, in essentially the same form, continued in use from the third century before Christ to the tenth century of the present era.

At the beginning of La Tene times, the torques were, in general, worn only by the women. About the third century B.C. they became a part of the male attire and were worn as marks of rank or honour. After its adoption by the men, the torque was seldom, if ever, worn by the women. It is known that the torque had reached the west as early as 361 B.C., for in that year Titus Manlius placed the torque of a gigantic Gaul, whom he had slain, about his neck, and thus acquired the cognomen Torquatus.

In the early forms in Europe as well as in the late forms in Britain, the torques terminated in ornamental knobs, some of which were beautifully decorated; in many later forms the ends were hooked together. A number of types were made (Fig. 148); some were made of two strands of twisted metal (it was from this form that the name torque, or twisted, was derived); some were formed of hollow rods; some consisted of a plain rod with the ends joined by a hook or rivet; and some had no opening. Some were richly engraved and some of the later ones were decorated with red coral or enamel. Beads and amulets were sometimes strung on them.

Herodian, writing about 238 A.D., stated that the Northern

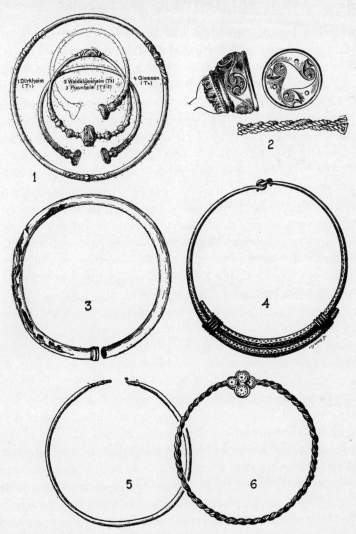

FIG. 148.—(1) Torques or neck rings ornamented with the Keltic scroll. In the early part of the period they were worn only by the women or rarely by the men. After Schumacher. (2) Portions of a beautifully moulded and engraved gold torque from England of late British development. Courtesy of the Trustees of the British Museum. (3) Tubular bronze torque without ornamentation (Alsace). After Ring. (4) Gold Scandinavian torque. After Gustafson. (5) Bronze torque of thin wire. The terminals are fastened with a catch (Marne). After Moreau. (6) Bronze torque of twisted metal (Marne). After de Baye.

321

tribes of Britain adorned their flanks and necks with iron, considering it an ornament and sign of wealth as other barbarians did gold.[5]

Fibulæ. Fibulæ (Fig. 149) were generally worn by both men and women to fasten their clothing and, as they were conspicuous objects, they are among the most artistic creations of the craftsmen. In Germany many of the fibulæ were strung with rings, and amber, and glass beads. The same type of fibula was used over wide areas with but slight variations

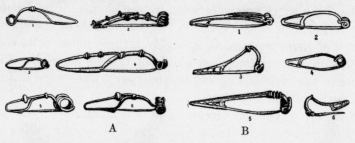

A   B

FIG. 149.—A. Bronze fibulæ from the middle of the period (La Tene II). (1) from Switzerland; (2) Baden; (3) Marne; (4) Sweden; (5) Switzerland; (6) France. After Déchelette. Much reduced.

B. Fibulæ from the Late La Tene (La Tene III). (1) and (2) from Stradonitz; (3) Carinthia; (4) Carthage; (5) Italy; (6) Germany. After Déchelette. Much reduced.

and new styles spread rapidly. Consequently, a study of these ornaments affords a ready means of dating objects found with them.

Bracelets. Bracelets have always been favourite ornaments for women and, until recently, of men as well. The goldsmiths and bronze workers of La Tene times did their best to satisfy the vanity of their patrons and produced delicate and artistic objects. A number of materials were utilised such as gold, silver, bronze, iron, jet, lignite, glass, and amber. In the graves of a few Keltic warriors of high rank bracelets—probably insignia of rank—have been found but, with rare exceptions,

[5] Read and Smith: "A Guide to the Antiquities of the Iron Age;" British Museum.

these ornaments were characteristically feminine adornments.

Finger-rings. Finger-rings of gold, silver, bronze, and iron were worn by men and women. The models differed considerably from time to time. The later ones especially show the effects of Greek and Italian influence.

Earrings. Earrings were worn by both the Germanic tribes and the Gauls. Some of them show a Greco-Roman influence but others are of native origin and are modifications of Hallstatt models.

Belts. Bronze chain belts with pendants were very popular in La Tene times and were worn by the women, from France to Czechoslovakia and Italy, in the second half of the epoch. Many of them were made of highly artistic links. Belts covered with thin, ornamented plates of bronze, somewhat like those of the Hallstatt epoch, but narrower, were worn during the early part of the period.

A grave at Dühren, Germany, affords an excellent example of the jewelry worn by a Gallic woman of the ruling or wealthy class who lived at the end of the second century before the Christian era.[6] It contained not less than seven fibulæ of gold, silver, bronze, and coral, an earring and finger-ring of gold, a necklace of amber, jet, and glass beads with pendants of bronze, four pressed glass bracelets, numerous ornamental pieces of bronze and bone, two bronze mirrors, an iron knife, shears, etc. These are not only the pious grave offerings of those left behind, but, according to other evidence, they are the ornaments and toilet articles used by the dead herself, just as the kettles, pans, bronze pitcher, and earthen pots give an accurate picture of the equipment of the kitchen.

Toilet Articles. The most conspicuous toilet article of the women was the bronze mirror, highly polished on one side for reflection and generally decorated on the other (Fig. 150). These mirrors came into use near the end of the period under discussion after a knowledge of them had penetrated from

[6] Karl Schumacher: "Siedelungs- und Kulturgeschichte der Rheinlande," p. 161.

Fig. 150.—One of the finest bronze mirrors yet discovered. The reflecting surface is of kidney form with its greatest diameter ten and one-quarter inches. It has a handle six inches long. On the back eccentric scrolls of La Tene design are engraved with a basket weave filling.

Courtesy of the Trustees of the British Museum.

the South. More common are the small toilet implements made of bronze and iron, such as tweezers for pulling out hairs. Some of these are miniature works of art remarkable for the delicacy of their ornamentation and workmanship. They are found more often in women's graves than in men's.

Other small implements such as scratchers and earspoons were more rarely used. Sets consisting of a tweezer, scratcher and earspoon, fastened to a ring or fibula, are sometimes found.

In the La Tene Epoch, iron razors were the rule. Some have the semicircular shape of those of the preceding epoch but most of them are more knifelike in form.

Fig. 151.—(2) Palmette from a Greek vase, and (1) details of a La Tene torque from Waldalgesheim, Germany. The palmette is thought by some authorities to have been the inspiration of the Keltic scroll and to have given rise to such designs as that shown in (1). On the top of this first figure is a leaf springing from the wedge which fills the angle of the volutes.

Courtesy of the Trustees of the British Museum.

Scissors or shears appear about the middle of the epoch and are found only in men's graves, often in association with swords and javelins, and with a razor or knife.

La Tene Decoration. The saying that La Tene artists would never use a straight line if a curved one was possible may not be literally true, but it emphasises the most characteristic feature of Keltic art; scrolls (Fig. 151), S-shaped figures, triskeles, palmettes and other curvilinear designs. A remarkable peculiarity of Keltic art is the rarity of human and animal forms. As many situlæ and other imported

bronzes were richly embellished with animal and human figures, the possibility that the absence of such figures was due
to some religious prohibition must not be disregarded. If no
such prejudice existed such representations would surely have
been made.

The beauty of the La Tene designs and the skill necessary
to produce them compare favourably with the best in Greek
and Roman art. This is well seen in a study of the shields,
scabbards, torques, pottery, fibulæ, mirrors, and other objects.
The ornamentation on some of the shields (Plate IV) and
scabbards is exquisite.

Curvilinear designs, however, were not used to the exclusion of geometric patterns. On carinate vases, for example,
curved lines were rarely used. However, La Tene pottery was,
in general, without decoration.

It is generally held that Keltic art was not created *de novo*
but that the graceful ornamentation which is so characteristic
was derived from the Greek palmette (see Fig. 151), not
from the whole palmette but from the curved lines at its
base. Simplified palmettes were also used but they did not
greatly influence Keltic art, and when used they are more
often a flowerlike figure of three petals which resembles the
fleur-de-lys. The artist seems to have been fascinated by the
scrolls of the palmette which he saw on the bronzes imported
from the South. With this beginning, he created the many
curvilinear designs with which he decorated his ornaments,
weapons, and other objects. He soon departed from the Greek
originals so far that it is difficult to trace any relation between
the two. In this sense, the Kelts created a new art.

The scroll designs were not only engraved but, where
possible, were cut in openwork designs in bronze. Toward the
close of the period, enamel was used in decoration, especially
in Britain. The life-giving coral was also set into ornaments.

The La Tene artistic influence (or Late Keltic as it is
called in Great Britain) lasted long in parts of Great Britain
and Ireland, and it was here that Keltic art reached its high-

est perfection. Long after the passing of the La Tene, scroll work continued to be used and reached its culmination in such illuminated manuscripts as the Book of Kells of the seventh century. In these manuscripts the interlaced ribbons, intricate knots, spirals and zigzag patterns, and entangled zoomorphic figures are examples of this art brought to the highest pitch of perfection.

"The artistic handwork of the La Tene with its exuberant and graceful ornaments, its love of costly materials and lively

Fig. 152.—The Kelts did not invent money but used and copied that of the Greeks and Romans. As a result of frequent copying, the coins departed more and more from the original designs until the later ones bore little or no resemblance to the Greek originals. This is well shown in this series. After R. Farrer.

colours (coral, enamel, coloured beads) as well as for artistic openwork metal objects, and with its inclination towards the stylising and conventionalising of organic forms—plant, animal, and human—is quite a new manifestation and by no means a short, half-barbaric prelude to provincial Roman artistic activity in the North."

Money. Until La Tene times trade was carried on by barter, but the Kelts early learned from the Greeks the importance of metallic money and soon made coins of their own. They first used Greek coins which probably came to

them by way of the Greek colony at Marseilles, but it was
not long before they were making gold and silver coins after
these models. As a result of frequent copyings the figures
and designs on the later coins (Fig. 152) came to have little
resemblance to the originals. The diesinkers may have used
worn coins for models and, being unfamiliar with the costumes
and customs portrayed, misunderstood some of the details.
This is well shown in the Gallic copies of the gold stater of
Philip II of Macedon which had on the obverse the head of
Apollo and on the reverse a chariot drawn by two horses and
the name of Philip. The first imitations quite faithfully repro-

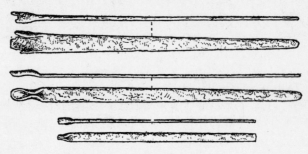

Fig. 153.—Iron currency bars. The units are 1, 2 and 4. After B. Farrer.

duced the design but the legend degenerated into a sort of
fret pattern which had somewhat the appearance of the
Greek letters. Later copies show the hair and laurel wreath
of the Apollo exaggerated to such an extent that the head has
the appearance of a Medusa. One horse with a human head
often replaces the two-horse chariot of the Greek coin and
the chariot itself is represented by a single wheel beneath
the horse. Later diesinkers departed still further from the
original: the charioteer is represented by dots and the horse
is hardly recognizable. In still later coins a vivid imagination
is required to detect a resemblance to the original model.

Many types of coins were made during this period. With
the spread of Roman influence new styles were introduced.

In addition to gold and silver, bronze, tin, an alloy of copper, zinc, lead, and tin, and one of one-fifth silver and four-fifths copper were used.

The Britains also used for money flat bars with rudely shaped handles (Fig. 153), which were graduated according to weight. No less than six denominations have been found of which the unit is 4777 grains or eleven ounces. The more common bar is the double unit or twenty-two ounces.

Trade and Commerce. The Rhone Valley route (Fig. 117, p. 258) carried on a considerable commerce in bronze objects, wine and oil in earthen jars (amphoræ), ornaments, glass, coral, etc. The quantities of fragments of wine and oil amphoræ in France, Switzerland, and the Rhineland, show the importance of the commerce in these two commodities. What constituted the return cargoes of the southern traders is not definitely known. In addition to metals, such as gold and bronze, food stuffs, skins, and salted meats may have been carried to the South. Diodorus, who lived in the first century of our era, that is, while Great Britain and Ireland were still in the La Tene epoch, probably gives a true picture when he says: "Traders buy tin from the natives (of England) and bring it to Gaul. Then it is carried by horses in about thirty days to the mouth of the Rhone."

Due to the trade in amber, salt, iron, and bronze in the Hallstatt epoch a network of communications had been developed (Fig. 117, p. 258) and, although the relative importance of the routes changed from time to time, they continued to be travelled throughout the La Tene.

The uniformity of the manufactured products over a wide region, from France to Czechoslovakia, and the mass production of pottery as well as metal objects in centres of industry, shows that the way for trade in the modern sense was well broken.

Druidism. The principal religion of the Kelts, and the chief underlying force at the time of the conquest of Gaul, was Druidism. The belief in the transmigration of the soul, and the practice of human sacrifice, usually of criminals, appear to have been prominent features of this religious cult. By means of the doctrine of the transmigration of the soul, the priests taught the warriors to hold death in contempt. The power of the Druids in temporal affairs came from the fact that while acting as arbiters and judges in disputes of every kind, they were enabled to enforce their decisions by the threat of excommunication which carried with it exclusion from citizenship as well as religious privileges. Writing was probably discouraged because of the insistence of the Druids that their body of doctrine should be transmitted by memory. As the priests were the intellectual leaders of the people their practice in this respect must have discouraged literary effort. Notwithstanding this opposition, however, the Kelts used writing for ordinary purposes.

Religion. The Kelts and Germans worshipped natural objects and forces such as the sun, moon, and stars, fire, plants, animals, and springs and brooks. Our knowledge of their religious ideas is confined to those which they possessed after they had come under Roman influence, and consequently the purely Keltic and Germanic gods are vague and ill-defined. We find a curious mixture of Northern and Southern religious ideas. The Northern ideas had an influence on the imported Roman ones and some of the Latin gods, Mercury, for example, absorbed the attributes and characteristics of several Gallic deities.

A few crude statues of Gallic gods have been preserved. Among their native divinities is "Sucellus," the god with the mallet: a bearded god, dressed in a tunic, who holds a vase in one hand and a long staff surmounted by a mallet in the other. He may have been the god of conviviality, for on several monuments a cask is shown at his feet. A triad of female deities seems also to have been an object of worship. In Germany, they are generally represented as seated and clothed in voluminous mantles and turbanlike head-dresses. They hold on their knees baskets heavily laden with fruit and sometimes a nursing baby. They would therefore seem to have been goddesses of fecundity or fertility. This is further indicated by a Gallic statue in which one figure has a double row of nipples. The Kelts and Germans probably considered them as divinities of the lower world, guardian goddesses of the towns, villages, and country, and perhaps the special protectors of women.

Belief in the power of amulets passed down through the ages to the Ages of Iron, and is astonishingly prevalent among the peoples of the world to-day. In addition to traditional objects, such as the canine teeth of strong carnivorous animals and boars, other objects were worn as a protection against the "evil eye," bad luck, sickness, etc. This is well shown in a necklace found in a tomb at Voulles (Marne), France, which should have protected the wearer against all evils if charms were efficient. This necklace was made of a hundred coral beads, an amber bead, a shell, a clay spindle whorl, a tooth of a wild boar, and a piece of human bone. Other objects of prophylactic or remedial value were human figures and parts of the human body, such as the foot. Figurines of the wild boar, horse, ox, and sheep have been found. The use of amulet axes continued from the Bronze Age. Whether this shows that the cult of the ax persisted, or that the original significance had long been forgotten and the axes were worn merely for traditional reasons, is not known.

A new material for amulets was glass, and a favorite charm against evil was a human face with large eyes.

Sepultures. Both inhumation and incineration were practiced in different places and at different times in the same region. The Germanic tribes, inhabitants of what is now North Germany, burned their dead throughout the period. The Keltic peoples buried their dead unburnt until the later part of the period (La Tene III), when the practice of incineration was introduced by invading Germanic tribes from the North and by the Romans from the South. In Central Germany, which was the boundary between the Kelts and the

Germans, the burial rites changed from time to time as one or the other of these peoples had temporary possession.

During the Early and Middle La Tene, the Kelts generally buried their dead in flat graves, that is, in the earth without conspicuous mounds or tumuli. The tombs are generally in cemetery-like groups. Tumuli were, however, raised for the dead in some Keltic regions. This is especially true of Southern Germany and Eastern Gaul, that is, in those regions where the traditions of the Hallstatt were firmly implanted. These tumular graves occupy an area which extends from Northern France through Southern Germany to Southwestern Czechoslovakia.

Exceptionally fine examples of La Tene tumuli have been discovered in the Rhineland where members of the ruling class—men and women—were buried with great care and with all their worldly goods and ornaments, and with the foods which they might require in order to occupy the same social station after death that they had enjoyed in this world. With them were buried a rich array of objects, and over the wooden or stone coffin was erected a large tumulus, some as much as 200 feet long, and eighteen or twenty feet high. The equipment of the men's graves consisted of weapons, sometimes with the long sword, but more often with the short slashing sword, beautifully decorated daggers, their war chariots, horse harness, etc. In addition to the equipment of the warrior, there were table utensils such as bronze and pottery vessels, Etruscan jars, Greek painted bowls, and bronze goblets. In a bronze vessel (stamnos) at Weisskirchen there is still the remains of white pitch, a favourite condiment for the wine of the ancients.

The women's graves (p. 323) contained rich ornaments of gold and bronze, some with coral inlay; fibulæ, disk-shaped ornaments, girdles, toilet articles, and mirrors (see also page 324).

These South German tumuli are on small elevations in the midst of broad, fertile plains or in regions which could support a large population. This would seem to indicate that these lands were great estates which belonged at one time to the occupants of the tumuli.

In many of the German incineration burials the swords are bent or broken intentionally. They may have been destroyed in order to "kill" the weapons so that they could be used by the spirit of the owner in the spirit world. There are, however, two other possibilities: they may have been bent in order to place them more easily in the sepulchral urn, or in order to render them useless to grave robbers.

In the Marne district of France a number of burials have been discovered in which the warrior was buried with his chariot and rich equipment. One of the richest of these chariot burials is that of La Gorge Meillet (Somme, Tourbe, Marne) which is now on exhibition in the museum of St. Germain-en-Laye. "The warrior lies between two iron tires and bronze axle trees; at his left side are iron spearheads, and an iron sword, and on his left arm is a gold bracelet; on his right side lay a knife with bronze blade and bone handle, and three vessels, one of which contained bones of animals, and egg shells. On his chest were four bronze buttons, and near his mouth a bronze fibula which no doubt fastened his cloak. Near his feet was a pointed helmet, rings, and iron disks. Beyond these were two horse bits, several buttons with heads of coral, two bronze ornaments in the shape of a cross ornamented with coral, and each provided with a fine chain for suspension. Between these objects and the body was a bronze vessel of the shape called by the Greeks œnochoë, which enables the date of the burial to be fixed at about the fourth century B.C. Another chariot burial, particularly rich in objects of the Iron Age (Fig. 154) was discovered at Somme Bionne, in the same department The horse trappings found here show beautiful open curvilinear bronze work exemplifying the art of this period, though the scroll designs are not so marked and characteristic as those of the Late Keltic period in Britain. Among the objects found with this interment was a dish with red

Fig. 154.—Plan of a chariot burial, Somme Bionne, Marne, France. The grave contained only one body, laid between the two wheels of a chariot. Another trench contained bridle bits and other trappings for two horses. The flagon (Œnochoe) at the right, the kylix (a flat drinking cup with two handles) and a much damaged third vessel of Keltic workmanship are seen near the feet. On the warrior's left are three iron spits, and a knife. On the right there is a long sword. A gold finger ring is shown.

Courtesy of the Trustees of the British Museum.

figures on a black ground, the Greek kylix, referable to the fifth or fourth century B.C., and thus affording evidence of the date of burial." [7]

THE CONTRIBUTIONS OF THE LA TENE TO CIVILISATION

The Keltic conquests had an important effect on the civilisation of Central and Northern Europe. In the Hallstatt, people had settled down to life in their communities and, in general, seem to have been contented with their lot. The La Tene brought about great changes. No longer were there isolated communities where bronze was used in preference to iron; no longer was free-hand work universal in pottery making; no longer were people content without writing; no longer were they willing to barter their products, but they demanded money; wooden plows did not satisfy them, but they had to have iron plowshares; no longer were they content with the old way of grinding grain, but used rotating hand mills. They increased the variety of their tools, invented new ones, and improved others until by the middle of the period the carpenter was well equipped and could, with patience, do nearly as good hand work as the modern wood worker. The Keltic industries flourished in well-fortified cities, and commerce, in the modern sense, had arisen.

The isolation of the North ended with the Roman conquest, except in distant regions, such as Ireland and parts of Britain. From the beginning of the La Tene until the present, uniformity has more and more replaced diversity of customs and dress and the peoples of the world are becoming more and more alike.

[7] E. A. Parkyn: "Prehistoric Art," pp. 272-274.

CHAPTER X

IN RETROSPECT

CIVILISATION is primarily the result of man's strivings for a constant supply of food; for protection against danger, human or other; for shelter; and for mating. In his million years' struggle, man slowly ameliorated the hard conditions under which he lived: he found means of reducing the horrors of famine; of lessening the discomfort of cold by making better garments; of sheltering himself in storm and winter in better habitations; of securing more adequate protection from human enemies and wild beasts. As an indirect result of these endeavours, religion and government arose.

The Paleolithic hunter depended chiefly on the chase for food and upon the nuts, wild fruits and herbs he could gather. He was a food gatherer, not a food producer. He depended entirely upon the bounty of nature. Lucretius (99-55 B.C.?) shows a remarkable insight into the life, habits and characteristics of primitive man but he paints too rosy a picture:

"The men that lived unhous'd in those far days
Were hardier, as beseemed an earthborn race.
Their bones were big and solid, and their thews
Knit in a sturdy frame. Nor heat nor cold
Could quickly weaken them, nor roughest fare,
Nor bodily disease; but like the beasts
They lived and roamed at large, and many suns
Passed over them. They had no skill, though strong,
To guide the plough, no use of iron tools
To work the land: saplings they planted none,
Nor used the hook to lop the antlered boughs
From lofty trees. What sun and rain might give,

And what the earth brought forth untill'd, were gifts
To satisfy their hearts. And thus they lived,
On acorns maybe, or on wilding fruits:
Those red-ripe berries of the winter time
Were more abundant then and larger too;
Their world was young and fertile, and brought forth
Enough hard fare to rear a suffering race." [1]

When the animals on which the men of the Old Stone Age fed were scarce, because of unfavourable climatic conditions, or because of disease, these ancestors of ours starved and they saw their women and children die for want of food. Few of the many children who were born to them grew to maturity as is shown by the sparse population of Europe in the Paleolithic, a population which probably consisted of not more than a few thousand souls. Moreover, man's life was short in those days and anyone who attained an age of forty or forty-five was very old.

To secure food and to protect himself from his enemies stimulated man to invent new tools and weapons. But at all times his progress was retarded by the restraints of tradition. It is for this reason perhaps that the hand-ax or *coup de poing* was used for tens of thousands of years. Nevertheless, in the process of time, more and more tools appeared but the variety in the Paleolithic was never large. After the Paleolithic new and better tools were made of flint, bone, and stone, a better technique of stone working was devised, and man finally ground and polished many of his stone implements.

The struggle for food eventually led to the invention of agriculture and the domestication of wild animals, and ushered in the Neolithic, that greatest of all ages in man's upward progress from savagery. With the invention of agriculture and the domestication of animals, one invention suggested another and stimulated man to new thought and energy unparalleled in his history. Although from necessity he made

[1] Lucretius V, 925-944. Translated by Denis Turner, *The Spectator*.

most of his clothing from skins, his active mind suggested that cloth could be made from wool and vegetable fibres and he invented the loom. The same inquiring attitude of mind led to the invention of methods of making pottery.

It was not until man had learned how to control fire and to make pottery that the invention of a method of smelting ores of copper, and of alloying copper with tin to make bronze became possible. The use of bronze, directly and indirectly, had an important influence in changing man's habits, in increasing his comfort, and in broadening his intellectual horizon. The sharper metal tools enabled him to prepare larger areas for cultivation and thus to push famine farther away. Metal weapons enabled him better to protect himself against enemies; gleaming metal ornaments gave him an opportunity better to satisfy his æsthetic longings. The desire for copper, bronze, and amber led to trade and thus to intercourse with other peoples and other civilisations. No longer was his knowledge confined to one cultural circle. The trader not only brought new tools, new weapons, and new ornaments, but new ideas as well, and man, for the first time in his history, began to be cosmopolitan. Ideas were spread in still another way, for with metal weapons organised warfare came into being. When bronze was in general use those tribes or villages which had a goodly supply of the superior metal weapons could not resist the temptation to despoil their less well-equipped neighbours. It was not, however, until the more abundant and better iron was adopted that ambitious leaders carried on war on a large scale. It was then that war parties conquered Mycenæ and other Ægean cities, destroyed them and their interesting civilisations, and replaced them with inferior cultures.

One of the greatest stimuli to progress in the past has been the leisure which a constant food supply gave. In early times such leisure was enjoyed by the few who thus had the opportunity to satisfy their desire to improve the condition of their families and themselves and to gratify their vanity by utilising the manual dexterity, and inventiveness of less fortunate persons to carry out their plans. They were thus enabled to design and make better and more artistic tools, to make better houses and household furniture, to make finer cloth for clothing, to make more artistic ornaments and, finally, to make the best equipment for war that could then be devised.

Attention has been called to the probability that agriculture was invented in an irrigable region and it was pointed out that the Valley of the Nile seems to afford more favourable conditions for this invention than any other region except that of Peru in South America.

As soon as man found it necessary to have permanent houses and to live in communities, a government of some kind became essential. This was especially true in regions depending upon irrigation, since water had to be distributed to many families. Not only this but channels and reservoirs for the water had to be prepared before the time of the rise of the river. As an outcome of this need, a means of counting time was of the utmost importance. "The Egyptians had at an early date elaborated a calendar for this purpose, and thereby had performed a very great service to mankind. It is in connection with the elaboration of a calendar, a work demanding great ability, that, . . . the kinship came into being.

"Whatever opinion be held with regard to this view of the origin of ruling families, there is no doubt that the earliest rulers were intimately concerned with the life of the community, and that they performed functions that, in the opinion of their subjects, were of direct importance to the welfare of the whole community. The whole of the ceremonial that was supposed to assure the growth of crops, the fertility of animals, and so on, was in their hands, and their chief function was, in the beginning, centered round such matters.

"In the course of time the ruling group began to constitute a definite class, distinct from the rest of the community.

A vested interest arose, and, as in the case of every such vested interest, it began to consolidate its own position and to acquire power for itself. The class system soon emerged. Thus we find in Egypt, by the time of the Fifth Dynasty, the rulers had so far distinguished themselves from the commoners that they had come to claim divine birth: they were the Sons of the Sun, they were mummified at death, while their subjects, with the exception of some favoured nobles, were buried in the ordinary way. The kings went, after death, to the sky, while their subjects went underground. In these and in many other ways did they mark themselves off from the rest of the community." [2]

It is difficult to evaluate the religion of Paleolithic man. Man at that time was full of the fear of natural forces, and of superstitions. The priests, or sorcerers, or "medicine men" worked upon this fear in order to gain power. The saving fact was that the priest must use his arts to prevent famine and disaster. If he failed, his power over the people disappeared or was lessened. The realistic cave art of the Upper Paleolithic seems certainly to have been created by sorcerers who believed in sympathetic magic. Later, after the adoption of agriculture, elaborate festivals and ceremonies designed to increase the yield of grain and the fertility of the flocks and herds were evolved. These festivals, under other names and with an entirely different significance, are celebrated to-day. The Early Christians at Rome modified the pagan springtime festivals, for instance, which in turn had had a beginning in the prehistoric past.

The result of man's struggles has been what we term civilisation. Is it an advantage or disadvantage?

There is no evidence that civilisation is producing a race with greater mentality. As far as one can judge from their works, no men with greater intelligence than those of Ancient Greece are living now,—and these men were working and teaching when the Kelts were conquering and spreading over

[2] W. J. Perry: "The Growth of Civilization," pp. 183 and 184-185.

Central Europe, and when a large part of the population of Great Britain and Ireland was in a state of savagery. Indeed, it is probable that never before has the majority of the population of the world needed so little brain in order to secure food, shelter, protection, and to mate. One anthropologist [3] goes so far as to state as his opinion that modern man does not use more than one-tenth of his brain power.

Unwise philanthropy is preventing the operation of natural selection—the elimination of the unfit—and it is possible that, for this reason, civilisation may be causing the physical and mental degeneration of the human race. This tendency is hastened by the too-large families of the unfit, and the too-small families of the able and industrious. A remedy for this unfortunate condition is not impossible and will doubtless be found.

One great benefit of modern civilisation, due indirectly to transportation and the interchange of ideas, is its effect on the religions of the world. Mankind has suffered sorely from dogmas. For ages his fears of present and future punishment have been worked upon in order to induce him to give a large part of the products of his labour to the Church. His days and nights have been filled with unreal dangers and his death has been made unhappy by the fear of a dreadful future. However, the worst in religion is slowly disappearing and the best of different religions is being adopted more rapidly than ever before in the history of the world.

We can probably learn a great deal about the life of the people of prehistoric times by a study of the life of the common people of 1000 A.D., that is, before modern commerce and trade were well developed.

"A village tried to produce everything it wanted, to be free of the uncertainty and expense of trade. We find, then, that almost all of the people of a village were agriculturists, and these raised the necessary food supply by methods which were always crude, and were very often cumbersome and

[3] Sir Arthur Keith.

wasteful. The stock was of such a poor breed that a grown ox seems to have been little larger than a calf of the present day, and the fleece of a sheep weighed often less than two ounces. Many of the stock had to be killed before winter, as there was no proper fodder to keep them, and those that survived were often so weak in the spring that they had to be dragged to pasture on a sledge. Insufficient stock meant insufficient manure, and although the fields were allowed to lie fallow every third year they were exhausted by the constant crop of cereals, and gave a yield of only about six bushels of wheat an acre, of which two had to be retained for seed. . . . Nearly every year was marked by famine in one part or another of the country, and famine was often followed by pestilence. Diseases now almost unknown to the civilised world, like leprosy and ergotism or St. Anthony's fire, were not infrequent. The food at best was coarse and monotonous; the houses were mere hovels of boughs and mud; the clothes were a few garments of rude stuff. Nothing better could be procured so long as everything had to be produced on the spot and made ready for use by the people themselves. Finally, these people were coarse and ignorant, with little regard for personal cleanliness or moral laws, and with practically no interests outside the narrow bounds of the village in which they lived. So we read of kings and princes being always on the road, travelling with court and retinue from one manor to another, eating up the surplus that had accumulated and then moving on." [4]

The greatest advantages of civilisation are those for which man has struggled so long. Never before has he been so free from the terrors of starvation and of cold. Modern slums and the horrors of modern warfare are less dreadful than the despairing poverty of the poor of Europe prior to the nineteenth century. The fear of the unknown which was ever present in primitive times, is disappearing with the increase of knowledge. If the happy man is the "man who has inter-

[4] Clive Day: "A History of Commerce," 1907, pp. 35-37.

esting thoughts," the applied sciences have been a great blessing to mankind.

If we term that civilisation modern which has been developed since the beginning of the Christian Era and compare it with the prehistoric civilisations of Europe, we find that the fundamental inventions were made by our prehistoric forebears. Our modern inventions—printing, electricity and its manifold applications, the steam and internal combustion engines, the telegraph and telephone, wireless telegraphy, etc., etc.—while not fundamental in the sense that those of the Neolithic were, have nevertheless enormously increased man's ability to secure greater results for his labour, that is more and better food, more and better clothing, better protection from the weather and from despoilers, and more leisure. In addition to these advantages they have increased man's pleasures, have embroidered the mantle of civilisation, and have thus made life less drab and much more interesting.

BIBLIOGRAPHY

The references included in this bibliography have been selected for the general reader. References to periodicals have been excluded except such as are especially helpful or such as contain important material not to be found in more general works. A list of the more important journals dealing with prehistory is at the end of this appendix.

GENERAL

AVEBURY, LORD (Sir John Lubbock), Prehistoric Times. 7th ed. London, 1913.

BEHN, F., Das Haus in vorrömischer Zeit. 1922; Das deutsche Bauernhaus. 1922; Hausurnen. *Vorgeschichtliche Forschungen.* I. 1924.

BROOKS, C. E. P., The Evolution of Climate. London, 1922; Climate Through the Ages. London, 1926.

BURY, J. B., The Cambridge Ancient History. 2nd ed. 1924.

CHILDE, V. Gordon, The Dawn of European Civilization. London, 1925. An excellent book dealing mainly with the Neolithic but including the Epipaleolithic and Bronze Ages. It assumes that the reader has already a knowledge of the subject.

CRAWFORD, O. G. S., Man and his Past. Oxford, 1921.

DAWKINS, W. BOYD, Early Man in Britain. London, 1880.

DÉCHELETTE, J., Manuel d'Archéologie. 3 parts. Paris, 1908, etc. This is still a standard work on the subject. It is especially valuable on the Bronze, Hallstatt, and La Tene Ages.

EBERT, MAX, (Ed.) Reallexikon der Vorgeschichte. Berlin, 1924, etc. This encyclopedia on Prehistory which is in the process of publication promises to be one of the best reference works on the subject. The various articles are written by leading prehistorians, are up-to-date and give excellent bibliographies. The illustrations are abundant and well chosen.

FRAZER, J. G., The Golden Bough. A Study in Magic and Religion. 2nd ed. London, 1900.

GRENIER, A., Habitations gauloises, 1906.

344

HOERNES, M.-MENGHIN, O., Urgeschichte der bildenden Kunst in Europa. Vienna, 1925.

HOERNES, MORITZ, Natur- und Urgeschichte des Menschen. Vienna & Leipzig. 2 vols. 1909.

HOOPS, J., Reallexikon der germanische Altertumskunde. Strassburg, 1911-19.

KOSSINNA, GUSTAF, Die deutsche Vorgeschichte. *Mannus-Bibliothek*. No. 9. 1912; (Ed.) *Mannus-Bibliothek*. Würzburg, 1911-etc. A collection of articles on prehistoric subjects by leading prehistorians.

MACALISTER, R. A. S., Ireland in Pre-Celtic Times. Dublin, 1921; The Archæology of Ireland. London, 1928.

MACCURDY, GEORGE GRANT, Human Origins. New York, 2 vols. 1924.

MACKENZIE, D. A., Ancient Man in Britain. London, 1922.

MORGAN, JACQUES DE, Prehistoric Man. A General Outline of Prehistory. Trans. by J. H. Paxton and V. C. C. Collum, New York, 1924.

MOSSO, SEN. ANGELO, The Dawn of Mediterranean Civilization. Trans. by M. C. Harrison, London, Leipzig, 1910.

PARKYN, ERNEST A., Prehistoric Art. London, 1915.

PEAKE, HAROLD, AND FLEURE, HERBERT JOHN, Volumes I-IV, *The Corridors of Time*. New Haven, 1927.

PERRY, W. J., The Growth of Civilization. London, 1924; Children of the Sun. 2nd ed. London, 1927; The Origin of Magic and Religion. London, 1923. These three books by Mr. Perry contain some very suggestive theories for the Neolithic and Bronze Ages.

REINACH, S., Repértoire de l'art quaternaire. Paris, 1913.

SCHUCHHARDT, CARL, Alteuropa in seiner Kultur- und Stilentwicklung. Strassburg and Berlin. 1919.

SCHUMACHER, KARL, Siedelungs- und Kulturgeschichte der Rheinlande von der Urzeit bis in das Mittelalter. vol. I. Mainz, 1921. Although this work is concerned chiefly with the Rhine district, it contains much excellent material on the general subject of Prehistory. The chapters on the Bronze and Iron Ages are especially good.

SOLLAS, W. J., Ancient Hunters. 3rd ed. New York, 1924.

VULLIAMY, C. E., Our Prehistoric Forerunners. London, 1925.

WILKE, GEORG, Die Religion der Indogermanen in archaeologischer Beleuchtung. *Mannus-Bibliothek*. 1923.

WINDLE, B. C. A., Remains of the Prehistoric Age in England. 2nd ed. 1909.

WINTER, F., Die Kämme aller Zeiten von der Steinzeit bis zur Gegenwart. 1906.

The guide books of the larger European Museums of Prehistory contain much valuable material. This is especially true of the remarkable guide books of the British Museum (listed separately in the chapters with which they deal) which give comprehensive discussions and are, in fact, treatises on prehistory.

CHAPTERS I AND II

PALEOLITHIC AND EPIPALEOLITHIC

ARANZADI, T. DE, BARANDIARÁN, J. M. DE, AND EGUREN, E. DE, Exploraciones de la Caverna de Santimamiñe, Bilbao, 1925.

BÉGOUEN, COMTE, AND BREUIL, ABBÉ H., Peintures et Gravures préhistoriques dans la Grotte du Mas-d'Azil. Toulouse, 1913.

BOULE, M., Fossil Men. Trans. by J. E. and J. Ritchie. 2nd ed. Edinburgh, 1923.

BREUIL, ABBÉ H., CAPITAN, L., AND PEYRONY, D. See the various articles in the *Revue Anthropologique, Revue Préhistorique*, and other French and foreign periodicals. See also under Capitan.

BURKITT, M. C., Prehistory. Cambridge, 1921; Our Forerunners. New York, 1924; Our Early Ancestors. Cambridge, 1926. Contains a discussion of the Epipaleolithic.

CAPITAN, L., La Préhistoire. Paris, 1922.

CAPITAN, L., BREUIL, H., PEYRONY, D., La Caverne de Font de Gaume. Monaco, 1910. This important monograph contains drawings and coloured plates of Paleolithic art and should be consulted by all students of Prehistory. Les Combarelles aux Eyzies, 1924. This is the last of the splendid monographs of cave art which are illustrated by the drawings and photographs of Abbé H. Breuil. All of these should be consulted.

CARTAILHAC, E., AND BREUIL, ABBÉ H., La Caverne d'Altamira à Santillane. Monaco, 1906. This important monograph contains superb illustrations of the cave art of Altamira.

CRAWFORD, O. G. S., Man and his Past. Oxford, 1921.

ELLIOT, G. F. SCOTT, Prehistoric Man and his Story. 2nd ed. London, 1917.

EVANS, JOHN, The Ancient Stone Implements of Great Britain. 2nd ed. London, 1897.

GEIKIE, JAMES, The Antiquity of Man in Europe. New York, 1914.

HERNÁNDEZ-PACHECO, E., Estudios de Arte Prehistórico. *Comisión de Investigaciones Paleontológicos y Prehistóricos.* No. 16. Madrid (1918).

JOHANSEN, K. F., Une station du plus ancien âge de la pierre dans la tourbière de Svaerdborg. *Mém. de la Soc. Roy. des Antiq. du Nord.* 1918-1919. Published 1920.

KEITH, SIR ARTHUR, The Antiquity of Man. 2 vols. 2nd ed. London, 1925.

KENDRICK, T. D., The Axe Age. London, 1925. This book contains a discussion of the Epipaleolithic and Neolithic.

LULL, R. S., and others. The Evolution of Man. New Haven, 1922.

MACALISTER, R. A. S., A Text-book of European Archaeology. Vol. I The Paleolithic Period. Cambridge, 1921.

MADSEN, A. P., and others, Affaldsdynger fra Stenalderen i Danmark. Pub. in 1900 for the National Museum at Copenhagen.

MOIR, J. REID, The Antiquity of Man in East Anglia. Cambridge, 1928.

MONRO, ROBERT, Paleolithic Man and Terramara Settlements in Europe. Edinburgh, 1912.

OBERMAIER, HUGO, Fossil Man in Spain. New Haven, 1924. This excellent work contains a discussion of the Paleolithic and Epipaleolithic of Europe, and a good bibliography of the Paleolithic to 1923.

OSBORN, HENRY FAIRFIELD, Men of the Old Stone Age. 2nd ed. New York, 1916.

PEAKE, HAROLD, AND FLEURE, HERBERT JOHN, Apes and Men, Vol. I, and Hunters and Artists. Vol. II of *The Corridors of Time.* New Haven, 1927.

PEYRONY, D., Eléménts de Préhistoire. Ussel, 1914.

READ, C. H.,-SMITH, R. A., A Guide to the Antiquities of the Stone Age, 3rd ed. British Museum, 1926.

SARAUW, G., En stenalders boplads i Maglemose ved Mullerup, sammenholdt med beslaegtede fund. *Aarbøger for nordisk Oldkyndighed og Historie.* Copenhagen, 1903.

SCHMIDT, R. R., Die Kunst der Eiszeit. Augsburg-Stuttgart. A folio containing illustrations of Paleolithic art. Die diluviale Vorzeit Deutschlands. Stuttgart, 1912.

SMITH, G. ELLIOT, Essays on the Evolution of Man. London, 1924.

SOCIEDAD ESPAÑOLA DE AMIGOS DEL ARTE. Catalogo de la Exposicion de Arte Prehistorico Español. Madrid, 1921.

SOLLAS, W. J., Ancient Hunters. 3rd ed. New York, 1924.

WOODWARD, A. SMITH, A Guide to the Fossil Remains of Man in the Department of Geology and Paleontology in the British Museum (Natural History). 3rd ed. London, 1922.

CHAPTER III

NEOLITHIC

ÅBERG, N., Das nordische Kulturgebiet in Mitteleuropa während der jüngeren Steinzeit. Uppsala, 1918; Die Steinzeit in den Niederlanden. Uppsala, 1916.

BUXTON, DUDLEY, Primitive Labour. 1924.

CLASSEN, K., Die Völker Europas zur jüngeren Steinzeit. Stuttgart, 1912.

FRANCHET, L., Céramique Primitive. Paris, 1911.

KOEHL, C., Die Bandkeramik der steinzeitlichen Gräberfelder und Wohnplätze in dem Umgebung von Worms. 1903.

MERTINS, OSCAR, Wegweiser durch die Urgeschichte Schlesiens. 2nd ed. Breslau, 1906.

OSBORN, HENRY FAIRFIELD, Man Rises to Parnassus. Princeton, 1928.

PARRY, T. W., Trephination of the living Human Skull in prehistoric times. *British Medical Journal.* March, 1923.

PEAKE, HAROLD, AND FLEURE, HERBERT JOHN, Peasants and Potters; Priests and Kings. Vols. III and IV of *The Corridors of Time.* New Haven, 1927.

PETRIE, SIR W. M. FLINDERS, Tools and Weapons. 1917.

PFEIFFER, L., Die steinzeitliche Technik. 1912; Die Werkzeuge des Steinzeit-Menschen. 1920.

READ, C. H.,-SMITH, R. A., A Guide to the Antiquities of the Stone Age. 3rd. ed. British Museum, 1926.

REINECKE, P., Zur Kenntnis der frühneolitischen Zeit in Deutschland. Mainz, Z. 3 (1908).

REINERTH, H., Chronologie der jüngeren Steinzeit. Augsburg, 1923.

SALMON, PH., D'AULT DU MESNIL, G., AND CAPITAN, L., Le Campignien. Rev. d'Anthrop. 8, Paris (1898).

SCHEIDT, WALTER, Die Rassen der jüngeren Steinzeit in Europa. Munich, 1924.

SCHLIZ, A., Das steinzeitliche Dorf Grossgartach. 1901.

SCHUMACHER, K., Materialen zur Besiedelungsgeschichte Deutschlands. 1913.

SEGER, H., Die keramischen Stilarten der jüngeren Steinzeit Schlesiens. 1916.

SPECIAL COMMITTEE, Report of the excavations at Grime's Graves. Prehist. Soc. of E. Anglia. March-May, 1914.

WUNDT, W., Elements of Folk Psychology. 1916.

CHAPTER IV

NEOLITHIC IN SCANDINAVIA

ÅBERG, NILS, Studier öfver den yngre stenåldern i norden och västeuropa. This work has a résumé in French. (1912); Das nordische Kulturgebiet in Mitteleuropa während der jüngeren Steinzeit. 1918.

ALMGREN, OSCAR, Sveriges Fasta Fornlämningar från Hednatiden. Uppsala, 1923.

ANTEVS, E., On the late-glacial and post-glacial history of the Baltic. Geographical Review. 12 (1922), pp. 602-612.

BALTZER, L., Hällristningar från Bohuslän. Göteborg, 1881.

GUSTAFSON, G., Norges Oldtid. Christiania, 1906.

HALLSTRÖM, G., Nordskandinaviska Hällristningar. Ur Forvännen. Stockholm, 1907.

LINDQUIST, SUNE, Nordens Benålder och en teori om dess stenålderraser. Rig. Bd. 1-2, 1918-1919.

MÜLLER, SOPHUS, Les poignards en silex de l'âge de pièrre en Scandinavie. Nordiska Fortidsminder, Heft 4, pp. 125-180.

1902; Les divisions de l'âge de la pièrre en Danemark. *Cong. Internat. d'Anthrop. et d'Arch.* X, p. 223 ff.

NORDÉN, ARTHUR, Brandskogs-skeppet. Vår bronsålders Märkligaste skeppsbild. *Ur Forvännen,* heft 3-4, Stockholm, 1925, pp. 376-391; Felsbilder der Provinz Ostgotland in Auswahl. 1923.

SCHNITTGER, BROR, En Hällristning vid Berga-Tuna i Södermanland. *Ur Forvännen.* Stockholm, 1922.

CHAPTER V

LAKE DWELLINGS

GUMMEL, HANS, Der Pfahlbau Moosseedorf bei Bern. Hanover, 1923.

HEIERLI, JAKOB, Urgeschichte der Schweiz. Zurich, 1901.

KELLER, F., Lake Dwellings of Switzerland. 2nd ed. London, 1878.

MONRO, R., The Lake-Dwellings of Europe. London, 1890.

REINERTH, H., Pfahlbauten am Bodensee. 1922.

SCHENK, ALEXANDRE, La Suisse Préhistorique. Lausanne, 1912.

SCHLAGINHAUFEN, OTTO, Die Anthropologischen Funde aus den Pfahlbauten der Schweiz. Zurich, 1924.

v. TRÖLTSCH, Die Pfahlbauten des Bodenseegebietes, 1902.

VIOLLIER, D., and others, Pfahlbauten. *Mittheilung der Antiquarischen Gesellschaft in Zurich.* Bd. XXIX, heft 4, Zurich, 1924.

VOUGA, P., Essai de classification du Néolithique lacustre d'après la stratification. Three articles in the *Anzeiger für Schweizerische Altertumskunde.* Band XXII, heft 4, 1920; and in same journal for 1921, and 1922; Zur kulturgeschichtlichen Stellung der westschweizerischen Pfahlbauten. Special publication of the *Wiener Praehistorische Zeitschrift.*

CHAPTER VI

MEGALITHIC MONUMENTS

BALL, GODFRAY, NICOLLE, RYBAT, La Hougue Bie. St. Helier, 1925.

BORLASE, W. C., The Dolmens of Ireland I-III. London, 1897. Nænia Cornubiæ. London, 1872.

CRAWFORD, O. G. S., Long Barrows of the Cotswolds. 1925.

COFFEY, G., New Grange and Other Incised Tumuli in Ireland. Dublin, 1912.

LEEDS, E. T., The Dolmens and Megalithic Tombs of Spain and Portugal. *Archæologia*, (20) 1920. pp. 201-202.

LUKIS, W. C., The Prehistoric Stone Monuments of the British Isles; Cornwall. London, 1885.

MORTILLET, A. DE, Distribution Géographique des dolmens et des menhirs en France. *Rev. d'École d'Anthropologie*, 1901.

PEET, T. E., Rough Stone Monuments and their Builders. 1912.

ROUZIC, Z. LE, The Megalithic Monuments of Carnac and Locmariaquer. 1908; Carnac Menhirs-statues avec signes figuratifs et amulettes ou idoles des Dolmens du Morbihan. Nantes, 1913.

ROUZIC, Z. LE, AND SAINT-JUST PÉQUART, M. AND MME., Carnac. Fouilles faites dans la Région. 1922, 1923.

ROUZIC, Z. LE, AND KELLER, C.; Locmariaquer. La Table des Marchands. Vannes, 1923.

SMITH, G. ELLIOT, The Ancient Egyptians. 1911; Evolution of the Rock-cut Tomb and the Dolmen. 1913; Migrations of Early Culture. 1915; Evolution of the Dragon. 1919.

SOCIÉTÉ JERSIAISE, La Hougue Bie. (Extract from the *Bulletin of the Society* for 1925). St. Helier, 1925.

STONE, E. HERBERT, The Stones of Stonehenge. 1924.

TROTTER, A. P., Stonehenge as an Astronomical Instrument, *Antiquity*, I, p. 927, p. 42-54.

VULLIAMY, C. E., Prehistoric Remains in West Penwith. St. Ives. 1921.

CHAPTER VII

BRONZE AGE

ABERCROMBY, JOHN, A Study of the Bronze Age Pottery of Great Britain and Ireland and Its Associated Grave-Goods. 2 vols. Oxford, 1912.

ÅBERG, NILS, La civilisation énéolithique dans la péninsule ibérique. Uppsala, 1921.

ANDRÉE, DR. J., Bergbau in der Vorzeit. *Vorzeit,* Band II, Leipzig, 1922.

ARMSTRONG, E. C. R., Catalogue of Irish Gold Ornaments in the Collection of the Royal Irish Academy. Dublin, 1920.

BELTZ, ROBERT, Die bronze- und hallstattzeitlichen Fibeln. *Zeitschrift für Ethnologie*. Berlin, 1913.

BLANCHET, J. ADRIEN, Les Souterrains-refuges de la France. Paris, 1923.

BREUIL, ABBÉ H., L'âge du bronze dans le bassin de Paris. *L'Anthropologie*. Paris, 1900-1905.

BUFFUM, W. A., The Tears of the Heliades, or Amber as a Gem. 3rd ed. London, 1898.

COFFEY, GEORGE, The Bronze Age in Ireland. Dublin, 1913.

COOK, SIR E. T., Handbook to the Greek and Roman Antiquities in the British Museum. 1903.

EVANS, SIR ARTHUR J., The Prehistoric Tombs of Knossos. *Archaeologia*. London, 1906.

FIMMEN, DIEDRICH, Zeit und Dauer der kretisch-mykenischen Kultur. Leipzig and Berlin, 1909; Die kretisch-mykenische Kultur. Leipzig and Berlin, 1921.

FRISCHBIER, ERIC, Germanische Fibeln im Anschluss an der Pyrmonter Brunnenfund. *Mannus-Bibliothek*. Leipzig, 1922.

GIRKE, GEORG, Die Tracht der Germanen in der vor- und frühgeschichtlichen Zeit. *Mannus-Bibliothek*. Leipzig, 1922.

GLOTZ, GUSTAVE, La Civilisation égéenne. Paris, 1923. An English translation is now available. 1925.

GOWLAND, WM., The Metals in Antiquity. *Journal of the Anthropological Institute of Great Britain and Ireland*. 1912. pp. 235-287.

HADDOW, J. G., Amber. *Cope's Smoke Room Booklets* No. 7, 1892.

HALL, EDITH H., The Decorative Art of Crete in the Bronze Age. *Univ. of Penn. Trans., Dept. of Arch.* 1907.

HALL, H. R. H., Aegean Archaeology. 1915; Ancient History of the Near East. London, 5th ed. 1920.

ISSEL, ARTURO, Liguria Preistorica. Genova, 1908.

KEITH, SIR ARTHUR, The Bronze Age Invaders of Britain, *Journal of the Anthropological Institute of Great Britain and Ireland*. XLV. 1915.

KOSSINNA, GUSTAF, Die Indogermanen. *Mannus-Bibliothek*. No. 26, 1921; Der germanische Goldreichtum in der Bronzezeit. 1913.

LINDQUIST, S., Äringsriter i Bohuslän under bronsåldern. *Göteborgs och Bohusläns Fornminnesforenings Tidskrift*. 1923.

MONTELIUS, O., Sur la chronologie de l'âge du Bronze. Paris, 1885; Die Chronologie der ältesten Bronzezeit in Norddeutschland und Skandinavien. *Archiv für Anthropologie*. Brunswick, 1898-99; Pre-Classical Chronology in Greece and Italy. London, 1897; La chronologie préhistorique en France et en d'autres pays celtiques. *L'Anthropologie*, 1901; Die vorklassische Chronologie Italiens. Stockholm, 1912; The Chronology of the British Bronze Age. *Archaeologia*, London, 1908; La civilisation primitive en Italie depuis l'introduction des Metaux. Stockholm, 1895-1910; Der Handel in der Vorzeit. *Praehistorische Zeitschrift*, Berlin, 1910; Kulturgeschichte Schwedens von den ältesten Zeiten. Leipzig, 1906; Sur les differents types des Haches en silex suedoises. Stockholm, 1874; Musée des Antiquitiés Nationales de Stockholm. 1899; Sur les Rochers sculptés de la Suede. Paris, 1875.

MORGAN, J. DE, Note sur les origines de la métallurgie *L'Anthropologie*, XXXII, 1922.

MORTILLET, A. DE, L'argent aux temps protohistoriques en Europe. *Revue mensuelle de l'École d'Anthropologie de Paris*. 1903; Classification des fibules d'après leur ressort. *Revue Anthropologique*. Paris, 1913.

MORTILLET, P. DE, Origine du Culte des Morts. 1914.

NAVARRO, J. M. DE, Prehistoric Routes between Northern Europe and Italy defined by the Amber Trade. *Geographical Journal,* Dec., 1925.

NEERGAARD, CARL, Dépots d'objets de l'Âge du Bronze. *Nordiske Fortidsminder*. Copenhagen, 1897.

PEAKE, HAROLD, The Bronze Age and the Celtic World. London, 1922.

PEET, THOMAS E., The Stone and Bronze Ages in Italy and Sicily. Oxford, 1909.

PETRIE, SIR W. M. FLINDERS, Tools and Weapons. London, 1917.

PIROUTET, MAURICE, Questions relatives a l'Âge du Bronze. *L'Anthropologie*, Paris, 1917.

READ, C. H.,-SMITH, R. A., A Guide to the Antiquities of the Bronze Age, 2nd ed. British Museum, 1920.

SADOWSKI, JAN VON, Die Handelstrassen der Griechen und Römer. Jena, 1877.

SAYCE, A. H., New Light on the Early History of Bronze. *Man,* XXI, 97, 1921.

SCHUCHHARDT, CARL, Der Goldfund vom Messingwerk bei Eberswalde. Berlin, 1914.

SCHUMACHER, K., Stand und Aufgaben der Bronzeitlichen Forschung in Deutschland. Frankfort-am-Main, 1917.

SIRET, L. Les Cassiterides et l'empire des Pheniciens. *L'Anthropologie,* XIX, 1908; XX, 1909; XXI, 1910.

STOPPANI, ANTONIO, L'Ambra nella storia e nella Geologia. Milano, 1886.

TSOUNTAS, C., and MANATT, J. I., The Mycenean Age. Boston and New York, 2nd ed. 1915.

VIOLLIER, D., Les Débuts de l'Âge du Bronze en Suisse. *Beitrage zur Anthr. Ethnol. und Urgeschichte.* Anniversary Volume to F. Sarasin, 1919.

CHAPTER VIII

HALLSTATT

ADAMS, LOUISE E. W., A Study in the Commerce of Latium.

BECK, L., Die Geschichte des Eisens. 1890.

BRYAN, W. R., Italic Hut Urns and Hut Urn Cemeteries. *Papers and Monographs of the Am. Acad. at Rome.* Vol. IV. 1925.

BUSCHOR, ERNST, Greek Vase Paintings. 1921.

DÉCHELETTE, J., Manuel d'Archéologie, Vol. II, Pt. 2. Though published in 1913 this is the best general discussion of this period.

HERTZ, MME., *L'Anthropologie.* Tome, XXXV, nos. 1, 2. Mme. Hertz gives the literary sources for archaeology of iron in the Near East.

HOERNES, M., Das Gräberfeld von Hallstatt, seine Zusammensetzung und Entwicklung. 1920.

JAHN, MARTIN, Die Bewaffnung der Germanen in der alteren Eisenzeit. 1916.

KELLER-TARNUZZER, K., and REINERTH, H., Urgeschichte des Thurgaus. 1925.

RANDALL-MACIVER, DAVID, Villanovans and Early Etruscans. Oxford, 1924.

READ, C. H.,-SMITH, R. A., Guide to the Antiquities of the Early Iron Age, 2nd ed. British Museum, 1925.

SACKEN, EDUARD VON, "Das Grabfeld von Hallstatt in Oberösterreich und dessen Altertümer. 1868; Hallstatt. *Internat. Zeitschrift für Metallographie.* 4 (1913).

SCHUMACHER, KARL, Siedelungs- und Kulturgeschichte der Rheinlande. 1921.

TREPTOW, E., Die Mineralbenutzung in vor- und frühgeschichtlicher Zeit. 1901.

CHAPTER IX

LA TENE

BEAUPRÉ, COUNT J., Contribution à l'étude de l'habitation aux débuts de la Tène. Nancy. 1912.

BELTZ, R., Die Latène Fibeln. *Zeitschrift für Ethnologie.* XLIII, pp. 664-817, 930-943. (1913).

DÉCHELETTE, J., Manuel d'Archéologie, Vol. II, Pt. 3, 1914. This is the standard work on the Second Age of Iron—La Tene.

FORRER, R., Studien zur keltischen Numismatik. 1926.

READ, C. H.,-SMITH, R. A., Guide to the Antiquities of the Early Iron Age, 2nd ed. British Museum, 1925. This volume contains excellent material.

SCHELTEMA, F. A. VON, Altnordischer Kunst. 1923.

SCHUMANN, Die Waffen und Schmucksachen Pommerns zur Zeit des La Tèneeinflusses.

VOUGA, P., La Tène. Leipzig, 1923. This monograph on the Station of La Tène, Switzerland, is beautifully illustrated.

PERIODICALS

There are numerous American and Foreign periodicals which from time to time contain excellent articles on phases of Prehistory. Those listed below, while not inclusive, are the ones which seem to be the most important.

American Journal of Archaeology, New York

American Journal of Physical Anthropology

Annales de paléontologie, Paris

L'anthropologie, Paris

The Antiquaries Journal
Antiquity, Gloucester. A new quarterly review of Archæology
Anzeiger für schweizerische Altertumskunde
Archæologia, London
Archæologia Cambrensis
Archiv für Anthropologie, Brunswick
Bulletin archéologique, Paris
Journal Royal Anthropological Institute of Great Britain and Ireland, London
Journal British Archæological Association
Man. A monthly record of anthropological science, London.
Nordiske Fortidsminder, Copenhagen
Praehistorische Zeitschrift, Berlin
Proceedings of the Prehistoric Society of East Anglia
Revue anthropologique, Paris
Revue archéologique, Paris
Revue préhistorique, Paris
Weiner Praehistorische Zeitschrift, Vienna
Zeitschrift für Ethnologie, Berlin

GLOSSARY

Acheulean. A Lower Paleolithic industry. It follows and is a direct descendant of the Chellean. The coup de poing or hand-ax of this stage is distinguished from that of the Chellean by better workmanship and more elegant shape.

Aeneolithic. See Eneolithic.

Alignment. A row of standing stones or menhirs. The finest alignments are in Brittany, France. They were erected in the Late Neolithic or Early Bronze Age.

Allée Couverte. See Hallcist.

Alpine Race. Characterised by small or medium stature, thick-set body and round (brachycephalic) head. The face is broad, the nose rather large, the eyes, brown, and the hair dark. It is a common type in Switzerland and the neighbouring regions and of the greater part of Russia.

Amber. A fossilised vegetable resin, called in mineralogy succinite. The ancient Greek name is elektron. (The word electrical is derived from electron because of the electrical properties of amber.) It occurs in all shades of yellow, tending to white and red or brown and black. The occurrence of amber on the shores of Denmark in Prehistoric times had an important effect on the spread of southern culture through trade. Later, the deposits of East Prussia were used.

Amulet. An object, generally an ornament, worn as a charm against bad luck, disease, accident, the "evil eye," etc. Amulets were probably the earliest ornaments worn by Prehistoric man.

Ancylus Lake. A lake formed by the shrinking of the Baltic due to the elevation of the neighbouring Scandinavian lands. It was contemporaneous with the Maglemose culture, the creation of a fisher folk who lived on its shores. The name is derived from a mollusk, *Ancylus fluviatalis*, that lived in the waters of the lake.

Anklet. An ornamental ring or band worn on the ankle.

Antennæ. A term applied to a type of sword handle (especially characteristic of the First Age of Iron) which is ornamented at the end with two metal appendages which recall the antennæ of insects.

Ape-Man. One of the earliest prehuman creatures, known as Pithecanthropus erectus. The term "ape-man" is also used, in general, for man's supposed ancestors who possessed many ape-like characteristics.

Artifact. Any object made or modified by human skill.

Asturian Culture. An Epipaleolithic culture of the North of Spain. It is next younger than the Azilian.

Aunjetitz Culture. The first, original Bronze Age civilisation of Central Europe. The name is derived from a great cemetery south of Prague.

Aurignacian. The oldest division of the Late Paleolithic. The Aurignacian of Africa is known as the Capsian.

Aurochs. Bos primigenius. Wild cattle of Europe.

Ax. This term is limited to the stone or metal cutting tool which is perforated for a handle. The *celt* is not perforated.

Azilian. A culture which takes its name from Mas d'Azil, in the foothills of the Pyrenees. The stratum in which the artifacts are found overlies the Magdalenian. The Azilian, Tardenoisian, Asturian, and Northern Maglemose industries are included in the Epipaleolithic.

Band Ceramics. Pottery decorated with ribbon designs arranged in spiral and meander patterns. It appears in the Neolithic and continued to be made in the Early Bronze Age.

Barrow. See Tumulus.

Bâton de Commandement. A ceremonial staff. Some, at least, of the so-called bâtons de commandement were shaft straighteners.

Battle-Ax. They are of many shapes. Some are double-bladed and some are blunt at one end and have an edge at the other. All are bored for hafting.

Battle-Ax Folk. A term applied to the people of the so-called separate graves of Scandinavia. The typical implement, the battle-ax, has been found over a great part of Europe and seems to indicate the wide extension of a warlike. Neolithic race.

Beehive Tomb. Chamber shaped like an old-fashioned beehive. See corbelled tomb.

Bell Beakers. These calyx-shaped cups, also called zoned beakers, and drinking cups, are of Late Neolithic and Early Bronze Age.

Bos primigenius. Or Aurochs. Wild cattle of Europe.

Bracer. A bowman's wrist guard used to protect the wrist when using a bow. They are rectangular in shape. Their use began in the Bronze Age or earlier.

Brachycephalic. Short-headed. See under Cephalic Index.

Bronze. An alloy of copper and tin. The best bronze contains ten percent of tin.

Bronze Age. This age began with the invention of metallurgy. Copper was first used and was later alloyed with tin to make bronze. The term Eneolithic is often used for the Age of Copper, and generally includes the later part of the Neolithic and the earlier part of the Bronze Age as defined in this book.

Bucket. See situla.

Buckler. A shield, especially a small round shield.

Bull, Cult of. The worship of the bull can be traced back to Early Minoan times. It later became widely spread.

Burial. See Collective, Contracted, and Extended Burials.

Burin. A graving tool, much used in Aurignacian and Magdalenian times.

Cache. The French *cacher* means to hide but it seems admissible to use the word cache not only for the hiding place but for the things hidden. The term "hoard" is misleading, as is also "find."

Calläis. A term applied by Pliny to, what is believed to be, turquoise. It is also used by Prehistorians for a greenish mineral, spotted with white and blue, which has been found in the form of beads in Late Neolithic or Early Bronze Age (Eneolithic) graves in Brittany, rarely in Southern and Central France and Spain. The calläis of Brittany is an hydrous phosphate of aluminum, nearly like turquoise in composition. It is now called callainite by mineralogists.

Campignian. A culture which is generally held to be contemporaneous with the Kitchen Midden or Ertebolle culture. It is placed in the Mesolithic by some authors and in the earliest European Neolithic by others.

Capsian. The Aurignacian culture of Africa is known as the Capsian. It immediately succeeded the Mousterian.

Carinate or Keeled Scraper. Grattoir Caréné. A thick flake which resembles an inverted boat. The base is flat and the back has the shape of a keel. The scraping end has a chisel edge.

Celt. The forerunner of the ax. It is never perforated for hafting but was attached to a handle by a thong, or was inserted in a bone or wooden handle or was held in place in other ways.

Celts. See Kelts.

Cephalic Index. The index is a number expressing the ratio of the length to the breadth of the skull, thus $\dfrac{\text{breadth} \times 100}{\text{length}} = \text{index}$. When the index is 80 or more the skull is brachycephalic (short-headed); when 75 or less, the skull is dolichocephalic; when between 75 and 80, it is mesaticephalic.

Chalcolithic. A synonym for Aeneolithic, Eneolithic, and the Copper Age.

Chape. The metal tip of a scabbard. As the style of these varied with time their form and ornamentation aid in determining the age of finds or caches.

Châtelperron Point. A curved, pointed knife-like blade characteristic of the Lower Aurignacian.

Chellean. One of the oldest cultures of the Lower Paleolithic. It precedes the Acheulean.

Cinerary Urn. An urn in which the burned bones of the cremated dead were placed.

Cist. Simple rectangular tomb made of slabs of rock. Hallcists (vid.) are of large size.

Collective Burial. A burial in which more than one body was placed in the same tomb or grave.

Compresseur. An anvil of bone used in chipping flints.

Contracted Burial. The knees are drawn to the chin and the arms are crossed over the breast. The body is held in this position by cords.

Corbelled Tomb. See also Beehive Tomb. The vaults of such tombs are made by an arrangement of stones in which successive courses project beyond those below.

Corded Pottery. Also termed *Schnurkeramik* or string ceramics.

The ornamentation was made by pressing twisted cords into the paste before firing. Neolithic.

Coup de poing or Hand-ax. The most characteristic flint tool of the Chellean and Acheulean stages.

Covered Gallery. See Hallcist.

Crannog. A crannog is an artificial island usually made of logs laid transversely with the addition of brushwood, stones, and earth, and surrounded by one or more stockades, the piles of which were held by branches of trees or even by mortised beams. It was often surrounded by a platform of timbers on which hearthstones were placed and wattle-and-daub huts erected, and was generally oval or circular with a diameter of at least sixty or seventy feet. There was a gangway of some kind connecting it with the shore. Crannogs are most numerous in Ireland and Scotland but are known in England and Wales. Most or all of them were fortresses. The Irish and Scottish crannogs continued in occupation right through the Middle Ages.

Cro-Magnon. An important Late Paleolithic race. It is characterized by great stature, large, long heads and rather short faces.

Cromlech. A circle of upright monoliths. The term is also locally used in Cornwall and Ireland for megalithic tombs.

Cypriote Dagger. An early form of dagger especially characterised by the shank which extended through the handle and which was held in place by bending back the end of the shank into the handle.

Danubian Culture. An important Neolithic culture of the Danube valley and neighbouring regions.

Dawn Men. Osborn holds that the human race was descended from an independent line of Dawn Men, ancestors springing from an Oligocene neutral stock, which also gave rise independently to the anthropoid apes.

Dolichocephalic. Having a long skull, the cephalic index being less than 75. See under Cephalic Index.

Dolmen. The dolmen consists of a few large, upright stones upon which a huge slab has been laid to form a roof. The whole was generally covered by a mound or tumulus. The term dolmen is often loosely used to include all megalithic tombs.

Double ax. An ax with two cutting edges. The double ax was the symbol of a wide-spread religious cult.

End scraper. Or Grattoir. A scraping tool with the chipped edge at the end of the blade.

Eneolithic. Aenolithic, Chalcolithic, or Copper Age. The last part of the Neolithic or beginning of the Bronze Age during which unalloyed copper was used.

Engraver. See Burin.

Eolith. One of the crude flints of the Eolithic.

Eolithic. The earliest part of the Stone Age. It is characterised by the rudest flints.

Ertebolle. Kitchen Midden, or Shell Heap culture. This culture is included in the Mesolithic by some authors and in the Neolithic by others. It is considered as earliest Neolithic in this work.

Extended Burial. The body rests on its back in an extended position.

Face Urn. An urn modelled in the shape of the human face. They were manufactured from the Bronze Age, throughout the Hallstatt, and in La Tene times.

Faience. A glazed pottery, generally highly decorated with colours.

Fibula. An ornamental brooch of the type of the safety pin. The fibula is one of the most important objects for determining the age of graves in Northern, Central, and Western Europe.

Find. A synonym for cache or hoard.

Food vessel. Pottery vessels which were deposited in English and Irish round barrows or tumuli to hold food for the dead. Some are lavishly ornamented and are the most attractive pottery of the Bronze Age in the British Isles.

Gaul. Ancient Gaul or Gallia embraced what is now Northern Italy, France, Belgium and parts of Holland, Switzerland, and Germany. Its boundaries varied from time to time.

Glastonbury Lake Village. The lake dwellings of England are all later in date than the Neolithic. The best known lake village is that of Glastonbury which is of the Iron Age.

Gouge. A Scandinavian flint or stone tool with a concave edge. Similar tools were made by the American Indians of New England and neighbouring states.

Grattoir or end scraper. A planing tool generally of flint.

Gravette Point. A knife-like flake with one edge completely retouched. It differs from the Châtelperron point in its greater straightness and narrowness as well as in its more acute point. Upper Aurignacian.

Great Mother. A deity worshipped at least from Early Neolithic times. It had several forms and attributes. Many of the clay figurines are steatopygous.

Grime's Graves. A Neolithic flint mine in England.

Haft. The handle of a cutting weapon or tool such as the haft or hilt of a sword, or of an ax.

Halberd or *Halbert.* The simplest and earliest form of a halberd was made by inserting a dagger blade in a shaft at right angles.

Hallcist. Covered gallery or long stone cist. A megalithic tomb which may be regarded as a degenerate form of a Passage Grave (*vid.*) in which the chamber has disappeared and the end of the passage is used as a burial place.

Hallstatt. The First Age of Iron. It follows the Bronze Age and precedes the La Tene. It receives its name from a cemetery at Hallstatt, Austria.

Hammer-ax. These axes have an ax edge on one end and are blunt on the other. They are bored for hafting. They are generally carelessly made and were used for domestic purposes. They are typical of Eastern Europe and were used in Scandinavia toward the close of the Neolithic.

Hand-ax. See coup de poing.

Heidelberg man. Homo heidelbergensis. This species is known from a jaw bone (Mauer jaw) found near Heidelberg, Germany.

Hoard. See cache.

Holed stones. In some countries hallcists or covered galleries were entered by a holed stone.

Holocene. (Greek *holos*, whole; *kainos*, recent.) Recent times, that is, the time since the Great Ice Age.

Incense cup. Small pottery vessels which had some part in the ceremonies associated with cremation in England and Ireland in the Bronze Age. They vary in shape but are generally perforated in one or more places.

Jade, Jadeite, and *Nephrite.* Extremely hard and tough minerals of varying composition. The colour varies from greenish-white to deep green. On account of their toughness and colour they were highly prized by prehistoric man who fashioned them into ornaments, tools and weapons.

Jet. A variety of coal, which being compact, taking a good polish, and having considerable strength, has been used for ornaments from Neolithic times to the present.

Kelts or Celts. Members of a race or any of the several races of Central and Western Europe called Celtæ by the Romans.

Kist, or Cist. A tomb formed of upright slabs of stone with a cover stone or stones. After Megalithic times such tombs were small.

Kitchen Middens, Ertebolle, Shell Heaps, Køkkenmøddinger, etc. Mounds composed of sea shells and bones, the kitchen refuse of shore dwellers. The Kitchen Middens of Denmark are extensive and are of Early Neolithic Age.

Lake Dwellings. See Pile Dwellings.

La Tene. The Second Age of Iron. The time of the domination of Central and Western Europe by the Kelts. The Age closed with the conquest by Cæsar. It receives its name from the station La Tène, Switzerland.

Les Eyzies. A village in the Dordogne, France. It has been called the capital of the Prehistoric world because of the large number of Paleolithic caves. It is the best center for Paleolithic art.

Levallois Flake. The Levallois flake was made from a flake struck off from a nodule. Its importance lies in the fact that in Acheulean times a new technique, which was later to be so important, was evolved.

Lignite. Brown coal. Compact varieties were manufactured into bracelets and other ornaments in Neolithic and later times.

Limhamn culture. A culture in Sweden parallel to the Ertebolle or Kitchen Midden culture of Denmark.

Littorina Sea. Ancylus Lake (*vid.*) gave place to a salt water sea in which a shellfish, *Littorina litorea,* was abundant. The Kitchen Midden or Ertebolle people lived on the shores of this ancient Baltic sea.

Long Barrow. The tumuli of England are of two kinds: long and round. The long tumuli or barrows are of the Neolithic and the round ones of the Bronze Age. The people buried under the long barrows are mostly long-headed and those under the round barrows short-headed.

Lunulæ. Flat, gold crescents with the terminals in a plane at right angles. They are of Irish origin and were carried to England and the continent. Early Bronze Age.

Magdalenian. The last Paleolithic culture of Europe. The Magdalenian peoples have been called the Paleolithic Greeks because of their remarkable cave art.

Magic. "The art or body of arts, which pretends or is believed to produce effects by the assistance of supernatural beings or departed spirits or by a mastery of secret forces of nature." (Webster.)

Maglemose. A Scandinavian culture similar to the Azilian and Tardenoisian. It is of Epipaleolithic Age.

Mastaba. The earliest type of Egyptian tomb. It covered the mouth of a sepulchral pit and was used as a mortuary chapel.

Mediterranean Race. Characterised by long (dolichocephalic) skull, long narrow face, small or medium stature, aquiline nose, dark eyes, dark hair, and swarthy skin. The characteristic type of the Mediterranean lands.

Megalithic Tomb. A tomb of the Neolithic and Early Bronze Ages made of huge rock blocks or slabs. See Dolmen, Passage Grave, Hallcist.

Megaron. A large hall of an Aegean or Greek dwelling, generally oblong in shape and subdivided by one or more longitudinal ranges of supports.

Menhir. A single, rough megalith.

Mesaticephalic. A skull with a cephalic index of 75 to 80 (see under Cephalic Index).

Mesolithic. A term used by some authors to include the cultures between the Paleolithic and the Neolithic. It is generally used to embrace the Azilian, Tardenoisian, Campignian, and Kitchen Midden cultures.

Microlith or Pygmy flints. Small flints, generally carefully shaped and worked. They are especially characteristic of the Epipaleolithic.

Minoan. A period covering the Bronze Age in Crete. It lasted approximately from 2500 to 1200 B. C. and produced one of the most striking and influential civilisations of antiquity.

Mousterian. A Paleolithic culture which is included in the Lower Paleolithic by some authors and in the Middle Paleolithic by others. It was followed in Europe by the Aurignacian. The Neanderthal race lived at this time.

Mycenæ. A prehistoric Greek city with a remarkable Bronze Age civilisation, called the Mycenæan.

Neanderthal Man. A wide-spread Lower Paleolithic race, Homo neanderthalensis.

Neolithic or New Stone Age. Stone and flint tools were ground as well as chipped, agriculture was practiced, and animals were domesticated.

Nordic Race. Characterised by long (dolichocephalic) skull, long, narrow face, straight aquiline nose, large stature, blue eyes, and fair hair. Widespread at present in the north of Europe.

Nøstvet Culture. A Swedish culture similar to that of the Kitchen Midden. Implements were made of bone, horn, slate and green-stone.

Notched flake. A flake with a curved depression on one or both edges. Probably used for smoothing arrow or javelin shafts.

Obsidian. Obsidian or volcanic glass made excellent stone tools and weapons, especially those used for cutting. Expeditions were sent to Melos for it as early as Neolithic times.

Ochre, red. A pigment made of hematite, the red oxide of iron, was used by Paleolithic man and is used to-day.

Ochre Graves. Graves in which the corpse had been covered thickly with a layer of red ochre. They do not belong to a single period. They are found principally north of the Caucasus in Russia.

Ostrich Shell ornaments and implements. Curved blades were made of ostrich eggs in Late Capsian (Late Paleolithic) times, and beads in the Late Neolithic or Early Bronze Age (Copper Age).

Painted Pebbles. Pebbles on which signs were painted. They are characteristic of the Azilian stage.

Paleolithic. The Old Stone Age, or age in which man chipped but did not grind and polish his stone implements. It includes the Prechellean, Chellean, Acheulean, Mousterian, Aurignacian, Solutrean and Magdalenian periods in Europe.

Palstave. A flanged bronze celt with a stop-ridge. Characteristic of the Middle Bronze Age.

Passage Grave. A megalithic monument consisting of a round, oblong or rectangular chamber which is reached by a covered passage.

Patina. A surface appearance produced on metals and stone by age. The term is more commonly applied to the green rust or ærugo on bronze. The patina of flint may be white, yellow, brown or reddish. The thickness and character of patina is an indication of the antiquity of an object.

Petroglyph. A rock carving. The petroglyphs of Scandinavia are the most interesting of any in Europe. Most of them depict the life of the Bronze Age.

Pick. A pointed stone implement typical of the Kitchen Midden and Campignian cultures.

Pile Dwellings. Huts or houses built on piles on the shores or in the shallow waters of lakes. The pile dwellings of the Swiss lakes were numerous. They were first built in the Early Neolithic. Pile dwelling villages of considerable size were in existence in the Bronze Age. The terms Lake Dwellings and Pfahlbauten are synonyms.

Piltdown Man (Eoanthropus dawsoni). An early man or manlike creature closely related to Homo sapiens.

Pit dwelling. A human habitation excavated partly or wholly underground. "The pit dwellings were formed by sinking a floor three to seven feet and throwing out the earth round the opening which was fourteen to twenty feet in diameter; on the bank thus formed were placed stakes leaning toward the centre and supporting a roof of turf, bracken, or other material." (Description of a Bronze Age pit dwelling. Read-Smith.)

Pithecanthropus. The so-called ape-man of Java. See Ape-Man.

Platform dwelling. See Pile dwellings.

Pleistocene. The glacial epoch which preceded recent times.

Plowshare, or "Shoe-last celt." These stone implements are flat on one side and curved on the other. Some are perforated for a handle. They were probably used as hoes.

Point. (Pointe.) The Mousterian point was possibly a javelin head. It has also been suggested that they were used for splitting large bones in order to extract the marrow.

Potter's Wheel. A horizontal disk revolving on a spindle used by potters for holding the prepared clay and whirling it. Without the wheel it is nearly impossible to make symmetrical pottery. The wheel was employed in the Mediterranean countries in the Bronze Age but was not known in Central and Western Europe until much later.

Prechellean. The human cultures which preceded the Chellean.

Propulseur. Spear thrower, generally of bone.

Rapier. A narrow sword adapted for thrusting rather than for cutting.

Retouch. To improve the shape or sharpness of an edge by flaking.

Ring Money. An early form of money in the shape of rings. No denominations giving a unit of weight have yet been determined. Ring money was sometimes strung on bracelets. Used in the Early Bronze Age.

Rock Carving. See Petroglyphs.

Rössen Pottery. A Neolithic pottery from Germany.

Scraper. The side scraper is equivalent to the French racloir, the end scraper to the grattoir.

"Separate Grave" Culture. A Scandinavian culture contemporaneous with the Megalith cultures. The dead were buried under tumuli without tombs.

Shoe-last Celt. See Plowshare.

Side Scraper or Racloir. A flint, as a rule worked on one side only, used for dressing skins and for other purposes.

Situla. A bucket-shaped bronze vessel with a bail, of the Bronze Age, is usually called a situla. A Greco-Egyptian vase shaped like a bucket and having two small handles near the top is the more usual shape.

Solutrean. A culture which followed the Aurignacian and preceded the Magdalenian. It is characterised by a remarkable flint technique.

Spindle Whorl. A disk of pottery or other material used as a balance wheel on the shaft of a spindle.

Spokeshave. Notched scraper (*vid.*).

Steatopygy. An accretion of fat on the buttocks. Some Hottentot women have this characteristic which is also shown on some Aurignacian statuettes.

Strepyan. A synonym for Prechellean.

String Ceramics. See Corded pottery.

Sympathetic Magic. It is based on the principle that like affects like, or that a desired result may be brought to pass by mimicking it, naming it in spells, etc.

Tardenoisian. The Azilian and Northern Maglemose industries are the descendants of the Paleolithic and are placed in the Epipaleolithic. The Tardenoisian is a similar industry.

Terramara Settlements. Villages built on piles over dry land. The typical terramara settlements were in the Po Valley. They are of the Bronze Age.

Torque, or *Torc.* A neck ring of bronze, gold, or iron, worn in the Bronze and Iron Ages. Some torques were made of twisted wire (hence the name), others were plain or engraved.

Tranchet. A typical Kitchen Midden (Ertebolle) and Campignian implement. Its broad cutting edge was produced by the removal of a single transverse flake, not by a number of flakes.

Transverse Arrowhead. An arrowhead with the edge at right angles to the shaft. Widely used in Epipaleolithic and Kitchen Midden times.

Trepanned Skull. A skull from which a portion of the bone has been removed. Trepanation was practiced in the Neolithic in Europe and in pre-Columbian America.

Troglodyte. A cave dweller.

Tumulus. A sepulchral mound. In Great Britain and Ireland such mounds are called barrows.

Urn Burial. In this form of burial the unburnt body was placed in a large urn and the urn was either sealed by a stone slab or by another urn placed over it mouth to mouth.

Votive Offering. Offerings made in fulfilment of a vow or in thanksgiving for a favour received. Some of the so-called votive offerings of the Bronze Age may have been made to bring good fortune.

Villanova Culture. An Early Iron Age culture named from the proto-historic cemetery of Villanova, near Bologna, Italy. The village was founded near the close of the Bronze Age.

Zoned Beaker. The Bell Beakers or "drinking cups," as the British Prehistorians call them, are generally ornamented in horizontal bands as zones. Hence the name.

INDEX

Acheulean man, 12, 13, 45-47
Acheulean period, 10-14, 46, 47, 51
Aegean Basin, Neolithic idols of, 126
Affaldsdynger, 80
Age, Dawn Stone, 4; Holocene, 4
"Age of Bone," 57
Agriculture, 56, 69, 73, 77, 84, 86, 93, 100-107, 122, 127, 130, 147, 150, 154, 163, 165, 213, 227, 263, 313, 315, 337
Alignments, 184, 188, 189
Allées couvertes (*see* hallcists)
Alphabet, invention of, 113
Alpine Race, 67, 119, 294
Altamira, cave of, 36
Altars, Druid (*see* dolmens)
Amber, 108, 109, 110, 117, 128, 139, 144, 147, 233, 237, 282, 283, 332; in megalithic tombs, 182; in trade, 260, 289
America, origin of agriculture in, 104-107
America, Paleolithic man in, 13
American Neolithics, 73, 87
Amphora, 95
Amulets, 109, 110, 126, 128, 298, 331
Anau Neolithic deposits, 79
Ancylus epoch, 134
Ancylus lake, 134, 135
Animals, domestication of, 69, 73, 77, 84, 93, 107, 122, 130, 213, 242, 337
Anklets, 237, 283
Anvils, 18, 224, 315
Ape, brain of, 8
"Ape man," 8, 9, 47
Aqueducts, 105
Arbor Low tumulus, 252
Arctic fauna, 46
Armour, of Bronze Age, 222; La Tene, 311
Arrowheads, 128, 129, 139, 143, 145, 155, 159; transverse, 81, 82, 84; Neolithic, 88; evolution of, 161; in

megalithic tombs, 182; Bronze Age, 222; Hallstatt, 276
Art, Paleolithic, 30-43; and dates, 47; Epipaleolithic, 59-61, 63; Neolithic, 78; Cretan, 211; Bronze Age, 240; Keltic, 325; of Upper Paleolithic, 340
Asia, place of man's origin, 3; in Tertiary times, 5
Asia Minor, 74, 78, 79, 102
Aunjetitz culture, 251
Aurignacian man, 21, 27, 29, 47
Aurochs, 160
Avebury monument, 194
Awls, 12, 17, 82, 83, 85, 128, 155, 157, 224; Neolithic, 88; La Tene, 315
Ax, invention of, 12; cult of, 128, 331
Axes, 12, 86, 126, 135; Scandinavian, 141-143; stone and bronze, 143, 223; Swiss pile dwellers, 155; Hallstatt, 277; La Tene, 315
Azilian period, 47, 57, 59

Baltic, 84, 135
Bandkeramik, 95, 97
Barley, 102, 103, 104, 132, 163
Barrows, 172, 183 (*see* also mounds)
Baskets, 93, 101, 149
Battle-axes, flint, 141; stone and bronze, 146; bronze, 222
Beads, 108, 128, 129
Bell Beaker culture, 77, 118; pottery, 97, 98
Bells, bronze, 283
Belts, Hallstatt, 284; La Tene, 323
Boars, 82, 84, 108; as a religious symbol, 255
Bone, Age of, 57
Bone and horn, use of by pile dwellers, 157
Bone implements, 25, 58, 59, 109, 128, 129, 131, 140, 141, 148, 157, 224

371